PLAY
IN THE
EARLY
YEARS

Sara Miller McCune founded SAGE Publishing in 1965 to support the dissemination of usable knowledge and educate a global community. SAGE publishes more than 1000 journals and over 800 new books each year, spanning a wide range of subject areas. Our growing selection of library products includes archives, data, case studies and video. SAGE remains majority owned by our founder and after her lifetime will become owned by a charitable trust that secures the company's continued independence.

Los Angeles | London | New Delhi | Singapore | Washington DC | Melbourne

PLAY

IN THE

EARLY YEARS

EDITED BY

KAY OWEN

Los Angeles | London | New Delhi
Singapore | Washington DC | Melbourne

Los Angeles | London | New Delhi
Singapore | Washington DC | Melbourne

SAGE Publications Ltd
1 Oliver's Yard
55 City Road
London EC1Y 1SP

SAGE Publications Inc.
2455 Teller Road
Thousand Oaks, California 91320

SAGE Publications India Pvt Ltd
B 1/I 1 Mohan Cooperative Industrial Area
Mathura Road
New Delhi 110 044

SAGE Publications Asia-Pacific Pte Ltd
3 Church Street
#10-04 Samsung Hub
Singapore 049483

Editor: Delayna Spencer
Assistant editor: Catriona McMullen
Production editor: Martin Fox
Copyeditor: Sharon Cawood
Proofreader: David Hemsley
Indexer: Gary Kirby
Marketing manager: Lorna Patkai
Cover design: Wendy Scott
Typeset by: KnowledgeWorks Global Ltd.
Printed in the UK

Library of Congress Control Number: 2020947440

British Library Cataloguing in Publication data

A catalogue record for this book is available from the British Library

ISBN 978-1-5297-1623-8
ISBN 978-1-5297-1622-1 (pbk)

At SAGE we take sustainability seriously. Most of our products are printed in the UK using responsibly sourced papers and boards. When we print overseas we ensure sustainable papers are used as measured by the PREPS grading system. We undertake an annual audit to monitor our sustainability.

For Robbie and William. Always.

CONTENTS

CONTENTS

ABOUT THE EDITOR AND AUTHORS

Kay Owen is a developmental psychologist, currently lecturing on the BA (Hons) Early Childhood Studies and MA Childhood degrees at the University of Derby. Her particular research interests are the development of cognition during the preschool period, and how play and early relationships impact development.

Christopher Barnes is a developmental psychologist and senior lecturer with a specialist interest in parenting and child development, particularly with regard to prematurity and the newborn period, food allergy, autism and nature connectedness. He teaches on the BSc (Hons) Psychology undergraduate programme, and is programme leader for the MSc in Applied Developmental Psychology at the University of Derby.

Jenny Boldrin is a senior lecturer on the BA (Hons) Early Childhood Studies degree at the University of Derby. She has a particular research interest in the early experiences of Previously Looked After children and the ways in which their unique needs can be met through educational provision.

Trevor Cotterill is programme leader for Special Educational Needs and Disability (SEND) and teaches on SEND, Education Studies and Further Education Collaborations programmes at the University of Derby. His research interests include autism, the role of neurobiology and cognition in relation to it, and attention deficit hyperactivity disorder (ADHD).

Marco Antonio Delgado-Fuentes has been researching early childhood for almost 30 years. He has been an advisor to UNICEF, the Inter-American Development Bank and various other agencies in Mexico and Latin America. He has also developed the National Curriculum for children under age 3 in Mexico. His lines of research include intercultural childhoods, social involvement in services for young children, the transition from preschool to primary school, and policy development for services for young children and their families. Currently, he is a senior lecturer at the University of Derby.

Carol Fenton is a senior lecturer on the BA (Hons) Early Childhood Studies programme at the University of Derby. Prior to joining the University, she worked as a primary school headteacher. Carol has undertaken research into colour vision deficiency and the effects on social and emotional development in children, and the importance of continuing professional development in developing quality education in Higher Education. She is a member of the Early Childhood Studies Degree Network (ECSDN) and has been instrumental in the development of new workforce initiatives.

Jenny Hallam is a senior lecturer in Psychology at the University of Derby, who specialises in qualitative methods. She has a long-standing research interest in the arts and exploring the ways in which the co-production of artwork in educational settings shapes children's understanding and experience of the visual arts. She currently adopts a community psychology approach to exploring the ways the roles that nature and the arts have in community projects are designed to support the wellbeing of children and young people living in areas of deprivation.

Julianne Harlow has a background in nursing, midwifery and health visiting. She has worked as a senior lecturer and programme lead in several UK universities, including the University of Derby. Her research interests include childcare law and children's rights as applied to play, safeguarding and deafness.

Sarah Roeschlaub is a lecturer on the BA (Hons) Special Educational Needs and Disability and Child and Youth Studies degrees at the University of Derby. Sarah is particularly interested in policy making, its implementation and impact on families, children and marginalised groups of our society. She is currently studying for a PhD in the identity of alternative families in relation to political and personal identity.

Martin Smith is a consultant in public health, currently working in the north-west of England. His background is in nursing, health visiting and higher education. He has held a number of leadership roles in relation to children and young people's services.

Alistair Turvill is a lecturer on the Early Childhood Studies programme at the University of Derby. His research interests include the impact of technological advance, and health psychology, particularly chronic pain and other conditions.

Su Wall is the assistant programme leader and a senior lecturer on the BA(Hons) Early Childhood Studies at the University of Derby. Su's background is in the early years and as a former advisor for the local authority. Her interests and research include outdoor learning, inclusive practice, creativity and child protection.

ACKNOWLEDGEMENTS

The whole writing team would like to thank:

Our colleagues at the University of Derby for their insights, support and patience.

Our friends and families for their love and forbearance.

Delayna Spencer and the team at SAGE for their professional wisdom and listening ear.

INTRODUCTION: THE PROBLEM WITH PLAY

Kay Owen and Alistair Turvill

CONTENTS

PLAY IS HARD TO DEFINE

Most people would agree that young children need to play and should be allowed to play. However, the problem is that understandings of *what* play is or *why* it may be important, differ sharply. Over the years, some have viewed it as a largely frivolous and inconsequential activity, although possibly of value in enabling children to burn off their excess energy. Others have suggested that play is important because childhood should be a time of fun and exploration prior to the angst of adolescence and the burden of adult responsibilities. The Oxford Dictionary combines the two, defining play as 'activity for enjoyment and recreation rather than a serious practical purpose' (Stevenson, 2010). To some extent, the authors of this book embrace these perspectives. We want children to utilise their personal capacities, we want them to be silly and creative; to play for the simple joy of it. However, to quote David Hockney (Gayford, 2016): 'People tend to forget that play is serious.' Whilst conducting research in a nursery, we met a child whose play behaviours highlighted this very principle (Owen, 2017). The child had lost their family in a devastating accident and their 'play' revolved entirely around the incident. They enacted phoning the emergency services, being the first responders and being the adult who broke the news. If we accept that this child was 'playing' when they depicted each of these events, then we must question whether children's play is always enjoyable or recreational.

Researchers such as Erikson (1963, 1977) and Hartley, Frank and Goldenson (1957) suggested that socio-dramatic play can sometimes provide a useful means of working through fears and reconciling difficult emotions. Contemporary theorists have supported this position. Ariel (2002), Koplow (1997) and Paley (1990, 1992) all suggest that such play provides insights into the emotional lives of children. Ideas such as these are explored in more depth in 'What Are We Playing At?' (Chapter 7).

So, from the outset we find ourselves in a vexed position. Despite two centuries of argument and counter-argument, there remains no agreed explanation as to what constitutes 'play', and even the apparently obvious, 'play is fun' is under question. However, Peter Gray (2009, 2013) synthesised previous attempts to provide a definition and concluded that there are five key components that unite all of the differing perspectives. Play is:

- self-chosen and self-directed
- intrinsically motivated
- guided by mental rules
- imaginative
- conducted in an active, alert, but relatively stress-free manner.

TIME TO CONSIDER

Table 0.1 on p. 6 details how some major theorists have approached and categorised play. Are all of the points in the table covered by Gray's (2009, 2013) five components?

According to Gray's criteria, can the behaviours of the child who had lost his family in an accident be counted as play?

Do you feel that anything needs to be added to Gray's list?

PLAY CHANGES

As soon as we begin to think about children's play, we start to recognise that it is not a fixed commodity, and that all sorts of factors influence how, when and where children play. 'The Changing Face of Play' (Chapter 1) and 'The Role of Play in Child Development' (Chapter 2) chart how play has changed throughout history and how play activities change throughout childhood. We can see real-world examples of this progression in 'Understanding Children's Play Behaviours' (Chapter 3) and in 'Digital Play in Early Childhood' (Chapter 5), where new play behaviours are seen to emerge as children age, whilst others fall away. The importance of environmental factors is also made apparent in 'Play in the Great Outdoors' (Chapter 4).

To a certain extent, this interplay of internal and extrinsic factors ties in with the suggestion that play can be seen as an evolutionary mechanism, enabling human adaptation to environmental demands:

> Play is an ancient, voluntary, 'emergent' process driven by pleasure that yet strengthens our muscles, instructs our social skills, tempers and deepens our positive emotions, and enables a state of balance that leaves us poised to play some more. (Eberle, 2014: 214)

This perspective also dominates theories and concepts of play, with some schools of thought framing play as 'children's inbuilt learning drive' (Palmer, 2017) or 'learning for the real world' (Rudolf Steiner, 1861–1925; Maria Montessori, 1869–1952; and Margaret Macmillan, 1860–1931). Such notions take us further and further from our original starting point of viewing play as a frivolous and inconsequential activity.

THE RELATIONSHIP BETWEEN PLAY AND DEVELOPMENT

There seems little doubt that play and development are somehow linked, but our next problem is to try and understand the nature of the relationship between them. Krasnor and Pepler (1980) suggest three possibilities:

1   Play and development are intertwined. Play *reflects* the developmental level of the child (and therefore can be used as a diagnostic tool).
2   Play *follows* development and provides an opportunity to practise skills.
3   Play *precedes* and is a causal agent in developmental change.

If we accept that play drives development, or that the two are mutually enriching, then maximising play opportunities for children would seem a sensible way to enhance development. However, instead of opening the gates for more child-led, free play, in recent times these beliefs have led to play being increasingly viewed as a vehicle to accelerate 'desirable' aspects of development. Consequently, play not associated with expanding developmental potential, or play forms which appear challenging/detrimental to typical progression (for example, the sedentary behaviours associated with digital play), lead to them being devalued or jettisoned.

THE RHETORIC OF PLAY IN EDUCATION

Furthermore, as 'Learning and Play' (Chapter 9) demonstrates, early years education has experienced a move towards escalating didacticism. Whilst policy frameworks (Wood, 2015) espouse a play-based curriculum, it is defined as being planned, purposeful and structured (Pescott, 2017), with child-initiated activities and free play seemingly secondary to play that is planned by practitioners, typically with curriculum goals in mind. As Krasnor and Pepler's first view shows, this play can then be used to assess children against predetermined 'norms' and expectations.

As a result of this discourse, play has become increasingly instrumentalised, with early years policy and curricula sharply in contrast to other discourses which value freedom and choice within play. Play, in Singer and Singer's (2006: 97) opinion, is now 'viewed as ephemeral, pointless albeit enjoyable, and counterproductive to the major task of early education, the acquisition of literacy and numerical skills'. This juxtaposition between the rhetoric of play within official documentation and the reality of play from the players' perspective, is a recurrent theme throughout the book.

THE EXPERIENCE OF PLAY

Besio (2016) considers play from a philosophical and intrinsic basis, rejecting such a prescriptive approach and asserting in 'The need for play for the sake of play':

> Play … cannot have extrinsic preordained goals – it lives, arises, develops, and stops, only for itself; it is free, but not without limits, and indeed seeks out and constructs by itself the constraint to become more exciting, compelling, and challenging. (Besio, 2016: 45)

Extending this approach, Eberle (2014) considers the psychological artefacts necessary for creating a 'play experience'. He argues that play is a subjective, transient occurrence, wherein engagement and pleasure are followed by understanding, strength or poise. The enjoyment derived from 'fun' events incentivises children to seek out further play experiences. If we make learning the by-product rather than the focus, children will instinctively drive and manage their own learning, differentiating activities in accordance with their own preferences and requirements.

Here, we are beginning to think about play from the perspective of the child's individual experience, rather than our external perspective of observing, interpreting and sometimes evaluating their visible behaviour. In 'Autism and Play' (Chapter 11), Cotterill considers the differing play behaviours of children with autism, whilst 'Intercultural Perspectives' (Chapter 10) and 'Play and Gender' (Chapter 6) highlight the folly of assuming that play behaviours are unwavering and universal. Whilst we can find points of commonality, we must never lose sight of children's intrinsic individuality or what the play experience means to them.

HOW TO APPROACH THIS BOOK

Some of the debates around the role and formats of play will inevitably continue and develop in the coming years. Readers should not, therefore, embark upon the book in the hope that it will provide definitive answers; instead, it aims to highlight the depth and variability in what might appear, on the surface, to be a relatively uniform category of behaviour. The expansive and diverse nature of the philosophical, biological, social and cultural arguments presented within the coming pages, are indicative of the need to adopt a critical approach when evaluating research, arguments and evidence in this area. We hope that through engaging with the theories and research evidence, readers will broaden their understanding and formulate their own opinions about the nature, function and importance of play for the developing child.

Over the last 200 years, theorists and commentators have offered a perplexing variety of definitions of and views on play. We list a number of them in Table 0.1. Whilst this list is by no means exhaustive, it should help you to navigate your way through some of the key points they have raised, and the ways in which they believed play could be sub-divided. Many of the modern theorists listed here have written excellent texts on the subject which you can investigate in order to find out more.

Table 0.1 Play pioneers and their ideas on play

Name	Year	View of play/Categories of play
Froebel	1825	Play as child-centred, educative, sensory, open-ended
Groos	1896–1901	Practice theory – play as a rehearsal for future adulthood Categories: experimental (rule-based games), socio-economic play (chasing and play fighting), imitative, social and family games (make-believe play)
Montessori	1900	Play develops inner life. Multi-sensory learning
Freud	1920	Play as a means of reconciling inner conflict
Parten	1932	Categories: solitary, parallel, associative, cooperative
Vygotsky	1936	Play for cognitive and socio-cultural learning. Play as a cultural tool
Piaget	1945	Play as intellectual development. Categories: practice, symbolic, games with rules
Isaacs	1951	Free play allows release and rehearsal. Play as 'the child's work'
Sullivan	1953	Peer relationships during play are essential in the development of cooperation, compromise, empathy and altruism
Smilansky	1964	Socio-dramatic play develops cognitive, creative and socio-emotional abilities Categories: functional, constructive, symbolic, games with rules
Plowden	1967	Play reconciles children's inner lives with external reality
Bruner	1966, 1972	Learning by doing. Play as rehearsal. Play as intellectual development
Takata	1974	Categories: sensorimotor, symbolic and simple constructive, dramatic and complex constructive, games with rules, recreational and competitive
Rubin	1976	Categories: sensorimotor, simulation, simulation with objects, simulation with substitution, socio-dramatic, role-play, games with rules
Bruce	1987–2002	The relationship between play and learning. Free-flow play. Froebelian
Athey	1990	Schema theory. Piagetian
Garvey	1990	Categories: play with motion and interaction, play with objects, play with language, play with social materials
Nutbrown	1996–2018	Play advocate. Schema theory. Froebelian
Hughes	2002	Categories: symbolic, rough & tumble, socio-dramatic, social, creative, communication, dramatic, locomotor, deep, exploratory, fantasy, imaginative, mastery, object, role, recapitulative
Broadhead	2003–12	Social play continuum. Play and learning
Whitebread	2012	Play supports a range of cognitive and emotional developments. Categories: physical play, play with objects, symbolic play, pretence or socio-dramatic play, and games with rules

REFERENCES

Ariel, S., (2002) *Children's Imaginative Play: A Visit to Wonderland*. Westport, CT: Praeger Publishers

Besio, S. (2016) The need for play for the sake of play. In *Play Development in Children with Disabilities*. Warsaw: Sciendo Migration, pp. 9–52.

Eberle, S.G. (2014) The elements of play: Toward a philosophy and a definition of play. *American Journal of Play*, 6(2), 214–233.

Erikson, E. (1963). *Childhood Society*. New York: Norton.

Erikson, E. (1977) *Toys and Reasons*. London: Marion Boyars.

Gayford, M. (2016) *A Bigger Message: Conversations with David Hockney*. London: Thames and Hudson.

Gray, P. (2009) Play as a foundation for hunter-gatherer social existence. *American Journal of Play*, 1, 476–522.

Gray, P. (2013) *Free to Learn: Why Unleashing the Instinct to Play Will Make Our Children Happier, More Self-reliant, and Better Prepared for Life*. New York: Basic Books.

Hartley, R.E., Frank, L., & Goldenson, R.M. (1957) *The Complete Book of Children's Play*. New York: Crowell.

Koplow, I. (ed.) (1997). *Unsmiling Faces: How Preschoolers can Heal*. New York: Teachers College Press.

Krasnor, L.R., & Pepler, D.J. (1980) The study of children's play, some suggested future directions. In K.H. Rubin (ed.) *New Directions for Child Development* (No 9). San Francisco: Jossey-Bass Inc., Publishers.

Owen, K. (2017) Automaticity and the development of categorisation in preschool children: Understanding the importance of play. PhD thesis, University of Derby, http://hdl.handle.net/10545/621649.

Paley, V.G. (1990) *The Boy Who Would Be a Helicopter*. Cambridge, MA: Harvard University Press.

Paley, V.G. (1992) *You Can't Say You Can't Play*. Cambridge, MA: Harvard University Press

Palmer, S. (2017) How Lego lost its innocence. *Guardian*, 8 August. Available at: www.theguardian.com/commentisfree/2014/aug/08/lego-child-play-big-business-marketing-toys-shell (accessed 8 May 2020).

Pescott, C. (2017) What can we learn from UK Early Years curricular? In A. Thomas & K. McInnes (eds) *Teaching Early Years: Theory and Practice*. London: Sage.

Singer, J.L., & Singer, D.G. (2006) Pre-schoolers' imaginative play as a precursor of narrative consciousness. *Imagination, Cognition and Personality*, 25(2), 97–117.

Stevenson, A. (ed.) (2010) *Oxford Dictionary of English*, 3rd edition. Oxford: Oxford University Press.

Wood, E. (2015) The capture of play within policy discourses: A critical analysis of the UK frameworks for early childhood education. *International Perspectives on Children's Play*, 187–198.

1

THE CHANGING FACE OF PLAY

Kay Owen

CONTENTS

This chapter is all about changes – how attitudes towards play have changed over the years and how children's play behaviours change as the child develops. The background it provides should help you to contextualise the information provided in later chapters.

 THIS CHAPTER WILL...

- Explain some historic perspectives on children's play
- Introduce some important figures who have contributed to thinking about play
- Explain how play behaviours change as children develop
- Introduce some of the different types of play children engage in
- Help you to start to consider the role and impact of adults.

KEY TERMS

play behaviours, taxonomy, zone of proximal development

INTRODUCTION

The young of every species are vulnerable and need the time and opportunity to prepare for the responsibilities of adulthood. In the majority of vertebrates, including humans, much of early life is given over to a mixture of independent and adult-guided play activities, with the play becoming increasingly complex as the individual develops. Across species, the most common play behaviours support physical development, whilst also introducing activities and behaviours that will be useful in adult life. Play therefore allows the young to explore the environment, discover their body's capabilities and try out new behaviours without undue risk or cost. Given that anything without purpose usually dies out during the evolutionary process, the prevalence of play amongst multiple species has led to claims that it must serve a vital function (Auerbach, Kanarek & Burghardt, 2015). This belief led the evolutionary biologist Karl Groos to propose: 'The animal does not play because he is young, he has a period of youth because he must play' (Groos, 1898: xviii). Our understanding of the role, importance and structure of play has been shaped over the years by the work of researchers and theorists. Some of the most notable and influential theorists are considered next, together with some basic contextual information about the time when they were alive and working.

HISTORIC PERSPECTIVES ON PLAY

1700–1910 key theorists: Froebel, Groos, Curtis, Spencer

Prior to the mid-1700s, children in Britain were raised predominantly in extended family groups located in rural communities. This pattern remained true for much of Western Europe and the United States until the 1800s. From an early age, children were encouraged to help with chores, meaning that any play activities were centred on these tasks and the materials they required. As the Industrial Revolution spread from Britain across Western Europe to North America and then to Eastern Europe and Asia, it increased urbanisation, fragmented the family and increased the chasm between rich and poor. As a result of this, the experiences of childhood and the opportunities to play began to differ more sharply from child to child. Whilst mon-eyed children had an option on play and education, working-class children faced greater constrictions, often working long hours with limited opportunities for free expression. In Britain in the early 19th century, the average age to start work was 10 years old. Whilst some adults regarded this as necessary to ensure family financial stability, the tide gradually turned due to campaigners such as Richard Oastler (1830) and Lord Shaftsbury (1842).

Attitudes towards play

During this period, adult perceptions regarding the necessity of play were also quite polarised, often reflecting their own social standing, philosophy or political beliefs. Thus, whilst idealists such as Froebel (1782–1852) believed play to be the highest expression of human development in childhood, others regarded play's only value as being an outlet for children's excessive energy. This idea was formalised and popu-larised by Curtis (1916) in the *surplus energy theory* and found favour amongst early psychologists such as Herbert Spencer (1872). Advocates of play, including Groos (1861–1946) and Erikson (1903–94), decisively refuted it, proposing instead that play developed skills and allowed children to practise social situations in prepara-tion for adult life. Groos (1901) and Isaacs (1885–1948) further postulated that play was 'critical' in shaping social, emotional and cognitive development. These notions were to influence and shape both Piaget's (1962) and Vygotsky's (1967) later seminal theories, and are discussed in more detail in Chapter 2.

The concept of early learning was relatively unexplored prior to this point but the late 1800s and early 1900s saw the emergence of a few influential pioneers who brought the topic to the forefront. Rudolf Steiner (1861–1925), Maria Montessori (1869–1952) and Margaret Macmillan (1860–1931) all presented a blueprint for early learning, shaped round their own notions of how children learn through play.

TIME TO CONSIDER

In what ways were attitudes towards play shaped by what was happening in society at the time? To what extent do you think current attitudes towards play reflect modern society?

1920–1970 key theorists: Parten, Isaacs, Piaget, Smilansky

Interest in children's **pretend play** emerged in the 1920s when Parten conducted her innovative observational research with preschool children. Initially, her findings were included in academic writings about child development, leading Isaacs (1929: 210) to propose that 'play is indeed the child's work, and the means by which he grows and develops'.

Parten (1932) subsequently produced a **taxonomy** that provided the foundation for many later classifications of children's play. She suggested that there are six different play formats:

- unoccupied
- solitary
- onlooker
- parallel
- associative
- cooperative/social.

We will consider how these reflect and link to development, both later in this chapter and in Chapter 2.

The role of early psychologists

During the 1940s, psychology (at this point a very young science) introduced new concepts such as personality theory and play therapy, which served to induce more widespread interest in the social and emotional benefits of play. Piaget's observations of his own children's play and his pronouncements regarding its significance drew particular attention. Piaget echoed the view of another influential theorist, Mead (1934), who proposed that interactions during play cause children to see themselves as others see them. This ability to reflect on your own behaviour and the views of other people is a crucial component of social development.

The following decades were largely dominated by the work of a handful of key theorists. Jean Piaget (1962) and Sara Smilansky (1968) developed Parten's nascent theories, suggesting that play changes in style and format as children develop.

Together, Piaget and Smilansky devised what they termed the three categories of play, these being:

- sensorimotor play
- symbolic play
- games with rules.

From a more theoretical perspective, Piaget proposed a perspective he termed *genetic epistemology* (broadly meaning 'a study of the origins of knowledge'), which states that human understanding progresses through a series of stages as the person develops. These stages always happen in the same order but the speed and extent of development can be impacted by what is going on around the child. The interaction between the child and their environment during play can therefore aid progression through the stages.

 **TIME TO CONSIDER**

Parten's way of categorising play is very different from that of Piaget and Smilansky. What would you consider to be the main point of difference between the two? Is it possible to accept these differing approaches as being equally valid?

 SPECIAL STUDY: LEV VYGOTSKY

Cultural tools

Between 1924 and 1934, Lev Vygotsky produced several works outlining differing aspects of his human development and learning theory. He is probably best known for the sections relating to child development. Vygotsky regarded the experiences of early childhood as being pivotal in allowing humans to move from being 'slaves to the environment' to becoming 'masters of their own behaviour' (Bodrova & Leong, 2015). He recognised that many of the processes that set humans apart from all other animals involve *cultural tools*. By 'cultural tools', he meant devices such as language, which aid psychological development and help transmit cultural norms. Once the child understands the norms and gains mastery of the tools, they are able to fit in to the culture that surrounds them. So, for example, an adult will use words and gestures to show an infant that they should not bite people. Both the words and the gestures are 'tools'. Through the interaction, the child begins to learn the words, the gestures and the socially acceptable behaviour that will aid their integration.

Play and the zone of proximal development

This transference of knowledge is necessarily conducted within a social context and typically involves parents, teachers and/or older children supporting the child's learning. These are also the individuals generally associated with Vygotsky's most famous concept, the **zone of proximal development** (ZPD). The ZPD explains how this 'more knowledgeable other' can help children move from what they can currently do unaided, to the next level of performance – a level they currently require help to achieve (Vygotsky, 1978). Vygotsky believed that children were most likely to understand and internalise new ideas if they were actively engaged in a joint activity that utilised their intrinsic interests and motivations. Ideally, this should incorporate both verbal and nonverbal communication. Each of these criteria, he suggested, is met when children play with someone who is more skilled in terms of experience, knowledge and understanding. Vygotsky (1967) therefore advocated play as the optimum means of enabling children to actualise their ZPD.

When he was talking about play, Vygotsky was generally referring to the sort of socio-dramatic or pretend play favoured by young children. He regarded socio-dramatic play as having three main features: (1) children construct a make-believe situation, then (2) they assign roles, before finally (3) acting out the situation. In their enactment, they follow the rules they believe govern their character's behaviour in that situation. The input offered by a child's playmates will serve to embellish and extend their understanding of social norms and behaviours and, therefore, in this context, the whole group assumes the role of 'knowledgeable other' and drives development through the ZPD.

In a seminal 1933 lecture, Vygotsky made clear his belief in the importance of play in childhood, saying:

> In play a child is always above his average age, above his daily behaviour; in play it is as though he were a head taller than himself. As in the focus of a magnifying glass, play contains all developmental tendencies in a condensed form; in play it is as though the child were trying to jump above the level of his normal behaviour. (1967: 16)

Developing Vygoskian perspectives

A number of theorists have subsequently extended and developed Vygotsky's work, most notably Jerome Bruner (1915–2016) and Barbara Rogoff. Bruner emphasised the social nature of learning and the importance of active support through 'scaffolding' (Wood, Bruner & Ross, 1976). The concept has achieved prominence within several teaching ideologies, often in conjunction with notions of guided play or playful learning (Hirsh-Pasek, Golinkoff, Berk & Singer, 2009) which stress the importance of supportive social interaction between the child and a 'more knowledgeable other'.

1970–2000 key theorists: Belsky, Bretherton, Bruner, Glickman – The impact of cultural change

Social

The calls for a more equal society which had begun to gain momentum in the 1960s, eventually led to major legal changes regarding women's rights. Unsurprisingly, these were accompanied by much public debate regarding differences between the sexes, which in turn generated research interest into whether sex differences were apparent in children's play (see Chapter 4). Similarly, changes to the ethnic composition of British society, during the latter part of the century, fostered an upsurge in interest in the links between play and culture.

Academic

The 1970s also saw a renewed focus on pretend play, specifically its stages (Rosenblatt, 1977; Watson & Fischer, 1977). Whereas prior to this time, exponents of play primarily relied on philosophical arguments, this period saw an increasing emphasis on research and so proponents attempted to demonstrate evidence of the relationship between specific play behaviours and precise developmental outcomes. Several influential researchers turned their attention towards studying aspects, such as the role of pretend play in developing language (Bates et al., 1979; McCune-Nicolich, 1981) or cognition (Saltz, Dixon & Johnson, 1977). However, methodological difficulties and weaknesses undermined a number of studies (Rubin, Fein & Vandenberg, 1983) and, thus compromised, interest in pretend play diminished and faltered for a time.

The late 1980s and early 1990s witnessed the emergence of some influential new psychological perspectives and research methodologies that were to influence thinking about human development. Pinker's (1994) language acquisition hypothesis, behavioural genetics (Loehlin, 1992; Scarr, 1986) and the rise of neuroimaging (Posner & Raichle, 1994) together offered new ways of thinking about the nature–nurture debate. This served to innervate developmental research with a particular emphasis on the relative importance of internal and external factors. With regard to play, interest focused on its potential contribution to cognitive development (Fisher, 1992; Kim, 1999; Krafft & Berk, 1998) and skill acquisition (Roskos & Neuman, 1998; Stone & Christie, 1996) as part of the drive to discover which aspects of human development are fixed and which are fluid.

Educational

Things were also changing in education throughout this period. The 1988 Education Act laid the groundwork for the **National Curriculum** and the introduction of Standard Assessment Tests (SATs). This was later mirrored in America's Standardized Tests (US Department of Education, 2008). The resultant emphasis on evaluating English, Mathematics and Science abilities, and the clear disparities in performance the tests revealed, promoted widespread debate regarding learning and the potential means of accelerating progress in both the UK and the USA. Research into the relative benefits of play, the role of play in educational institutions and the potential means of assessing play therefore began to proliferate. By and large, academics and practitioners favoured supported play as the cornerstone of a happy and productive childhood, but successive governments' desire to 'drive up standards' led to an increasing formalisation of the early years curriculum.

In 1988, Rogers and Sawyers argued that 'this hurried, structured, work-oriented approach is based on several unwarranted and faulty beliefs:

(1) earlier is better,
(2) children are not interested in learning unless they receive rewards,
(3) success and winning are more important than effort,
(4) teacher-directed work is the most efficient way for children to learn, and
(5) play has little value'. (Rogers & Sawyers, 1988: vi)

Their suggestion that child-led play was ultimately more beneficial than structured teaching illustrates well the dichotomy that was beginning to re-open regarding play in early childhood.

2000–2015 key theorists: Bergen, Fromberg, Moyle – The formalisation of early learning

Whilst the **Early Years Foundation Stage** (DfE, 2014) stressed play as the gateway to learning, it specified 'planned, purposeful play' wherein 'the balance will gradually shift towards more activities led by adults to help children prepare for more formal learning, ready for Year 1' (DfE, 2014; 2017: 9). The increasingly didactic nature of early years education (Broadhead, 2009) thus led many play researchers to focus on intellectual development (Cheng & Johnson, 2010) in order to better understand its educational benefits. Whilst some researchers considered generalised enhancement (Alfieri, Brooks, Aldrich & Tenenbaum, 2011), others focused on specific components including maths (Nath & Szucs, 2014), problem solving (Russ, 2003), language (Orr & Geva, 2015) and cognitive competencies (Uren & Stagnitti, 2009).

However, some theorists, academics and practitioners have argued that the emphasis on accountability and measurable learning outcomes that are so apparent within current educational ideology (see Chapter 9), not only restrict learning, they have also misinterpreted play (Weisberg, Hirsh-Pasek & Golinkoff, 2013) as the format on offer lacks the joy and spontaneity that characterise true play. Furthermore, it is asserted that play has an intrinsic value far in excess of pedagogical fashions (Whitebread, Basilio, Kuvalja & Verma, 2012), and to manipulate it 'instrumentalises' play (Lester & Russell, 2008) and ignores its true value.

The debates surrounding play remain open, with contributions from some prolific authors including Fromberg and Bergen (2006), Broadhead (2009), Baines and Blatchford (2011) and Moyles (1989, 2012, 2015) being well worthy of the reader's attention. There are also a number of groups in the UK and beyond who actively campaign regarding children's right to play. A child's right to play is fully discussed in Chapter 7.

THE CURRENT POSITION: SOME FACTORS TO CONSIDER

Attitudes towards children, childhood and children's activities do not exist in a vacuum. As this first section has shown, they are enmeshed with other things that are happening in society. Politics determine funding priorities and educational philosophies and drive social attitudes – all of which impact upon children. Changes to the structure or functioning of the family unit affect the children growing within it. We are therefore in a time of flux with regard to children's play. This section considers some of the changes that are having a particular impact on how, where and when children play.

Urbanisation

Young people, families with children and people without a car are the most likely to visit urban green spaces. However, over the 13 years between 1992 and 2005, some 34,000 sports pitches were lost to development in the UK, and the amount of farmland, forest, gardens and greenfield sites given over to housing development increased by 58 per cent between 2014 and 2018. There are therefore fewer green spaces for children to play in than there were a generation ago (Comer & Forbes, 2016). Urbanisation has been accompanied by an increase in car ownership, with both moving and stationary vehicles causing a further reduction in safe outdoor areas for children's play.

CASE STUDY 1.1

Jack lives in a two-bedroom flat in Handsworth, Birmingham with his parents and two sisters. His dad is an HGV driver and his mum works part-time in hospitality. In 2018, Birmingham had a population of about 1.26 million, growing from 1.02 million in 2011. It is one of the most populated cities in Britain, with some 10,391 people per square mile. Birmingham is also one of the most youthful cities in Europe, with some 40 per cent of the population being aged under 25.

Archie lives in Eden, Cumbria with his parents and his twin brother. They have a four-bedroom detached house with a large garden. His parents run their own business from home. Eden has a population density of around 64 per square mile. It has the greatest proportion of green space in England, and also has very little land given over to roads.

Reflective question

How do you imagine Jack and Archie's play experiences will differ? See Figure 1.1.

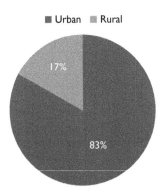

Figure 1.1 UK urban–rural divide (2017)

Social changes

As Britain has increasingly moved away from being a manufacturing nation towards being a service economy, the nature and patterns of work have changed, with fewer workers contracted to a 'Monday to Friday, 9–5' job than previously. Increased gender equality has also meant more women are in employment than a generation ago. Together, these factors have caused changes in childcare arrangements, with implications as to where, when and how children play.

Education

The changes within early years education that we have already discussed have served to reduce the opportunities for free play (Whitebread, Basilio, Kuvalja & Verma, 2012). Young children are now more likely to experience formalised instruction and to have their play shaped by adults.

Additional factors

Technological developments (see Chapter 5), the loss of play spaces and parental anxiety (Boyd, Lee & Holt, 2013) have progressively changed the nature of play. Modern children are increasingly likely to play indoors and to be involved in less vigorous play (see Chapter 4).

Play as apprenticeship

Elkonin (1978), a post-Vygotskian scholar, points out that, historically, play had a role in preparing children for pre-determined adult responsibilities. Children there-fore re-enacted adult jobs, using scaled-down adult tools. However, in the present day, tools used by adults may be too complex, too dangerous or too transitory for children to engage with. Many of the tools used in the workplace two decades ago are now outmoded or even obsolete. Elkonin suggests that children's play has therefore changed, now being more concerned with general competencies, understandings or behaviours that will help them acclimatise to the tools of the future.

Sections of the public, some educators and members of the academic community have expressed concern at the current trajectory, provoking a resurgence of debate regarding the place of play in modern childhood.

 TIME TO CONSIDER

Can you think of any other factors within modern society that you believe are having an impact on children's play?

Would you regard these as being changes for the better, or are you concerned by recent changes?

Could it be argued that we are returning to a time when children worked long hours instead of enjoying the freedoms of play, or is this overstating the case?

What do you think we need to do as a society to safeguard children's play?

THE DEVELOPMENT OF PLAY BEHAVIOURS

This second section of the chapter will consider how play behaviours change during the first years of life, and also look at some of the reasons underlying these changes. It will provide you with a basic introduction to the concepts that will be further developed in Chapter 3.

It is important to note that when considering any form of development, the order is generally fixed but the timings and the level of proficiency will vary from child to child. So, whilst for all typically developing children, play involving simple object manipulation will come before complex games of pretend, some children will hit those milestones sooner than others. Some will also devise incredibly complex play behaviours, whilst others remain happy with relatively uncomplicated scenarios. Each child is an individual with their own mix of interests, skills and talents. One of my sons could form three word sentences by 12 months but did not walk until he was 17 months old. The other could run with a ball by 17 months but barely spoke. Now in their early 20s, they both enjoy very similar levels of physical and linguistic ability, although the talker still likes to talk and the runner plays more sport!

Early infancy

Humans are essentially social animals, born with an innate desire to communicate and interact. Similarly, those who surround the baby have a natural inclination to engage with it and establish the beginnings of a relationship. Most humans automatically pitch their language and interactions at a level slightly above the child's current competencies, thus supporting progressive development through the ZPD. With regard to play, most adults and older siblings will engage with the baby in a manner and at a level designed to aid development by encouraging them to participate in 'games' that are marginally above their present abilities. From the first weeks of life, therefore, children are encouraged to become involved in play activities by the adults who care for them. As Gessell (1880–1961) noted, developmental change is particularly rapid early in life. We shall therefore concentrate on the first three years of life. See Table 1.1 for the infant's developmental stages by age in months.

Table 1.1 Development stages by age in months

Approx. age in months	Developmental stage	Toys and games	Points to consider
0–3	Visually tracks objects. Interested in hands	Mobiles	Mobiles help to direct and focus visual attention and augment the child's desire to reach, grasp, swipe and to bring objects to the mouth.
0–12	Increased control over hands	Likes to hold and explore items	Object manipulation provides the baby with new sensory information regarding texture, weight, malleability, taste, sound and smell. Special toys with safe moving parts are of interest, but everything is new and interesting to a small child, so many everyday items constitute appropriate 'toys' during this stage.
0–10	Increasing social awareness and bodily control	Games with other people	The games are necessarily repetitive and need to be played with someone who understands the 'rules'. Games of tickle, peek-a-boo and give-and-take are the most common. We shall see in Chapter 2 that they also aid development.
10–15	Increasing cognitive maturity	Starts to pretend, e.g. using a toy car as a telephone or a bath sponge as a cake	Children may like toys but they are not vital to the development of play behaviours. Montessori recommended the use of real objects where safe and practicable – proper pans rather than plastic ones, empty packets instead of child-sized replicas. Indeed, the Montessori philosophy advocates 'Real toys. Mostly wood. Not too many' (see Lillard, 2013).
8–15	Development of pincer grip. Increased physical control	Toys and games that allow this skill to be practised and perfected	Toys with buttons and strings enable the child to effect an instant change in something beyond their body and this sense of mastery creates great joy.
12	Increased social awareness. Improved categorisational ability	Play starts to involve dolls or soft toys and then other people	Items are initially grouped indiscriminately (e.g. a spoon and a train may form the components of a 'game'). However, as understanding improves, objects are used in a more conventional manner (Owen & Barnes, 2019).
8–24	Understanding of object permanence	Pop-up and pop-out toys and books	Babies have no initial concept of object permanence, believing that things simply cease to be when they are not in view. Thus, peek-a-boo and pop-ups seem almost magical. Theorists disagree as to exactly when this happens.
15	Emergence of cooperative play	Shared games and activities	An interest in others, particularly other babies, begins early. Interactions start with a look but gradually develop into the exchange of smiles and then objects. Children thus start to engage in the sort of complementary and reciprocal behaviours that form the foundations of social interaction (Muller & Carpendale, 2004). Before they can engage in coordinated play, individuals must have the facility to recognise themselves as separate beings.

(Continued)

Table 1.1 (Continued)

Approx. age in months	Developmental stage	Toys and games	Points to consider
12–24	Symbolic and pretend play develop	Objects and items to facilitate pretend play	Initially, it is conducted in parallel and focuses on the manipulation and exploration of objects (Vondra & Belsky, 1989). The emergence of pretend play occurs universally when children are aged between 18 and 24 months old, regardless of whether it is modelled or actively discouraged, fostering claims that it is innate and adaptive (Taylor & Carlson, 2000).
24–36	Substantial increase in physical and cognitive abilities and in social awareness	Play dough, paint, building blocks, creatures and dolls. Pretend play	Play behaviours move from repetitious to individual and creative. Pretend play shows increasing awareness of social roles (Howes, Unger & Seidner, 1989) and an ability to combine sequences of play (Hughes, 2009). Whilst play retains some vestiges of earlier stages, for instance in the use of symbolic tools, they are utilised in an increasingly sociable manner (Fromberg & Bergen, 2006).

CASE STUDY 1.2

The following excerpt is taken from some research I undertook at a nursery. The children who are mentioned here were all 3 years old:

> Ms H is in the book corner reading the *Three Billy Goats Gruff* to a group of children.
>
> Makayla and Daisy-Mae go to the Small World table. Makayla has a lift-the-flap book and is alternating between looking at it in her hand and in the mirror. She is making sound effects to go with the story. Daisy-Mae points out that there are pictures of goats in Makayla's book and that she has goats in her hands. Daisy-Mae wants Makayla to join her in playing with the toy goats but she turns back to the beginning of the book and starts looking through it again.
>
> Tyreese and Viktor put some train track on the floor and pretend they are balancing on a wobbly bridge. Ms H re-tells parts of the story. Other children come to join in. Daisy-Mae says, 'We need a bigger bridge'. Ms H goes to find some big blocks.
>
> Makayla picks up a goat mask and puts it on. The children construct a bridge with the big blocks and hide the troll figure underneath. Children start to walk over the bridge pretending to be the goats.
>
> Ms H picks up the troll figure who tries to gobble up the 'goats'. The children all laugh and shout 'No!' Ms H continues to talk through the story. Makayla throws the troll in the air and all the children laugh.
>
> Olly puts the troll back under the bridge and asks Ms H to start the story again.

Reflective question

What examples can you find in the case study of children being at different points in their development?

True socio-dramatic pretend play emerges when the child is around 4 years old, although it may be apparent earlier if the child has a more proficient playmate such as a parent or an older sibling (Dale, 1989; Farver & Wimbarti, 1995; Fiese, 1990; Haight & Miller, 1993). You can see an example of this in Chapter 2 case study 2.1 where the children care for 'the baby'. Imaginative pretend-play peaks during the late preschool period but declines as the child approaches 6 years of age (Kelly & Hammond, 2011; Rogers, 2011; Singer & Singer, 2006).

It can be seen that as children develop, their play becomes more flexible and creative. It evolves from the exploration of the sensory properties of objects to simple repetitive play, and from there to relational and constructive play with objects, to functional play, and finally to play that is symbolic in nature. As Garner and Bergen (2006: 126) note: 'As significant developmental changes occur during the first four years of life in children's social, emotional, physical and cognitive domains, concomitant progressive changes occur in play.'

FINAL REFLECTION

Social attitudes towards childhood, and subsequently towards play, have changed substantially over the years. To a large extent, these reflect broader changes happening within society and evolving expectations of juvenility. Our understanding of play has been augmented by the work of influential theorists, reformists and practitioners who have acted as advocates and exponents.

We have also considered how play behaviours change and investigated simultaneous changes happening as part of the maturation process. We will consider Garner and Bergen's assertion that the two are interlinked in greater detail in the next chapter.

KEY POINTS

- Attitudes towards play have changed over the years, often as part of more general social and political shifts.
- Academic theory and research into play have also been subject to changes according to social and academic trends.
- Attitudes towards childhood and play are currently in a state of flux.
- Children's play behaviours progress in line with other developmental changes.

QUESTIONS TO CONSIDER

1   Refer back to the case studies of Jack and Archie and their differing play experiences. Which of the differences would you consider to be the most important? Do you think these differences will have any lasting impact on them?
2   Vygotsky stated that 'in play, a child is always … a head taller than himself' (Vygotsky, 1967). What do you understand by this phrase and to what extent do you agree?
3   Do you consider children's play to be in a better or worse place than it was 200 years ago? 100 years ago? What changes would you hope to see in the next 100 years?

4   What would you consider to be the most important changes that happen in children's play behaviours during the first three years of life?
5   To what extent do you agree with the call for 'Real toys. Mostly wood. Not too many'? What are your views on the range, type and number of toys available for babies and young children?

FURTHER READING

You can read more about Play England, including its manifesto for children's play, at www.playengland.org.uk. The organisation considers play in schools, open places and on the streets. The site also provides links to other groups and to a variety of resources.

The National Trust also provides information regarding play areas throughout the country, at www.nationaltrust.org.uk.

A useful overview of how play behaviour develops is provided in Bergen, D. & Fromberg, D.P. (eds) (2006) *Play from Birth to Twelve: Contexts, Perspectives and Meanings*, 3rd edition. New York: Routledge.

REFERENCES

Alfieri, L., Brooks, P.J., Aldrich, N.J., & Tenenbaum, H.R. (2011) Does discovery based instruction enhance learning? *Journal of Educational Psychology*, 103, 1–18.

Auerbach, J., Kanarek, A.R., & Burghardt, G.M. (2015) To play or not to play? That's a resource abundance question. *Adaptive Behavior*, 23(6), 354–361.

Bates, E., Benigni, L., Bretherton, I., Camaioni, L., & Volterra, V. (1979) *The Emergence of Symbols: Cognition and Communication in Infancy*. New York, London: Academic Press.

Baines, E., & Blatchford, P. (2011) Children's games and playground activities in school and their role in development. In A.D. Pellegrini (ed.) *The Oxford Handbook of the Development of Play*. New York: Oxford University Press.

Bodrova, E., & Leong, D.J. (2015) Vygotskian and post-Vygotskian views on children's play. *American Journal of Play*, 7(3), 371–388.

Boyd, K.A., Lee, H., & Holt, N.L. (2013) Family members' perceptions of changes in children's active free play: An intergenerational study. *Journal of Exercise, Movement and Sport*, 45(1), 24–36.

Broadhead, P. (2009) Conflict resolution and children's behaviour: Observing and understanding social and cooperative play in early years educational settings. *Early Years*, 29(2), 105–118.

Cheng, M.-F., & Johnson, J.E. (2010) Research on children's play: Analysis of developmental and early education journals from 2005 to 2007. *Early Childhood Education Journal*, 37, 249–259.

Comer, A., & Forbes, K. (2016) Urbanisation in the UK: The need for a more focussed approach on city infrastructure. *Proceedings of the Institute of Civil Engineers – Civic Engineering*, 169(2), 53–53.

Curtis, H.S. (1916) *Education through Play*. New York: Macmillan.

Dale, R. (1989) *The State and Education Policy*. Milton Keynes: Open University Press.

DfE (2014) *The national curriculum in England Key Stages 1 and 2 framework document*. Available at: www.gov.uk/government/publications/national-curriculum-in-england-primary-curriculum (accessed May 2020)

DfE (2017) *The Early Years Foundation Stage*. London: DfE.

Elkonin, D.B. (1978) Psychologija igry [The psychology of play]. *Journal of Russian and East European Psychology* 43: 22–48.

Farver, J.A.M., & Wimbarti, S. (1995) Indonesian children's play with their mothers and older siblings. *Child Development*, 66(5), 1493–1503.

Fiese, B.H. (1990) Playful relationships: A contextual analysis of mother–toddler interaction in symbolic play. *Child Development*, 61(5), 1648–1656.

Fisher, E. (1992) The impact of play on development: A meta-analysis. *Play and Culture*, 5(2), 159–181.

Fromberg, D.P., & Bergen, D. (eds) (2006) *Play from Birth to Twelve: Contexts, Perspectives and Meanings*, 2nd edition. New York: Routledge.

Garner, B.P., & Bergen, D. (2006) Play development from birth to age four. In D.P. Fromberg and D. Bergen (eds) *Play from Birth to Twelve: Contexts, Perspectives and Meanings*, 2nd edition. New York: Routledge.

Groos, K. (1898) Author's preface. In *The Play of Animals* (trans. E.L. Baldwin). New York: Appleton.

Groos, K. (1901) *The Theory of Play: In The Play of Man* (trans. E.L. Baldwin). New York: Appleton, pp. 361–406.

Haight, W.L., & Miller, P.J. (1993) *Pretending at Home: Early Development in a Sociocultural Context*. New York: SUNY Press.

Hirsh-Pasek, K., Golinkoff, R.M., Berk, L.E., & Singer, D.G. (2009) *A Mandate for Playful Learning in Preschool: Presenting the Evidence*. Oxford: Oxford University Press.

Howes, C., Unger, O., & Seidner, L.B. (1989) Social pretend play in toddlers: Parallels with social play and with solitary pretend. *Child Development*, 60(1), 77–84.

Hughes, F.P. (2009) *Children, Play and Development*, 4th edition. London: Sage.

Isaacs, S.S. (1929) *The Intellectual Growth of Young Children*. London: Routledge & Kegan Paul.

Kelly, R., & Hammond, S. (2011) The relationship between symbolic play and executive function in young children. *Australian Journal of Early Childhood*, 36(2), 21–27.

Kim, S.-Y. (1999) The effects of storytelling and pretend play on cognitive processes, short-term and long-term narrative recall. *Child Study Journal*, 29(3), 175–191.

Krafft, K.C., & Berk, L.E. (1998) Private speech in two preschools: Significance of open-ended activities and make-believe play for verbal self-regulation. *Early Childhood Research Quarterly*, 13(4), 637–658.

Lester, S., & Russell, W. (2008) *Play for a Change: Play, Policy and Practice – A Review of Contemporary Perspectives*. London: National Children's Bureau.

Lillard, A.S. (2013) Playful learning and Montessori education. *NAMTA Journal*, 38(2), 137–174.

Loehlin, J.C. (1992) *Genes and Environment in Personality Development*. Newbury Park, CA: Sage.

McCune-Nicolich, L. (1981) Toward symbolic functioning: Structure of early pretend games and potential parallels with language. *Child Development*, 52(3), 785–797.

Mead, G. (1934) *Mind, Self, and Society*. Chicago: University of Chicago Press, pp. 173–178.

Moyles, J. (1989) *Just Playing? Role and Status of Play in Early Childhood Education*. Buckingham: Open University Press.

Moyles, J. (2012) *A–Z of Play in Early Childhood*. Maidenhead: Open University Press.

Moyles, J. (2015) *The Excellence of Play*, 4th edition. Maidenhead: Open University Press.

Muller, U., & Carpendale, J.I.M. (2004) From joint activity to joint attention: A relational approach to social development in infancy. In J.I.M. Carpendale & U. Muller (eds) *Social Interaction and the Development of Knowledge*. New York & Hove: Psychology Press.

Nath, S., & Szucs, D. (2014) Construction play and cognitive skills associated with the development of mathematical abilities in 7-year-old children. *Learning and Instruction*, 32, 73–81.

Orr, E., & Geva, R. (2015) Symbolic play and language development. *Infant Behaviour and Development*, 38, 15–22.

Owen, K., & Barnes, C. (2019) The development of categorisation in early childhood: A review. *Early Child Development and Care*, 191(6), 1–8. DOI: 10.1080/03004430.2019.1608193.

Parten, M.B. (1932) Social participation among preschool children. *Journal of Abnormal and Social Psychology*, 27(3), 243–269.

Piaget, J. (1962) *Play, Dreams, and Imitation in Childhood*. New York: Norton.

Pinker, S. (1994) *The Language Instinct*. New York: Harper.

Posner, M.I., & Raichle, M.E. (1994) *Images of Mind*. New York: Lawrence Erlbaum Associates.

Rogers, C.S., & Sawyers, J.K. (1988) *Play in the Lives of Children*. Washington, DC: National Association for the Education of Young Children.

Rogers, S. (2011) Play and pedagogy: A conflict of interests? In S. Rogers (ed.) *Rethinking Play and Pedagogy in Early Childhood Education*. London: Routledge.

Rosenblatt, D. (1977) Developmental trends in infant play. In B. Tizard & D. Harvey (eds) *The Biology of Play*. Philadelphia, PA: Lippincott, pp. 33–44.

Roskos, K., & Neuman, S. (1998) Play as an opportunity for literacy. In O.N. Saracho & B. Spodek (eds) *Multiple Perspectives on Play in Early Childhood*. Albany, NY: State University of New York Press, pp. 100–115.

Rubin, K.H., Fein, G., & Vandenberg, B. (1983) Play. In E.M. Hetherington (ed.) *Handbook of Child Psychology, Vol 4: Socialisation, Personality and Social Development*. New York: Wiley.

Russ, S.W. (2003) Play and creativity: Developmental issues. *Scandinavian Journal of Educational Research*, 47(3), 291–303.

Saltz, E., Dixon, D., & Johnson, H. (1977) Training disadvantaged preschoolers in various fantasy activities: Effects on cognitive functioning and impulse control. *Child Development*, 48(2), 367–380.

Scarr, S. (1986) *Understanding Development*. New York: Harcourt Brace Jovanovich.

Singer, J.L., & Singer, D.G. (2006) Pre-schoolers' imaginative play as a precursor of narrative consciousness. *Imagination, Cognition and Personality*, 25(2), 97–117.

Smilansky, S. (1968) *The Effects of Socio-dramatic Play on Disadvantaged Preschool Children*. New York: John Wiley & Sons.

Spencer, H. (1872) *The Principles of Psychology*, 2nd edition. London: Williams and Norgate.

Stone, S.J., & Christie, J.F. (1996) Collaborative literacy learning during sociodramatic play in a multi-age primary classroom. *Journal of Research in Childhood Education*, 10(2), 123–133.

Taylor, M., & Carlson, S. (2000) The relation between individual differences in fantasy and theory of mind. *Child Development*, 68, 436–455.

United States Department of Education (2008) Standardised Tests. Enacted by 107th United States Congress.

Uren, N., & Stagnitti, K. (2009) Pretend play, social competence and involvement in children aged 5–7 years: The concurrent validity of the child-initiated pretend play assessment. *Australian Occupational Therapy Journal*, 56, 33–40.

Vondra, J., & Belsky, J. (1989) Lessons from child abuse: The determinants of parenting. In D. Cicchetti & V. Carlson (eds) *Child Maltreatment: Theory and*

Research on the Causes and Consequences of Child Abuse and Neglect. New York: Cambridge University Press, pp. 153–202.

Vygotsky, L.S. (1967) Play and its role in the mental development of the child. *Soviet Psychology*, 5, 6–18.

Vygotsky, L.S. (1978) *Mind in Society: The Development of Higher Psychological Processes.* Cambridge, MA: Harvard University Press.

Watson, M.W., & Fischer, K.W. (1977) Development of social roles in elicited and spontaneous behaviour during the preschool years. *Developmental Psychology*, 16(5), 483–494.

Weisberg, D.S., Hirsh-Pasek, K., & Golinkoff, R.M. (2013) Guided play: Where curricular goals meet a playful pedagogy. *Mind, Brain and Education*, 7(2), 104–112.

Whitebread, D., Basilio, M., Kuvalja, M., & Verma, M. (2012) *The Importance of Play: A Report on the Value of Children's Play with a Series of Policy Recommendations.* Brussels: Toy Industries of Europe.

Wood, D., Bruner, J., & Ross, G. (1976) The role of tutoring in problem solving. *Journal of Child Psychology and Child Psychiatry*, 17, 89–100.

2

THE ROLE OF PLAY IN CHILD DEVELOPMENT

Kay Owen and Christopher Barnes

CONTENTS

This chapter explores the changes that take place in children's play and questions the direction of influence. Does play drive development? Do innate, biological factors cause changes in the way children play? Or do play and development perhaps complement and mutually enrich one another?

 THIS CHAPTER WILL...

- Investigate the links between play and social and emotional development
- Consider the relationship between play and cognitive development
- Consider the associations between play and language development
- Introduce ideas about how play may impact neurology
- Question whether play can promote school-readiness.

KEY TERMS

cognitive development, decentration, empathy, meta-cognition neurology, social and emotional development

INTRODUCTION

For many years, academics and educationalists have debated the benefits of play and questioned whether there is a link between particular sorts of play and specific areas of development. Whilst both classic (Bruner, 1961; Piaget, 1945; Vygotsky, 1962) and more modern theorists (Bergen, 2002; Moyles, 2015) generally agree that play aids development, some notable academics have suggested that there is actually remarkably little research evidence to support their claims (Lillard et al., 2013). The UK Government (DfE, 2017), parents and the public all broadly support the idea that children can and should be learning through play; however, their individual perceptions of what this involves appear to differ sharply. Indeed, some have gone so far as to question whether what some educationalists term 'learning through play' is really play at all (Whitebread, Basilio, Kuvalja & Verma, 2012).

This chapter will consider each of these controversial issues. It will also discuss some of the ways in which play and child development interrelate and consider how potential benefits can be maximised.

As claims concerning a relationship between play and **social and emotional development** are the most widely accepted (Holmes, Romeo, Ciraola & Grushko, 2015;

Orr & Geva, 2015), we shall start with these, before moving on to consider the more complex and contentious claims regarding **cognitive development**.

SOCIAL AND EMOTIONAL DEVELOPMENT
Early infancy

As noted in Chapter 1, the human desire for interaction drives both babies and those around them to playfully communicate from very early on in the child's life. Initially, this involves the exchange of looks and noises but gradually expands to incorporate exchanging objects, leading to games of give and take. This sort of 'serve and return' behaviour is arguably the beginning of both social interaction and playful behaviour (Muller & Carpendale, 2004). However, young babies think they are part of their mother and in order to play agreeably with others, infants must have grasped that they are separate, individual beings and that other people are individuals too. Once this is achieved, they can begin to understand reciprocal behaviours and cooperate more fully.

The emergence of cooperation and pretending

Around 18 months of age, children show a natural inclination to engage in pretend play, often re-enacting social situations. This happens regardless of whether such play is modelled or discouraged (Bretherton & Bates, 1984; Tamis-LeMonda & Bornstein, 1991). Initially, the infant will play alone before starting to include dolls, teddies and toys, and then ultimately other people. Both pretend and truly cooperative play also depend on the child recognising that other people know different things from them. This is referred to as **theory of mind** and, because it does not emerge until children are at least 3 years old (Wang et al., 2017), genuinely cooperative play cannot emerge before this point.

Nature and nurture

Clearly, a child needs to have had some experience of situations to re-enact them. However, these examples show that they also need to have reached a certain level of cognitive maturity. Pretend play is therefore dependent on both experiential and biological factors. The universal nature of these developments would also suggest some play behaviours are the result of inbuilt instinctual drives. Not only do lived experience and cognitive development shape play, games that incorporate other players also help to develop children's awareness of self and of 'otherness' – and this encourages both social and cognitive development. In this respect, therefore, play, cognition and social understanding are mutually beneficial.

PRETEND PLAY AND SOCIAL AWARENESS

As the child's cognitive capacity and understanding of the world increases, play becomes more creative, complicated and individualised. Developments in language, cognition and social understanding, enable increasingly detailed enactment of roles and situations. For example, a few months ago my children (CB) used boxes to create and symbolise a spaceship, pillows as moon rocks and their teddies as aliens. My 4-year-old son explained to me that the rug was moon rock, but a red blanket was lava – watch out, it's hot!

Pretend play like this aids development in several important ways:

- It allows children to experience how it feels to be someone else or to function in new situations, including trips to the moon and encounters with aliens!
- Children may use it to test out character traits or behaviours and to trial or rehearse different social behaviours.
- Creating social situations in play allows a child to safely explore responses and consequences.
- Pretend play allows children to control the emerging situation and to escape if necessary.
- It aids the development of abstract thought (Nicolopoulou, Barbosa, Ilgaz & Brockmeyer, 2010).
- It provides new insights into other people's thinking and reasoning.
- It helps children to develop appropriate social dialogue.
- It aids the emergence of **decentration** – meaning children start to consider multiple aspects of a situation (Lillard, 2012; Piaget, 1945).
- Together, decentration and theory of mind aid the development of **empathy** and emotional regulation (Galyer & Evans, 2001).

These developments involve conscious cognitive effort; so, in this respect, play is always a learning activity for the very young (Nicolopoulou, Barbosa, Ilgaz & Brockmeyer, 2010).

We can notice some of these factors within case study 2.1. The excerpt is taken from some research we did in a community nursery.

CASE STUDY 2.1

All of the children mentioned here are 3–4 years old. We join them at afternoon story time where the leader is reading *We're Going on a Bear Hunt*. Saffron has a new baby sister and has spent most of the afternoon pretending to be a baby.

The children think the bear looks sad. They stroke and kiss the picture so 'he feels better' and 'has friends'.

Everyone gets ready and goes outside.

Saffron starts making crying baby noises again. Jacob says, 'She's being the baby from the bear hunt. We need to get some food'. Sam strokes her hair, whilst Aarav and Nikolai watch.

Ms N and a group of children arrive with a crate of pots and pans. Sam gets a pan and spoon. He says, 'Here comes the big aeroplane', and tries to feed Saffron.

Drew is being a bear, so Ms N and some children go off on a bear hunt.

Adam is feeding Saffron from a plate. Sam has a bowl of mud. Saffron pretends to go to sleep, then wakes and cries. Sam offers her a ladle of grass.

The 'baby' cries again. Sam offers more grass. She refuses it and he leaves. Saffron is now alone and still pretending to cry.

Ms N returns and asks what will make the baby happy. Saffron says she needs a rattle. Ms N suggests she could make one. Saffron goes inside to the craft table.

She returns with a 'rattle' she has made. She wants Ms N to come to the shelter to 'play house'. Ms N says, 'We could make a house'. Ms N goes to get some plastic bread crates and is quickly joined by Galina and Elise who start stacking crates. Seth arrives, dressed as Buzz Lightyear. Ms N says, 'We have a mission for you!' Reuben and Seth join in carrying crates. Buzz Lightyear says he is going to 'make this house secure'. They build the walls up 'so the baby can't get out'.

Noah knocks on 'the door' and says he has brought baby food. Seth offers the baby a cup of tea and a sausage. Noah says, 'Babies can't have cups of tea!'

Ms N spots a hole in the 'wall' and says, 'Look, Buzz, there's a problem, the baby could escape, what could we do?' Seth suggests, 'Fix it!' He gets a crate to fill the space. The baby is crying. She is not well.

Kayla-Kate says, 'We need the doctor.' Clementine declares herself a doctor and gives Saffron medicine from a spoon.

Ms N says, 'In a minute we're going to finish this game to tidy up. We can leave our house out for tomorrow'.

Reflective question

Look back at the ways in which pretend play aids development. Is there any evidence that Saffron, Sam and Seth may be experiencing any of those points?

The role of 'more knowledgeable others'

Pretend play of this intensity generally emerges when children are around 4 years old and peaks during the following two years. The participation of more proficient playmates (in this case, the nursery staff) helps to extend the play. Assuming new roles in play and the personal benefits children derive from receiving the attention of more socially skilled individuals, form a potent combination, leading to the assimilation and acceptance of socially normative roles (Broadhead, 2009). Pretend play with a supportive and knowledgeable 'other' also helps the growing child to understand how the world works and how they can participate within it. In this way, playing 'shops' with a regular shopper may boost understanding of the processes, meaning the child can later approach a real situation with greater knowledge and confidence.

Vygotsky (1978) stressed that play has two essential and interrelated components:

1   the imaginary situation
2   the rules governing the imaginary situation.

So, when playing 'Mummies and Daddies', children are trying to act out adult behaviours as they understand them. This involves reflection on their lived experience, applying these experiences to the game and, potentially, modifying their previous understanding. We once observed some 3-year-olds setting up a game of 'Weddings'. In assigning roles, one boy said, 'You be the bride, you be the groom and I'll be the policeman who comes to break the fight up'. Following discussion with his playmates, he came to realise that police intervention was not a feature of all weddings!

During social play, children can be supported by having appropriate responses and socially accepted norms 'scaffolded' by more competent individuals ('Babies can't have cups of tea!'; 'Policemen don't come to weddings!'), allowing social understanding and performance to move to a more sophisticated level (Nicolopoulou, Barbosa, Ilgaz & Brockmeyer, 2010; Stone & Stone, 2015; Sutherland & Friedman, 2013).

 **TIME TO CONSIDER**

How do you think adults can best support social development during pretend play?

Theory and research appear to suggest that pretend play boosts development in several important areas, including those detailed in Table 2.1.

All of these factors in combination led Vygotsky to conclude that play 'is the leading source of development in the preschool years' (1967: 16).

Table 2.1 Contribution of play to specific areas

Area	Contribution of play
Emotional understanding	Vygotsky proposed that through socio-dramatic play, children also learn about generalised emotions and enact how they believe all individuals would behave in a given situation, rather than focusing exclusively on their own emotions.
Emotional regulation	Play, and particularly pretend play, helps children to recognise social signals and manage their own emotional responses. (Lillard, 2017)
Social understanding	Bussey and Bandura (1999: 695) propose that 'much early role-learning occurs in play', as socially competent participants guide the behaviours of other children (Xu, 2010), increasing their social awareness and competency (Uren & Stagnitti, 2009).
Social behaviours	During play, negotiations and discussions expose children to a world outside their own and are therefore influential in the development of social cognition (Kelly & Hammond, 2011).
Maturity	Children show greater functional maturity in their pretend play than in their normal social interactions (Uren & Stagnitti, 2009).
Impulsivity	Highly impulsive children have shown significant gains in self-regulation and inhibitory control following socio-dramatic play interventions (Elias & Berk, 2002).
Immediacy	Playing with peers is generally the means by which children learn deferred gratification, as they must suppress their desire for instant gratification in favour of fulfilling the rules of the game.
Imagination	The use of substitute items during play (e.g. using a banana as a phone) and the acting out of scenarios during role play, are involved in the development of imagination (Diachenko, 2010).

RESILIENCE

At the time of writing, there is considerable concern regarding the development of resilience in young children. 'Resilience' may be broadly defined as the maintenance of healthy development despite adversity. The hallmarks of a resilient individual are an ability to:

- self-regulate
- manage their emotions and behaviour
- implement impulse and behavioural control
- demonstrate an awareness of the rules.

It is also generally agreed that resilience can be bolstered in early childhood by positive relationships (Sciaraffa, Zeanah & Zeanah, 2018). It is apparent from the evidence considered in this chapter that, not only does play encourage children to develop relationships, it also aids the development of many aspects of these hallmarks. Pretend play, particularly with a supportive and knowledgeable 'other', would therefore appear potentially beneficial in the development of resilience (Sciaraffa, Zeanah & Zeanah, 2018). This is considered further in Chapter 7.

 TIME TO CONSIDER

It could be claimed that play, and particularly pretend play, helps children to develop (i) personally and (ii) as members of society. To what extent do you agree with this statement? What evidence is there to support your opinion? If these were the only benefits that play had to offer, would they still be sufficient to warrant young children spending most of their time engaged in play?

 SPECIAL STUDY: LANGUAGE DEVELOPMENT

Given the centrality and importance of language, it is unsurprising that much theoretical and research interest has centred on language acquisition and development (Golinkoff et al., 2000). Bruner (1983: 65) contended that 'the most complicated grammatical and pragmatic forms of language appear first in play activity', suggesting that children try out new linguistic formats in play before using them in daily life. This assertion appears to be supported by research evidence. Pellegrini and Galda (1990) discovered that during pretend play, preschoolers use more complex mental-state verbs (these are terms such as 'understand', 'wish', 'expect' and 'prefer') that can have very different meanings and are therefore easily misused. Play, being somewhat removed from reality, allows for greater freedom to experiment and make mistakes. Once successfully trialled, the language can then be confidently utilised in everyday life.

Language is often fundamental to play activities, so its development is naturally incorporated within an activity that is both pleasurable and relevant to the child. As a result, play helps to boost vocabulary, syntax and linguistic awareness (Holmes, Romeo, Ciraola & Grushko, 2015; Orr & Geva, 2015; Pellegrini, 1980), particularly, as we have noted, during socio-dramatic play which usually involves a lot of talking.

Whilst conducting our research, we have noted children using language in various ways during play. They use it to:

- establish the parameters of the play ('Let's pretend that I've brought my baby to hospital and you're the doctor')
- label and describe elements of the situation ('I've done it! I've mended the plug hole!')
- negotiate and maintain the play (Child A [sitting in a cardboard car]: 'Who wants to go to the seaside?'; Child B [climbing into the car]: 'Me!').

It is therefore unsurprising that research has discovered the amount of time infants spend engaged in pretend play (Tamis-LeMonda & Bornstein, 1991) and talking to peers during play (Dickinson & Moreton, 1991) correlates positively with their subsequent linguistic understanding and use (Holmes, Romeo, Ciraola & Grushko, 2015). Furthermore, the use of symbolic representations during play provides a staged introduction and functional basis for later success in reading.

 TIME TO CONSIDER

Observe a child or a group of children involved in pretend play (either in real life or on video). Note how and when they use language. Are there any notable differences between their language during the play activity and at other times? Are there, for instance, differences in tone, pitch, vocabulary, sentence length or structure? Share your observations with other group members. Does what you have seen lead you to any conclusions regarding play and language?

COGNITIVE DEVELOPMENT

In Chapter 1, we considered Groos's (1898) suggestion that play is fundamental to human development, and explored how this view was expanded and qualified by several influential psychologists:

- Piaget (1945) proposed that play:
  - aids the development of symbolic thought
  - promotes autonomy and control.
- Vygotsky (1978) went further, suggesting that:
  - play promotes social competence
  - interaction with older, more experienced playmates aids the development of cognition and language.

- Research in the area supports these theories. During play, children demonstrate high levels of:
  - o verbal communication
  - o creative thinking
  - o imagination
  - o problem solving. (Wood & Attfield, 1996, 2005)

Symbolism and abstraction

Play also helps with what Vygotsky deemed to be the other major accomplishment of the preschool years – the child's growing proficiency in the use of symbols. Symbolic representation enables humans to move away from the constraints of the here and now towards abstraction (Bergen, 2002) and control over their own thinking (Smith, 1978). This in turn facilitates the growth of **meta-cognition** (Lillard, 2012) and independent, internalised thought (Nicolopoulou, Barbosa, Ilgaz & Brockmeyer, 2010).

Play is therefore the catalyst that enables children to move from lower-level, 'real world' concrete thinking, towards high-level abstract thought. Whereas it had been largely accepted that imagination was a necessary precursor to play, Vygotsky claimed that it is actually the other way around – imagination is able to develop and thrive in humans because we engage in socio-dramatic play. He stated: 'The old adage that children's play is imagination in action can be reversed; we can say that imagination in adolescents and schoolchildren is play without action' (1967: 8). In much the same way that counting on fingers and working things out on paper are necessary precursors to complex mental maths, so children need to physically engage in pretend play before they can visualise a reality outside their own lived experience.

 **TIME TO CONSIDER**

To what extent would you agree that when you are using your own imagination, you are actually engaging in play but without any physical action?

Brain development

Things like our ability to plan, organise our thoughts and make decisions, develop very slowly and in a set order (Raznahan et al., 2012). The process is helped by exposing the child to suitable learning experiences as these boost the development of the brain's neural circuits. In order to bolster cognitive development, the right stimulus needs to be presented at the right developmental point (Soto, Waldschmidt, Helie & Ashby, 2013). If a child has insufficient mental stimulation, the brain's circuits become dulled and may start to decay (Alvarez & Sabatini, 2007). On the other hand, excessive demands give the immature brain more than it can cope with (Baddeley, Eysenck & Anderson, 2015) and in order to manage this, babies will simply shift their attention to something less demanding (Swingler, Perry & Calkins, 2015).

As we have seen, developmentally appropriate play aids advancement in many areas, including social cognition, self-regulation and language. Together, these boost the construction of **executive function** (the set of mental skills that help us to plan and to learn) and a prosocial brain (Yogman et al., 2018). As well as teaching discrete skills and enhancing a child's understanding, play thus ensures the brain's architecture is ready and able to respond to future learning opportunities.

Neurological insights into the importance of play

Advances in **neurology** suggest the interaction between play and learning is more complicated than had previously been assumed (Weisberg, Hirsh-Pasek & Golinkoff, 2013). The indications are that, in many instances, play creates a 'domino effect', with each small change creating further changes in processing or structure. For instance, we already knew that playing with a simple activity toy can help a baby's motor control and visual attention (Squire, Noudoost, Schafer & Moore, 2013). However, within the brain, both of these have neuronal links with working memory (Ullman, Almeida & Klingberg, 2014). So, whilst these are still early days, research appears to link this simple early object play to a whole range of other skills and functions including reasoning (Leisman, Braun-Benjamin & Melillo, 2014) and certain forms of learning (Foerde & Shohamy, 2011). In a nutshell, it would seem that play triggers a ripple effect that ultimately aids various aspects of cognitive development. Indeed, our own research into the development of emergent memory structures found that, over a 12-week period, children who participated in child-led play made greater gains in categorisational ability than children who followed a formal academic curriculum.

PLAY AND LEARNING: SCHOOL READY?

Recent years have seen considerable debate regarding 'school readiness' and how best to prepare children for the academic challenges ahead. We have shown that children's learning in the early years is both driven and constrained by a combination of biological, neurological and environmental factors. This next section therefore draws on ideas we have already considered in each of these domains, to evaluate whether play provides suitable preparation for schooling.

PLAY IN SCHOOL: THE LAST 50 YEARS

Educational ideology has always both reflected and driven social, philosophical and political research and theory. The influential Plowden Report (DES, 1967) drew on the (then new) work of Piaget and his assertions that children are independent, individual learners who should not be constrained through too tight and formal a curriculum:

> Adults who criticize teachers for allowing children to play are unaware that play is the principal means of learning in early childhood; it is the way through which children reconcile their inner lives with external reality. In play children gradually develop concepts of causal relationships, the power to discriminate, to make judgments, to analyse and to synthesise, to imagine and to formulate. (CACE in Plowden Report, DES, 1967; also cited in Brock, 2009: 26)

Some radical and much publicised responses (e.g. what has become known as the William Tyndale Affair) swung education sharply back towards greater regulation and accountability (Gillard, 2011). As noted in Chapters 1 and 9, the 1988 Education Act subsequently prepared the way for the National Curriculum and a **pedagogy** which emphasised rigorous assessment of traditional skills and knowledge. In the years that have followed, increasingly, nursery and preschool education have come to be viewed primarily as preparation for school (Rogers & Lapping, 2012; Stirrup, Evans & Davies, 2017). Whilst the EYFS recognised the need for play, it recommended that play should be increasingly adult led 'to help children prepare for more formal learning, ready for Year 1' (DfE, 2014: 9). Play during the preschool and Foundation Stage is thus contextualised as being purposeful and instructive rather than autonomous (Rogers & Evans, 2008).

Research into play and learning

Researchers have subsequently largely focused on the educational benefits of play (Cheng & Johnson, 2010), or investigated how play-based classroom activities can be used to boost maths (Nath & Szucs, 2014), problem-solving (Russ, 2003), language (Orr & Geva, 2015) and cognitive abilities (Uren & Stagnitti, 2009), in order that children can achieve politically defined norms. Others, however, have argued that the increasingly formal nature of early years education (Singer & Singer, 2006) both restricts learning and misrepresents play (Bartlett, 2011; Lester & Russell, 2008; Whitebread, Basilio, Kuvalja & Verma, 2012). It is argued that current trends have increased teacher-directed activity and driven real play from early years classrooms. Much of what is referred to as being play, they would claim, is actually academic instruction using more child-friendly objects.

To a large extent, therefore, an individual's attitude towards what is happening in early years education is shaped by that person's definition of 'play' (see Introduction) and their beliefs about how children learn and develop.

 CASE STUDY 2.2

The following two observations are taken from research work we did in nurseries. All the children are 3 years old.

Nursery 1

Ms M: 'We're going to do some counting.'

Small plastic bears are put out on a tray.

Ms M: 'I want you all to take two bears.'

James does this straight away, whilst the others take longer.

Ms M: 'Put them down in front of you and count them.' She goes round the children in turn and every child counts how many bears they have.

Ms M: 'We're going to get three now.'

Katie: 'Like this?' (She holds up three fingers.)

Ms M: 'That's right, Katie.'

Jayden and Katie both get four bears. Jayden says, 'I haven't got enough'.

Ms M: 'Have you got more than three or have you not got enough? Put them in front of you and count them.'

Jayden doesn't respond.

Ms M gives herself six bears and asks, 'Have I got three? Let's count them'.

Everyone counts to 6 together.

Ms M: 'Have I got too many or do I need more?'

James: 'Too many.'

Ms M: 'When we get to three, we need to stop. 1, 2, 3. We had too many, didn't we?'

They start to count Katie's: '1–2–3.'

Ms M: 'We don't need these, do we?' She returns the excess to the tray.

They work round the group, counting together, until everyone has three bears.

All bears are put back on the tray and Ms M again asks them to get three each, saying, 'Count to 3 and then stop'.

James gets three bears; everyone else has too many.

Katie has six, then two, then none. She looks tearful.

James pats her arm and gives her three purple bears.

Nursery 2

Lewis is waiting for Mason. He is tracing the shape of all the big numbers on the wall with his finger. Olga, Ayaan and then Mason all join in. They talk about the best place to start each number.

Mason, Lewis and Ethan put on waterproofs and go out to the water play area.

They pour water down a hollowed-out tree trunk, catch it at the bottom and then pour it into the guttering pipes.

Lewis goes and finds some toy boats. They sail them down the tree trunk and laugh.

The guttering comes out of its fitting. Mason replaces it.

They fill the big buckets using a hosepipe.

Ethan fetches a tea set. They transfer water between buckets using the jug, saucer and sugar bowl. Lewis says, 'This saucer's no good. It doesn't hold enough'.

Mason gets a big paint brush and starts splashing water at Mia. Ms H tells him to splash it at the big plants because they want a drink.

Mason and Lewis tip the water from the bucket into the watering can and water the plants.

Reflective question

What do you particularly notice about the two approaches? Do you think that the children are learning in both?

The psychology of early learning

Cognitive development is enhanced when children are at ease, positively engaged and receiving appropriate information in a manner they can process and understand. They remember best if the task and context are meaningful and if they have had time to think and ask questions (Roediger & Pyc, 2012). Play successfully garners and utilises natural interest and cognitive capabilities, allowing a breath of learning to take place. Furthermore, play leads to substantial and sustained improvements in attention, with instances of ADHD being markedly lower amongst children who did not start formal schooling until age 6 (Gokce & Yazgan, 2017).

Formal learning, on the other hand, particularly for the under-5s, frequently requires skills and behaviours beyond the child's natural capabilities (Hampton Wray et al., 2017). It may emphasise areas children have no interest or investment in and will therefore fail to engage the learners (Whitebread, 2012). Additionally, whilst instructional activities serve to teach clear-cut and specific skills or concepts, play helps to develop the cognitive architecture and a greater breadth of cognitive abilities.

When play activities include an element of adult guidance and support, additional sociocultural aspects are introduced which help boost children's understanding and internalising of social norms (Hirsh-Pasek, Golinkoff, Berk & Singer, 2009). During the preschool period, play, particularly play with supportive adults, would therefore appear to be strongly associated with the skills and abilities that ultimately lead to academic success.

FINAL REFLECTION

In this chapter, we have addressed two major questions: whether play promotes development, and whether the current forms of play available within UK education are beneficial to all young children. The evidence presented suggests that play encourages positive social and emotional development, including strong childhood relationships and resilience. There is also some evidence to support the assertion that play benefits children's cognitive structures, particularly in the development of abstract thought and symbolic systems such as language and gestures. Whilst some academics have questioned the robustness of historic studies into play, recent research has been both rigorous and of good quality. There would therefore appear to be an increasing body of evidence demonstrating that play benefits children's holistic development. We therefore conclude that children may profit from increasing interactive play within the early years curriculum. This is considered further in Chapter 9.

KEY POINTS

....

- Biological development and changes in play behaviours run parallel to one another. It appears plausible that they are mutually enriching.

- The link between play and development is complex and multi-faceted.
- Play with a supportive and more knowledgeable 'other' helps maximise the benefits of play.
- Pretend play helps children to develop their understanding of (and subsequently their ability to participate in) social situations.
- Although there is no clear causal link, play would appear to be associated with developments in memory and in cognitive processing.

QUESTIONS TO CONSIDER

1 Thinking about the time when you were a child, can you think of ways in which your parents, siblings, relatives or teachers helped scaffold your play? Using one or two examples, and with information in this chapter, in what ways do you think the play helped you and might help other young children develop?

2 Infographics are graphic visual representations of information, data or knowledge intended to present information quickly and clearly. They are quick and easy to do and all you need is paper and a pen. Have a go at designing a poster to promote play to parents using only the information in this chapter: what key information would you provide, what do parents need to know, and how might they use the information effectively with their own child?

3 Using the information above about the major theoretical approaches to play and cognitive development, consider how you might design and measure development during a play-based scenario that you have created. How would you go about this, what imaginary scenarios do you think would work best, how would you encourage children to use verbal communication, creative thinking, imagination and problem solving, and how would you know if your scenario has worked?

4 Now that you have read about resilience in the early years, think about the contexts in which children find themselves. How do you think play may differ and in what ways do you think the development of the child might be impacted by different environmental or individual factors? Have a go at listing answers to these questions for the following contexts:

   i   A child with a low to moderately severe developmental disorder such as autism
   ii   An only child or a child within a single-parent household
   iii A child with a chronic health condition.

FURTHER READING

Hirsh-Pasek, K., Golinkoff, R.M., Berk, L.E., & Singer, D.G. (2009) *A Mandate for Playful Learning in Preschool: Presenting the Evidence.* Oxford: Oxford University Press. (A brief but passionate and highly informative consideration of the relationship between play and cognitive development.)

Sciaraffa, M.A., Zeanah, P.D., & Zeanah, C.H. (2018) Understanding and promoting resilience in the context of adverse childhood experiences. *Early Childhood Education Journal*, 46(3), 343–353. (A wide-reaching consideration of how adults working in the early years can help children to build resilience. The importance of play is particularly highlighted here.)

Suzanne Zeedyk provides useful insights into early childhood development. Her website contains a wealth of information and can be found at www.suzannezeedyk.com.

REFERENCES

Alvarez, V.A., & Sabatini, B.L. (2007) Anatomical and physiological plasticity of dendritic spines. *Annual Review of Neuroscience*, 30, 79–97.

Baddeley, A.D., Eysenck, M.W., & Anderson, M.C. (2015) *Memory*, 2nd edition. London: Psychology Press.

Bartlett, T. (2011) The case for play. *Chronicle of Higher Education*, 57(25), B6–B9.

Bergen, D. (2002) The role of pretend play in children's cognitive development. *Early Childhood Research and Practice*, 4(1), 1–6.

Bretherton, L., & Bates, E. (1984) The development of representation from 10 to 28 months: Differential stability of language and symbolic play. In R.N. Emde & R.J. Harmon (eds) *Continuities and Discontinuities in Development*. New York: Plenum.

Broadhead, P. (2009) Conflict resolution and children's behaviour: Observing and understanding social and cooperative play in early years educational settings. *Early Years*, 29(2), 105–118.

Brock, A., Dodds, S., Jarvis, P., & Olusoga, Y. (2009) *Perspectives on Play: Learning for Life*. Harlow: Pearson.

Bruner, J.S. (1961) The act of discovery. *Harvard Educational Review*, 31, 21–32.

Bruner, J. (1983) Play, thought and language. *Peabody Journal of Education*, 60(3), 60–69.

Bussey, K., & Bandura, A. (1999) Social cognitive theory of gender development and differentiation. *Psychological Review*, 103(4), 676–713.

Cheng, M.-F., & Johnson, J.E. (2010) Research on children's play: Analysis of developmental and early education journals from 2005 to 2007. *Early Childhood Education Journal*, 37, 249–259.

DfE (2014) *The National Curriculum in England Key Stages 1 and 2 Framework Document*. London: DfE

DfE (2017) *The Early Years Foundation Stage*. London: DfE.

Department of Education and Science (DES) (1967) *The Plowden Report: Children and their Primary Schools*. Available at: www.educationengland.org.uk/documents/plowden/plowden1967–1.html (accessed 5 May 2020).

Diachenko, O.M. (2010) On major developments in preschoolers' imagination. *International Journal of Early Years Education*, 19(1), 19–25.

Dickinson, D.K., & Moreton, J. (1991) Predicting specific kindergarten literacy skills from three-year-olds preschool experiences. Paper presented at the biennial meeting of the Society for Research in Child Development, Seattle, WA, April.

Elias, C.L., & Berk, L.E. (2002) Self-regulation in young children: Is there a role for sociodramatic play? *Early Childhood Research Quarterly*, 17(2), 216–238.

Foerde, K., & Shohamy, D. (2011) The role of the basal ganglia in learning and memory: Insight from Parkinson's disease. *Neurobiology of Learning and Memory*, 96(4), 624–636.

Galyer, K.T., & Evans, I.M. (2001) Pretend play and the development of emotion regulation in preschool children. *Early Child Development and Care*, 166(1), 93–108.

Gillard, D. (2011) *Education in England: A Brief History*. Available at: www.educationengland.org.uk/history.

Gokce, S., & Yazgan, Y. (2017) Association between age of beginning primary school and attention deficit hyperactivity disorder. *Journal of Developmental and Behavioural Pediatrics*, 38(1), 12–19.

Golinkoff, R.M., Hirsh-Pasek, K., Bloom, L., Smith, L.B., Woodward, A.L., Akhtar, N., Tomasello, M., & Hollich, G. (2000) *Becoming a Word Learner: A Debate on Lexical Acquisition*. Oxford: Oxford University Press.

Groos, K. (1898) Author's preface. In *The Play of Animals* (trans. E.L. Baldwin). New York: Appleton.

Hampton Wray, A., Stevens, C., Pakulak, E., Isbell, E., Bell, T., & Neville, H. (2017) Development of selective attention in preschool-age children from lower socioeconomic status backgrounds. *Developmental Cognitive Neuroscience*, 26, 101–111.

Hirsh-Pasek, K., Golinkoff, R.M., Berk, L.E., & Singer, D.G. (2009) *A Mandate for Playful Learning in Preschool: Presenting the Evidence*. Oxford: Oxford University Press.

Holmes, R.M., Romeo, L., Ciraola, S., & Grushko, M. (2015) The relationship between creativity, social play, and children's language abilities. *Early Child Development and Care*, 185(7), 1180–1197.

Kelly, R., & Hammond, S. (2011) The relationship between symbolic play and executive function in young children. *Australian Journal of Early Childhood*, 36(2), 21–27.

Leisman, G., Braun-Benjamin, O., & Melillo, R. (2014) Cognitive-motor interactions of the basal ganglia in development. *Frontiers in Systems Neuroscience*, 8, 16.

Lester, S., & Russell, W. (2008) *Play for a Change: Play, Policy and Practice – A Review of Contemporary Perspectives*. London: National Children's Bureau.

Lillard, A.S. (2012) Pretend play and cognitive development. In U. Goswami (ed.) *Blackwell Handbook of Child Development*. Oxford: Blackwell.

Lillard, A.S. (2017) Why do the children (pretend) play? *Trends in Cognitive Sciences*, 21(11), 826–834.

Lillard, A.S., Lerner, M.D., Hopkins, E.J., Dore, R.A., Smith, E.D., & Palmquist, C.M. (2013) The impact of pretend play on children's development: A review of the evidence. *Psychological Bulletin*, 139(1), 1–34.

Moyles, J. (2015) *The Excellence of Play*, 4th edition. Maidenhead: Open University Press.

Muller, U., & Carpendale, J.I.M. (2004) From joint activity to joint attention: A relational approach to social development in infancy. In J.I.M. Carpendale & U. Muller (eds) *Social Interaction and the Development of Knowledge*. New York & Hove: Psychology Press.

Nath, S., & Szucs, D. (2014) Construction play and cognitive skills associated with the development of mathematical abilities in 7-year-old children. *Learning and Instruction*, 32, 73–81.

Nicolopoulou, A., Barbosa, A., Ilgaz, H., & Brockmeyer, C. (2010) Using the transformative power of play to educate hearts and minds: From Vygotsky to Vivian Paley and beyond. *Mind, Culture and Activity*, 17, 42–58.

Orr, E., & Geva, R. (2015) Symbolic play and language development. *Infant Behaviour and Development*, 38, 15–22.

Pellegrini, A.D. (1980) The relationship between kindergarteners' play and achievement in prereading, language and writing. *Psychology in the Schools*, 17(4), 530–535.

Pellegrini, A.D., & Galda, L. (1990) Children's play, language, and early literacy. *Topics in Language Disorders*, 10(3), 76–88.

Piaget, J. (1945) *Play, Dreams and Imitation in Childhood*. London: Heinemann.

Raznahan, A., Greenstein, D., Lee, N.R., Clasen, L.S., & Giedd, J.N. (2012) Prenatal growth in humans and postnatal brain maturation into late adolescence. *Proceedings of the National Academy of Sciences of the United States of America*, 109(28), 11366–11371.

Roediger, H.L., & Pyc, M.A. (2012) Inexpensive techniques to improve education: Applying cognitive psychology to enhance educational practice. *Journal of Applied Research in Memory and Cognition*, 1, 242–248.

Rogers, S., & Evans, J. (2008) *Inside Role-Play in Early Childhood Education*. Oxon: Routledge.

Rogers, S., & Lapping, C. (2012) Recontextualising 'play' in early years pedagogy: Competence, performance and excess in policy and practice. *British Journal of Educational Studies*, 60(3), 243–260.

Russ, S.W. (2003) Play and creativity: Developmental issues. *Scandinavian Journal of Educational Research*, 47(3), 291–303.

Sciaraffa, M.A., Zeanah, P.D., & Zeanah, C.H. (2018) Understanding and promoting resilience in the context of adverse childhood experiences. *Early Childhood Education Journal*, 46(3), 343–353.

Singer, J.L., & Singer, D.G. (2006) Pre-schoolers' imaginative play as a precursor of narrative consciousness. *Imagination, Cognition and Personality*, 25(2), 97–117.

Smith, E.E. (1978) Theories of semantic memory. In W.K. Estes (ed.) *Handbook of Learning and Cognitive Processes*, Vol. 6. Potomac, MD: Erlbaum, pp. 1–56.

Soto, F.A., Waldschmidt, J.G., Helie, S., & Ashby, F.G. (2013) Brain activity across the development of automatic categorization: A comparison of categorization tasks using multi-voxel pattern analysis. *Neuroimaging*, 71, 284–297.

Squire, R.F., Noudoost, B., Schafer, R.J., & Moore, T. (2013) Prefrontal contributions to visual selective attention. *Annual Review of Neuroscience*, 36, 451–466.

Stirrup, J., Evans, J., & Davies, B. (2017) Early years learning, play pedagogy and social class. *British Journal of Sociology of Education*, 38(6), 872–886.

Stone, S.J., & Stone, B.A. (2015) Play and early literacy: An analysis of kindergarten children's scaffolding during symbolic play transformations. *The International Journal of Holistic Early Learning and Development*, 2, 3–16.

Sutherland, S.L., & Friedman, O. (2013) Just pretending can be really learning: Children use pretend as a source for acquiring generic knowledge. *Developmental Psychology*, 49(9), 1660–1668.

Swingler, M.M., Perry, N.B., & Calkins, S.D. (2015) Neural plasticity and the development of attention: Intrinsic and extrinsic influences. *Development and Psychopathology*, 27, 443–457.

Tamis-LeMonda, C.S., & Bornstein, M.H. (1991) Individual variation, correspondence, stability and change in mother and toddler play. *Infant Behaviour and Development*, 14(2), 143–162.

Ullman, H., Almeida, R., & Klingberg, T. (2014) Structural maturation and brain activity predict future working memory capacity during childhood development. *The Journal of Neuroscience*, 34(5), 1592–1598.

Uren, N., & Stagnitti, K. (2009) Pretend play, social competence and involvement in children aged 5–7 years: The concurrent validity of the child-initiated pretend play assessment. *Australian Occupational Therapy Journal*, 56, 33–40.

Vygotsky, L.S. (1962) *Thought and Language*. Cambridge, MA: MIT Press.

Vygotsky, L.S. (1967) Play and its role in the mental development of the child. *Soviet Psychology*, 5(3), 6–18.

Vygotsky, L.S. (1978) *Mind in Society: The Development of Higher Psychological Processes*. Cambridge, MA: Harvard University Press.

Wang, Z., Kwok, R., Wong, S., Wong, P., Chuen Ho, F., & Pui Wah Cheng, D. (2017) Play and theory of mind in early childhood: A Hong Kong perspective. *Early Child Development and Care*, 187(9), 1389–1402.

Weisberg, D.S., Hirsh-Pasek, K., & Golinkoff, R.M. (2013) Guided play: Where curricular goals meet a playful pedagogy. *Mind, Brain and Education*, 7(2), 104–112.

Whitebread, D. (2012) *Developmental Psychology and Early Childhood Education*. London: Sage.

Whitebread, D., Basilio, M., Kuvalja, M., & Verma, M. (2012) *The Importance of Play: A Report on the Value of Children's Play with a Series of Policy Recommendations*. Brussels: Toy Industries of Europe.

Wood, E., & Attfield, J. (1996) *Play, Learning and the Early Childhood Curriculum*, London: Sage.

Wood, E., & Attfield, J. (2005) *Play, Learning and the Early Childhood Curriculum*, 2nd edition. London: Sage.

Xu, Y. (2010) Children's social play sequence: Parten's classic theory revisited. *Early Child Development and Care*, 180(4), 489–498.

Yogman, M., Garner, A., Hutchinson, J., Hirsh-Pasek, K., & Golinkoff, R.M. (2018) The power of play: A pediatric role in enhancing development in young children. *Pediatrics*, 142(3), e20182058.

3

UNDERSTANDING CHILDREN'S PLAY BEHAVIOURS

Jenny Boldrin

CONTENTS

This chapter introduces you to some of the ways in which we can observe, interpret and support children's play behaviours. We will consider how a recognition and an understanding of children's common play behaviours, such as schematic patterns, play cycles and play preferences, can shape our responses to children and build further opportunities for development.

 THIS CHAPTER WILL...

- Introduce you to schema theory and the play cycle as methods of understanding the play behaviours you might see in young children
- Explore how you can use an understanding of play behaviours to shape your responses to children
- Consider how you can see children's play differently
- Explore tensions between children's play behaviours and current educational policy
- Critically consider the contested nature of quality within early childhood education.

KEY TERMS

cognitive constructivism, pedagogy, play cues, play cycles, play frames, quality, schemas

INTRODUCTION

According to early childhood pioneer Susan Isaacs:

> By patient listening to the talk of even little children, and watching what they do, with the one purpose of understanding them, we can imaginatively feel their fears and angers, their bewilderments and triumphs; we can wish their wishes, see their pictures and think their thoughts. (Isaacs, 1929: 15)

Isaac's reflections encompass the principle underpinning this chapter. To understand children's many and varied play behaviours is to endeavour to become more attuned to their worlds and thus build a truly child-centred pedagogy. By refocusing our attention on the close observation of children's play behaviours, we aim to bring the child back to the centre of our pedagogical thinking. Throughout this chapter, we aim to critically discuss **schema theory** and the **play cycle** as ways in which we can observe, interpret and respond to children's play. We will also consider the relationship between the pedagogy of child-centred play and current policy and practice.

Before we begin…

Let us begin by outlining some definitions to support your navigation of this chapter. We will be predominantly exploring schemas and play cycles as behaviours we may observe in babies and young children. An understanding of such behaviours can support our work with children and enable us to become more closely attuned to them:

> Schema: In the context of this chapter, a schema is a repeated pattern of play or behaviour. As we will go on to explore, this may be expressed in a number of ways, for example through physical action, language or thought. Schemas are thought to allow children to make sense of their world through active exploration, building on existing ideas and adding new meaning. For example, a child exhibiting a rotation schema will use repeated experiences connected with this fascination to build on their knowledge of the concept of rotation, wheels, balls, cogs, properties of shape, and so on. By acknowledging and facilitating children's schemas, we can therefore support their continuous drive to make meaning in the world. This chapter provides some insights into schemas as well as practical considerations for observing and responding to them.

> Play cycle: The play cycle was first introduced by Sturrock and Else in 1998 within the professional sphere of play work. It is based on developing a conceptual understanding of play as a process. Acknowledging the stages of the play cycle requires professionals to interpret action within play in a more considered and reflective way. For example, how do we know a child with limited verbal communication skills wants to initiate play? Throughout this chapter, we will consider the theory of the play cycle and reflect on ways we can utilise this understanding to support developments in our practice.

OBSERVABLE PLAY BEHAVIOURS

Schemas

Schemas represent possibly the most commonly understood play behaviour we will explore in this chapter. Piaget is widely reported to be the first to identify the role of schemas within children's development. As a **cognitive constructivist**, Piaget (1962) proposed that children adapt their thinking to their immediate environment, using an innate need to make sense of the world as a biological motivation to construct meaning from experience (Arnold, 2018). Piaget alluded to the systematic nature of children's learning, with the young brain assimilating meaning and accommodating the unexpected through ordered patterns of action within play (otherwise known as schemas), with repetition being key to building on existing understanding to construct and secure new meaning (Louis et al., 2008). For example, a baby experiencing an early trajectory schema may drop an item from their highchair repeatedly in an endeavour to construct an understanding of linear movement.

Understanding schemas within play requires the practitioner to become conceptually attuned to children, not simply to observe what children are doing but also to make a leap and analyse what they may be thinking (Atherton & Nutbrown, 2013). Through close observation of children's fascinations in this way, the practitioner can facilitate the child's own articulation of their understanding and promote further opportunities for assimilation. Responding to children's strong exploratory impulses also requires a skilled appreciation of how environments can be shaped by practitioners to allow for a rounded engagement with schemas through play. Nutbrown (2006) has been particularly influential within this thinking. Her work linking the use of books to enable children to explore concepts such as journeys, connection and separation, is a powerful reminder of the flexibility and adaptability of resources.

Ten commonly observed schemas

It is worth noting here that children's presentation of schematic behaviours will be unique to the individual, depending on their interests and dispositions. Table 3.1 provides an overview of what you *may* see within children's play; however, this should not be considered an exhaustive list. It is also worth noting that whilst many children will exhibit a strong propensity for one schema, many will show a combination of two or more, showing milder signs.

Despite our efforts to label and outline schemas and their features, as we have above, observing schematic behaviours is not simple. As children grow, so do their schemas, becoming more sophisticated and complex in the way they are exhibited. Our ever-evolving understanding of patterns within children's play behaviours must shape our pedagogy and, as such, professionals working with young children must adopt a reflective and reflexive approach to teaching and learning, a subject further explored later within this chapter. By acknowledging and responding to the strong exploratory drives of children, we promote deep-level learning and higher-order thinking within play (Laevers, 2000).

Since Piaget's (1962) early work schemas have been widely researched – most extensively by Chris Athey through the Froebel Early Education Project (1973–78) and

Table 3.1 An overview of children's schematic behaviours

Schema	A fascination with...	You may observe...	Consider
Trajectory	Lines and linear formations	Children lining up toys and materials through their play; Drawing lines or linear structures on pictures; Using construction materials to create linear structures; An interest in linear patterns within nature or the environment, e.g. train lines.	This is considered one of the first schemas babies may exhibit, largely as a result of their own physical experience of trajectories, for example being pushed in a buggy or being elevated into a highchair. As babies track objects visually, they are beginning one of their first journeys into the trajectory schema.
Rotation	Spinning	Children physically spinning their bodies; An interest in objects that spin such as wheels and spinning tops; Parents feeding back that their children enjoy watching the washing machine!	Children who are fascinated with rotation will often enjoy the process of engineering: cogs turning, using screwdrivers, exploring the mechanics of how things work, etc.
Transporting	Moving objects from one place to another	Children using bags, buckets, pushchairs, wheelbarrows and other equipment to transport objects around their environment.	Again, this may be thought of as a schema which emerges early, born from experiences of being transported themselves prior to more physical independence emerging.
Enveloping	Covering things over, including themselves	A fascination with being physically enveloped themselves, through wearing dressing-up clothes or covering themselves up with fabric; Covering over objects or enveloping artwork by painting over it.	Have you ever considered that children who envelop themselves or objects are processing a need to understand a future sibling's arrival? After all, our first experience of enveloping is in the womb.
Enclosure	Creating boundaries	Children creating borders for their artwork; Barriers and borders being used through play, e.g. creating fences around animal structures; Creating clear physical spaces for play, using objects or furniture.	Consider how you might provide loose materials for enclosing small-world play or allow children to create frames for their artwork. The pictures we see at home are often in frames, so let's help children make connections by allowing for schematic fascinations to be fulfilled.

(Continued)

Table 3.1 (Continued)

Schema	A fascination with...	You may observe...	Consider
Connecting	Joining items together	An interest in construction materials or the process of constructing; Children joining materials together in a range of ways, using materials such as sticky tape, or simply with their hands.	When children experience disconnection in their life, we might potentially see a developing need to connect materialistically. (See Jessica's story in case study 3.1 for further thoughts on this.)
Transforming	The capacity for change	A fascination with the transformative power of materials, e.g. mixing paint or baking; Children mixing materials in their free play, e.g. sand and water.	To what extent do we allow children to transform? For example, children will gain as much from being a part of the process of making play dough as they will from exploring the final product.
Separation/ Scattering	Objects and materials disconnecting	Children spreading toys or emptying boxes without necessarily following up by *playing* with the contents; An interest in objects or play involving an outwards trajectory, e.g. scattering seeds, watering flowers, blowing bubbles.	This schema has the potential to be a messy one! Channelling children's fascination will be important – ways to scatter through play can be facilitated to support children to work through their interests.
Orientation	The way they are positioned in the world or the way the world can be viewed	Children experimenting with their own physical positions, e.g. lying on the floor or hanging upside down; An interest in toys which alter the way the world is seen, for example binoculars, a telescope or a kaleidoscope.	Provide opportunities for children to play at different levels and consider how flexible you are with children in the way they position themselves, for example lying on the floor to listen to a story.
Positioning	Arranging and ordering objects and materials	Children ordering objects or materials, e.g. lining them up or creating patterns; A desire to have toys or objects ordered or organised in a certain way; An interest in sequences.	This is a schema which has the potential to last into adulthood – how many of us arrange our cupboards in a certain way or colour-code our wardrobes?

through the fundamental work of early years experts such as Cath Arnold, Tina Bruce and Cathy Nutbrown, who have written extensively on the subject – developments in our understanding of schemas have thus evolved and, by no means exclusively, include extensions such as:

- An appreciation that schemas can and will be exhibited in different ways (Athey, 2007):
  - statically (through shape or objects)
  - dynamically (through movement);
- Building on Piaget's stage model, schematic play may be observed evolving through stages (Athey, 2007), including:
  - sensori-motor – through actions
  - symbolic representation – one thing standing for another
  - functional dependence – the relationship between action and effect
  - thought – recalling and representing ideas and events;
- Symbolic representation may then present in different ways, through:
  - graphic representation – as observed through visual mediums such as artwork
  - speech representation – as observed through speech
  - action representation – as observed through movement (Athey, 1990, cited in Arnold, 2007);
- The link between schemas and other areas of learning and development such as literacy (Brierley, 2018), maths, language and reading (Nutbrown, 2006).

 SPECIAL STUDY: CHRIS ATHEY (1924–2011)

The name Chris Athey has become synonymous with the development of schemas as an intrinsic part of our understanding of how children learn. Following many years teaching in challenging areas, Athey was invited to teach at Ibstock Place, the demonstration school connected to the Froebel Educational Institute at Roehampton. Athey was then supported to undertake the Froebel Trainers' Diploma by principal Molly Brearley and joined the college lecturing staff (Scott, de Keller & Bruce, 2011).

It was from here that, prompted by the findings of the Plowden Report (DES, 1967), Athey took the lead of the Froebel Education Project (1973–78), the findings of which she recorded and published in her seminal work *Extending Thought in Young Children* (1990).

The project was considered unique for two reasons:

- It specifically focused on observations of 2–5-year-olds, a group which was largely ignored by cognitive research at the time.
- It included children and families from two distinct sociocultural groups. Athey had found that prior research had largely centred on the experiences of more affluent children and families, and so was driven to explore the sociocultural influences of differing economic contexts.

Amongst the projects aims were predominantly a desire to:

- Explore the cognitive patterns and processes underpinning children's actions and experiences, documenting the journey from spontaneous sensorimotor movement to thought.
- Explore the impact of collaboration between parents and professionals, with an emphasis on communities of differing socio-economic status.

Athey argued against a deficit approach to our view of children, with a focus on what children can do. As discussed, parents were a central component of her work and she found that they had a profound influence when encouraged to participate in children's learning. Through Athey's further exploration of schemas as a means by which children build cognitive structures, she noticed that children develop understanding from their home and environment by building on existing knowledge. She encouraged adults to view the patterns in children's play and, instead of seeing actions as arbitrary and in isolation, suggested that perception can be altered by asking what these actions have in common (Arnold, 2007).

Schema theory was extended and developed as Athey further exemplified the ways schemas can develop, as discussed earlier in this chapter.

Athey passed away in 2011 but her legacy remains as a current and constant reminder that the child is a complex and unique learner to be placed firmly at the centre of pedagogical thinking.

Schemas and emotions

Within this chapter, we have previously identified schemas as patterns of thought, representative of children's ideas and experiences. As such, it is therefore also important that we consider the social and emotional nature of schematic expression. Researchers such as Athey (2007), Shaw (1991, cited in Arnold, 2010) and Arnold (2010) have explored the social and emotional dimension of schematic play, with Shaw specifically alluding to the role of schemas as a 'symbolic vehicle' for children's emotional expression. Shaw goes on to assert that the child is not consciously aware of the schema, rather that it forms a fundamental component of the unconscious mind. This allows us to consider the genesis of thought itself, as being created and sustained in context. According to Cole (1996: 136, quoted in McVee, Dunsmore & Gavelek, 2005), cognition cannot therefore be viewed in isolation but, instead, must be considered as a 'bio-social-cultural process' (see Chapters 1 and 2).

Recent research has seen a growing recognition of the potential development of schemas which may be exhibited as a result of children's negative early life experiences. After all, if patterns of thought and symbolic representation are influenced by experiences and environment, we must undoubtedly acknowledge that those children whose early life has been dominated by feelings and experiences of neglect and abuse may develop schemas related to feelings of fear, abandonment and mistrust (González, Florida, Wheeler & Daire, 2017). According to Lili and Lillard (2017), play behaviours are first gained from early attachments and the experience of serve-and-return interactions with parents. This understanding has led to an acknowledgment of early maladaptive schemas and given way to a rise in schema therapy.

 CASE STUDY 3.1

Jessica is 18 months old and lives with her adoptive parents. She transitioned to her *forever* family at 11 months old, having lived with a foster family from 6 weeks old. As a foster child, she had regular contact visits with her birth parents which came to an end once she was adopted. Jessica displays strong connection and separation schemas through her play. She is observed peeling labels off toys, connecting and disconnecting construction materials, and repeatedly emptying baskets and bags in order to scatter toys. Jessica is adept at fastenings and shows a strong interest in poppers and zips, using them as a means to separate herself physically from her clothes.

Reflective question

Do you feel Jessica's experiences of transition and regular connection and disconnection within her life have led her to develop her schematic behaviours? Is she using play as a means to work through her experiences to date and process her feelings? How can Jessica's adoptive parents best support her at this time?

Limitations

Schema theory has become a resilient staple of early childhood pedagogy and is widely acknowledged as a useful means by which to interpret and support children's learning. However, we must also take time to consider its potential limitations.

As previously discussed in this chapter, modern schema theory is often based on, and rooted in, the work of Piaget, who theorised that children's active and self-driven engagement with their immediate environment leads to cognitive assimilation and therefore new understanding. Criticism of Piaget's early theory predominantly derives from its lack of acknowledgement of the social nature of children's early experiences. Much is given to the systematic and structured nature of cognitive process without consideration of the role of the adult or peer within the learning and development process. Theorists such as Bruner became frustrated with the representation of the mind as being 'self-contained' and 'computational', with an apparent disregard for the cultural nature of meaning making (Shanker & Bakhurst, 2001). In its simplest form, we might argue that schema theory reduces children's play to a series of systematic cognitive actions, woven together to construct ideas, with not enough emphasis given to the relationship between the child and the sociocultural situation in which they exist – what we might call their situatedness.

McVee, Dunsmore and Gavelek (2005) argue that the problem may lie in the way schemas are understood and interpreted. They suggest that it is clear that individuals engage in repeated patterns in order to construct cognitive meaning. However, what is also clear is that these engagements are culturally mediated, or, to put it another way, are interwoven with the environment the child is situated in. We therefore cannot dismiss cultural and societal influences from our understanding of schemas as a means of observing behaviour. Early, but not widely recognised, proposers of schema theory such as Bartlett (1932, cited in McVee, Dunsmore & Gavalek, 2005) acknowledged the transactional nature of schemas with cultural experiences, a fact which must work in partnership with independent cognitive process. We touched on this when discussing the suggested link between schema and emotion earlier in the chapter. This is perhaps a good example of a model enabling practitioners to look beyond merely the action being observed and to take the imaginative leap required to consider alternatives – to not stick rigidly to a formulaic representation of theory, but to recognise and celebrate the unique, messy and often chaotic nature of any child development theory.

 TIME TO CONSIDER

- Do you feel that using an understanding of schema theory might support your facilitation of children's play?
- Do you find schema theory persuasive or do you feel it is too simplistic and limited?
- Do you feel adults *should* be interpreting children's play behaviours?

THE PLAY CYCLE

In 1998, Sturrock and Else presented their paper 'The playground as therapeutic space: Playwork as healing', otherwise known as the 'Colorado paper'. Sturrock and Else used their paper to introduce the theoretical concept of the play cycle within the discipline of playwork, a concept which now underpins the principles of the profession.

The play cycle itself outlines six distinct stages which play follows as a child searches for playful engagement within their immediate environment. According to Sturrock and Else (1998: 4), this conceptual understanding of play rests on the suggestion that 'prior to each act of creativity of the child lies an imaginal realm or zone that is playful (ludic) and symbolically constituted', ludic referring to what might be seen as spontaneous or undirected playfulness (King & Temple, 2018). As such, play can originate or exist on both a conscious and subconscious level. To understand and accept the play cycle (see Figure 3.1) requires professionals to attune to the child and work towards a symbolic understanding of play. As with schemas, the heart of this

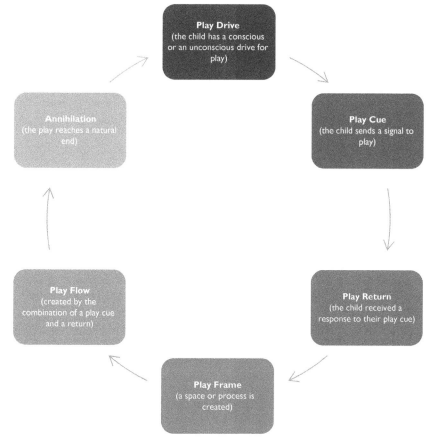

Figure 3.1   An example of a play cycle

Source: adapted from Sturrock and Else (1998)

concept is the ludic context which underpins the action, a full acceptance that play is a process rather than an outcome, and a desire to preserve the true meaning of each playful encounter.

Implications for the play cycle within early years education and care

In 2019, King and Newstead conducted research with childcare workers to explore their understanding of the play cycle and consider the transferrable nature of the approach between professions. Amongst their conclusions were that a greater under-standing of the play cycle was needed amongst childcare professionals, and that there was, at times, a tension in participants' perception of both the purpose of play and their role within it. Within playwork, the outcome of play is considered of second-ary importance to the process of play itself. King and Newstead (2019) assert that the prevailing discourse connecting play and learning within the early years could lead professionals to dismiss the importance of play for play's sake, favouring the notion of an outcomes-based approach. Sturrock and Else (1998: 4) originally referred to this as professionals 'polluting the ludic', allowing our drive to educate to muddy the waters of children's play drive. Should we therefore be cautious within early years about the coupling of play with learning? Does it place play at the mercy of becom-ing a tool for social control, a means by which to monitor and regulate experiences, perhaps losing the essence of what makes play so valuable? (Gibbons, 2007).

Later within this chapter, we go on to consider a broader exploration of the ten-sions between educational policy and our ability and preparedness to respond to play behaviours within practice.

 TIME TO CONSIDER

Take time to use Table 3.2 to navigate through some reflective considerations for each stage of Sturrock and Else's (1998) play cycle. What implications can you see for your professional practice?

Table 3.2 An overview of play cycle stages

Play cycle stage	Description	Reflections and considerations
Play drive	The unconscious or conscious thought and impulse which drive play	Sturrock and Else (1998) claim that professionals attuned to children through the play cycle are often engaged with children on a deeper level of unconscious thought and are there when they emerge to conscious action. What is required to reach this level of connectiveness with children?

Play cue	The signal to play, whether verbal or nonverbal; this might be seen through gestures, facial expressions, changes in behaviour or verbal expressions	How can practitioners use an understanding of play cues to shape their response to children? How might a play cue be misinterpreted as inappropriate behaviour that is disciplined? See Jakub's story in case study 3.2.
Play return	The response to the play cue: from another child, an adult, the environment or from themselves within solitary play	We can perhaps trace the notion of the play return back to our understanding of early attachments being formed with primary caregivers. The child throws out a serve (eye contact, a gesture, verbal communication, etc.) with the aim of it being met with a response from an attuned adult, thus reinforcing and validating the child's attempts at early communication and relationship building.
Play frame	The environment or situation which the play exists within, whether it be physical boundaries, rules, narrative or themes	How often do you feel the play frames children create are adulterated for adult purposes? What role could the adult play within the play frame? Within playwork, there is often a necessity for the adult to support the child to both physically and emotionally contain their play. Practitioners might consider the need to support children's play frames to be maintained for the child to fulfil their play cycle.
Play flow	The continuous 'flow' of play created by cues and returns	This will be unique for each play scenario; it could be as simple as turns in a turn-taking game, or narrative contributions to role play. It calls for a reflexive understanding of pedagogy to be embedded within environments.
Annihilation	The natural or destructive end to play	How often do practitioners force the annihilation of play? Is play always stopped for the right reasons? What impact could it potentially have when play is ended prematurely?

 CASE STUDY 3.2

Jakub is 4 years old and he and his parents have recently moved to England from Poland. Jakub has just started in Reception at his local primary school and he has very little English. Jakub is an only child and has not attended an early years setting previously. His mother used to take him to a local playgroup in Poland but he has not been for several months. Jakub's teacher begins to notice him pushing other children, mostly boys. The instances appear unprompted and without malice or aggression. His parents report no problem of him pushing in the home.

Reflective questions

Pause and reflect on the play cycle ... What do you think is prompting Jakub's behaviour?

Jakub's teacher begins to observe him regularly, noting down the times he is pushing and what precedes the action. It is noted that Jakub regularly approaches the same child and pushes during free play opportunities, particularly when the child is playing with the football outside:

- Do you think Jakub's language barrier is preventing him from forming a socially appropriate **play cue**?
- Could he be pushing as an attempt at gaining the attention of the other child to initiate a play return and enter into a **play frame**?
- How could his teacher support him to be successful in his play cues in future?
- What other support might the child need within the play cycle? Consider the reflections in Table 3.2.
- How might Jakub's teacher have responded had she not stopped to critically reflect on and question what was leading to his behaviour?

Parry (2018) explores the many ways children use to initiate play when not able to verbalise their intentions, including standing close, offering help, copying actions or touching. In order to avoid a misunderstanding of behaviour, it is vital that practitioners practise an analytical approach to their support of play, having an understanding of the range of ways children use cues, both verbal and nonverbal, to initiate play interactions, recognising that the entry point of play may not be representative of a child's interests and exists merely on a continuum to be extended and further explored (Hedges, 2012). Jensen (2017: 283) asserts that professionals working with children need to be able to operate with 'relational competency, defined by the ability to "see" the individual on his or her own terms and adapt one's own behaviour accordingly'. Here, Jensen is acknowledging the essential skills necessary of the early years practitioner – the ability to attune to the child's behaviour and adapt to respond to individual needs, ensuring an understanding that not all play behaviour conforms to socially accepted norms.

PEDAGOGIES FOR PLAY: TENSIONS IN POLICY AND PRACTICE

So far throughout this chapter, we have discussed the nature of children's play behaviours and questioned the attitudes we, as professionals, hold towards the value of children's play. As a final consideration for this chapter, we will be exploring some critical questions within the pedagogy of play (see Chapter 9), with a particular focus on the discourse of power and quality within early childhood education and care.

As you read, take time to consider the following questions:

- What role do the dynamics of power play in early childhood provision? What impact does this have on the way we understand and interpret children's play?
- How do we measure quality and what is important for children?

Power and our view of the child

According to Dahlberg, Moss and Pence (2013), pedagogical practice is subjective, shaped by the individual, societal or cultural lens through which the child is seen. McNamee (2016) affirms this position, believing that the fundamental question of *'what* is a child?' will depend on *who* is looking at the child, making reference to the social and cultural context the child exists within. The changing view of the child is therefore fundamental in exploring the evolution of play as a pedagogical tool.

Earlier on in this chapter, we questioned whether, by closely linking play with learning, we usurp its true meaning and therefore devalue its purpose. Perhaps at the heart of this debate is a question of power, of whom the play belongs to and what purpose it holds. This has been a central component of our discussions so far – a call to question our own view of children at play and a reminder that, by tuning in to the child's innate intent, we can alter our responses and reflect on the state of play as we have come to understand it.

Wyness (2012) asserts that children's invisibility is a key feature of a dominant discourse, where institutions, and therefore adults, regulate their lives. Historical writing within early years will often trace back to Locke's notion of the empty vessel as an early example of this. Locke's view of the child created a clear example of a power dynamic where children represented a passive being, prepared, by adults, for an adult world. While undoubtedly perceptions of the child have evolved over time, issues surrounding the discourse of power arguably remain. McNamee (2016) asserts that children have always been judged on their output and contribution to adult-determined outcomes and success criteria. Can we perhaps consider that, where philosophies regarding *how* children learn and develop have evolved, whilst adults still control *what* children learn, we are still perpetuating power and a sense of adult ownership over children's lives? Children will perhaps always be judged by what we, as adults, regard as impressive (McNamee, 2016).

Standards, accountability and testing

According to Rogers (2011), pedagogy has become increasingly concerned with economic terms and the inclusion of standards, accountability and testing as key components to what has become commonplace pedagogical practice. As a result, the coupling of play as a teaching and learning tool becomes problematic, potentially resulting in it being highjacked from its core purpose for children's autonomous expression. Rogers believes that, as a result, there exists a tension between adult and child objectives, with play often being managed and staged to achieve certain outcomes. Dockett (2011) agrees and asserts that a challenge has arisen in the relationship between play and pedagogy, whereby play has become a vehicle for teaching as well as learning, arguably handing over the power to adults in what should be a child-initiated form of exploration.

Wood (2010: 11) explores the dynamics of power within play through a simple means of perspective:

- 'Outside in': Power is exercised from outside the play by the adult.
- 'Inside out': Control rests with the child inside the play space.

Kuschner (2012: 247) goes so far as to argue that 'once play is put into the service of achieving the academic goals of the curriculum, it is no longer play'.

Quality and early childhood education and care

Our final thought within this chapter will rest with the contested nature of quality within early childhood education. We arrive at this point as a concluding reminder that our role in working with children is layered and complex. As we debate the ways in which we can better attempt to *see* and respond to the child at play, we must also remember that professionals may often feel bound by the practice they feel obliged to demonstrate and value, regardless of how attuned they are to the children in their care.

Quality is a problematic concept for many reasons, largely because, as a concept, it is rooted in positionality and paradigm (Moss, 2019). By this we mean that there are many truths associated with a view of quality – what parents value as quality provision may well differ from professionals, which in turn may differ from policy makers or children themselves. It begs the question: whose truth is the most valuable?

According to Laevers (2005: 20), 'it is quite ambitious or even hazardous to try to define the criteria for good practice in a way that would find universal approval'; however, this is arguably what policy and curriculum strive for. Quality over time has become inextricably linked with good educational outcomes, with economically focused, often data-driven benchmarks dominating the discourse. The Department for Education (2013: 6) itself stated that 'more great childcare is vital to ensuring we can compete in the global race, by helping parents back to work and readying children for school and, eventually, employment'. There exists a clear tension between the government's data-driven view of quality and what is widely accepted as quality practice within the early years community. According to Lewis (2018), this has led to national policy drivers that are focused on performance data and competitiveness at the expense of young children's rights and educational experiences. As Athey (2007) suggested, very few people are able to combine contrasting pedagogies, and so we are left in an often messy reality of conflicting ideas.

Moss (2019) uses the analogy of storytelling to explore the discourse of quality and notions of truth. In his analogy, each discourse (or opinion) becomes a story, a way of thinking or talking about a subject. When discourse becomes dominant, 'fictional stories become non-fictional statements, presenting themselves as natural, unquestionable and inevitable' (2019: 5).

 SPOTLIGHT ON RESEARCH

Stirrup, J., Evans, J., & Davies, B. (2017) Learning one's place and position through play: Social class and educational opportunity in early years education. *International Journal of Early Years Education*, 25(4), 343–360.

Objective

The researchers aimed to explore how learning is structured and organised through play across three early childhood settings.

Method

The research involved ten months of ethnographic fieldwork, taking place across the three settings. The researchers gathered participant and non-participant observations, field notes and conversations with children and practitioners to gather data.

Across the settings, the researchers observed 80 children and 15 practitioners by spending one morning per week in each setting.

Data analysis

The researchers report that the data was initially analysed ethnographically to identify the categories and concepts within each setting. Second, a 'sociological frame of reference' was applied in order to ensure equity. Finally, the third layer explored transactions through case studies, and interactions between staff and children and between children. All transactions were contextualised in time and place.

Results

The research found that, in many cases, play which had a performative element and was rooted in academic achievement and discourse, was valued more. This was found to be influenced by expectations from the EYFS, the expectations of school and those of parents. The findings also suggest a tendency to expect children to possess a level of understanding about social norms and compliance when entering an early years environment for the first time.

Conclusion

The research lends support to the perception of classed assumptions within early years settings, and explores practitioner implications that children will share the same values and behaviours within their play. The research supports the suggestion that the function of education in society is to produce individuals with appropriate social values.

FINAL REFLECTION

This chapter has given you some tools to *begin* to see children's play behaviours differently. We have considered schemas and the play cycle as examples of more informed and responsive ways in which to interpret play.

We have also critically considered what influences our responses as professionals and questioned whether the political landscape within the sector allows us the autonomy to choose our responses as often as we might like to. Critical reflection of our own behaviour might lead us to question the rhetoric on which our profession has built itself. When is *free play* truly free?

KEY POINTS

- Children's play can, and should, be viewed in a multi-dimensional way.
- The way we see and therefore value children and their play will have a direct impact on our response as professionals.
- Play begins with thought at a subconscious level before being exhibited at a conscious level.
- Pressure resulting from policy and accountability can lead to professionals disregarding children's play behaviours in favour of perceived standards and quality.

QUESTIONS TO CONSIDER

I   To what extent do you feel we allow play for play's sake within our early childhood education practices? This is a very loaded question and the answer will differ greatly depending on the setting, so take time to reflect on your own experiences. Do we hijack play for adult purposes? And, if so, how can we begin to turn the tide on this behaviour?

2   Following on from the previous question, how can we begin to attune more to children's play behaviours, in an attempt to recognise and respect the true drive behind the play and inform our own response (or perhaps even lack of response!)?

3   What impact might this chapter have on our behaviour management practices? To understand play behaviour is to see children's actions differently and begin to consider alternative explanations to what we might immediately perceive negatively. Take this as a professional challenge to critically reflect on what you see in front of you and question your assumptions. Use language such as 'I wonder' and 'what if' as you evaluate what you see!

FURTHER READING

Arnold, C. (2010) *Understanding Schemas and Emotions in Early Childhood*. London: Sage. (An important text in understanding the potential relationship between children's emotional experiences and their observable behaviours. Arnold shines a new light on children's action and provides practitioners with new ways to interpret and support their schematic behaviours.)

Athey, C. (2007) *Extending Thought in Young Children*, 2nd edition. London: Paul Chapman Publishing. (The second edition of Athey's seminal work in which she shared the findings of the Froebel Early Education Project, is explored through this chapter. A core text for anyone interested in understanding the role of schemas in children's play, learning and development.)

King, P., & Newstead, S. (2019) Childcare workers' understanding of the play cycle theory: Can a focus on 'process not product' contribute to quality childcare experiences? *Child Care in Practice*, DOI: 10.1080/13575279.2019.1680532. (An exploration of the role of the play cycle in understanding children's play behaviours. King and Newstead take a critical look at whether early years practitioners have the tools and agency to focus on the process of children's play rather than the end product.)

Moss, P. (2019) *Alternative Narratives in Early Childhood: An Introduction for Students and Practitioners*. Oxon: Routledge. (A critical exploration of perspectives in early childhood in a social context. Moss explores the political forces at play in early years education, particularly in relation to discourses of quality and practitioner agency.)

REFERENCES

Arnold, C. (2007) Young children's representations of their emotions and attachment in their spontaneous patterns of behaviour: An exploration of a researcher's understanding. PhD thesis, University of Coventry. Available at: http://eprints. worc.ac.uk/464/1/Complete_Thesis_cArnold.pdf (accessed 2 April 2020).

Arnold, C. (2010) *Understanding Schemas and Emotions in Early Childhood*. London: Sage.

Arnold, C. (2018) How action schemas are reflected in young children's early language. *Early Child Development and Care*, 189(12), 1999–2004.

Atherton, F. and Nutbrown, C. (2013) *Understanding Schemas and Young Children*. London: Sage.

Athey, C. (1990) *Extending Thought in Young Children*. London: Paul Chapman Publishing.

Athey, C. (2007) *Extending Thought in Young Children*, 2nd edition. London: Paul Chapman Publishing.

Bartlett, F.C. (1932) *Remembering: A Study in Experimental and Social Psychology*. Cambridge UK: Cambridge University Press.

Brierley, J. (2018) Are we underestimating 2-year-olds? Recognising the links between schema and mark making – implications for future pedagogy. *Journal of Early Childhood Research*, 16(2), 136–147.

Cole, M. (1996) *Cultural Psychology: A Once and Future Discipline*. Cambridge, MA, Belknap Press of Harvard University Press.

Dahlberg, G., Moss, P., & Pence, P. (2013) *Beyond Quality in Early Childhood Education and Care: Languages of Evaluation*. London: Routledge.

Department for Education (DfE) (2013) *More Great Childcare: Raising Quality and Giving Parents more Choice*. Available at: https://assets.publishing.service.gov.uk/ government/uploads/system/uploads/attachment_data/file/219660/ More_20Great_20Childcare_20v2.pdf (accessed 5 May 2020).

Department of Education and Science (DES) (1967) *The Plowden Report: Children and their Primary Schools*. Available at: www.educationengland.org.uk/ documents/plowden/plowden1967–1.html (accessed 5 May 2020).

Dockett, S. (2011) The challenge of play for early childhood educators. In S. Rogers (ed.) *Rethinking Play and Pedagogy*. Oxon: Routledge, pp. 32–47.

Gibbons, A. (2007) The politics of processes and products in education: An early childhood metanarrative crisis? *Educational Philosophy and Theory*, 39(3), 300–311.

González, O., Florida, O., Wheeler, N., & Daire, A. (2017) Exploratory analyses of cognitive schemas for child and adolescent sexual abuse survivors: Implications for the research to practice gap. *Journal of Mental Health Counselling*, 39(1), 25–38.

Hedges, H. (2012) Vygotsky's phases of everyday concept development and the notion of children's 'working theories'. *Learning Culture and Social Interaction*, 1(2), 143–152.

Isaacs, S. (1929) *The Nursery Years*. London: Routledge.

Jensen, H. (2017) Friendships, empathy and mindfulness in children's groups: Developing children's natural capacities. In S. Hart (ed.) *Inclusion, Play and*

Empathy: Neuroaffective Development in Children's Groups. London: Jessica Kingsley Publishers, pp. 281–301.

King, P., & Newstead, S. (2019) Childcare workers' understanding of the play cycle theory: Can a focus on 'process not product' contribute to quality childcare experiences? *Child Care in Practice*, DOI: 10.1080/13575279.

King, P., & Temple, S. (2018) Transactional analysis and the ludic third (TALT): A model of functionally fluent reflective play practice. *Transactional Analysis Journal*, 48(3), 258–271. DOI: 10.1080/03621537.2018.1471292.

Kuschner, D. (2012) Play is natural to childhood but school is not: The problem of integrating play into the curriculum. *International Journal of Play*, 1(3), 242–249.

Laevers, F. (2000) Forward to basics! Deep-level learning and the experiential approach. *Early Years*, 20(2), 20–29.

Laevers, F. (2005) The curriculum as means to raise the quality of early childhood education: Implications for policy. *European Early Childhood Education Research Journal*, 13(1), 17–29.

Lewis, Z. (2018) Policy and the image of the child: A critical analysis of drivers and levers in English early years curriculum policy. *Early Years: An International Research Journal*. DOI: 10.1080/09575146.2018.1501552 (accessed 20 May 2020).

Lili, M., & Lillard, A. (2017) The evolutionary significance of pretend play: Two-year-olds' interpretations of behavioural cues. *Learning and Behaviour*, 41, 441–448.

Locke, J. (1989) [1693] *Some thoughts concerning education*. J.W. Yolton & J.S. Yolton (ed.). Oxford, UK: Clarendon Press; New York: Oxford University Press.

Louis, S., Beswick, C., Magraw, L., Hayes, L., & Featherstone, S. (2008) *Understanding Schemas in Young Children: Again! Again!* London: Featherstone.

McNamee, S. (2016) *The Social Study of Childhood*. Basingstoke: Palgrave Macmillan.

McVee, M., Dunsmore, K., & Gavelek, J. (2005) Schema theory revisited. *Review of Educational Research*, 75(4), 531–566.

Moss, P. (2019) *Alternative Narratives in Early Childhood: An Introduction for Students and Practitioners*. Oxon: Routledge.

Nutbrown, C. (2006) *Threads of Thinking*, 3rd edition. London: Sage.

Parry, J. (2018) Making connections: Young children exploring early friendships through play. In G. Googliff, N. Canning, J. Parry & L. Miller (eds) *Young Children's Play and Creativity*. Oxon: Routledge, pp. 113–127.

Piaget, J. (1962) *Play, Dreams, and Imitation in Childhood*. New York: Norton.

Rogers, S. (2011) Play and pedagogy: A conflict of interests? In S. Rogers (ed.) *Rethinking Play and Pedagogy*. Oxon: Routledge, pp. 5–19.

Scott, W., de Keller, S., & Bruce, T. (2011) *Learning and Development: Education Pioneer – Chris Athey, 27.1.1974–27.11.2011*. Available at: www.nurseryworld.

co.uk/features/article/learning-development-education-pioneer-chris-athey-27-1–1924–27–11–2011 (accessed 5 May 2020).

Shanker, S., & Bakhurst, D. (2001) *Jerome Bruner: Language, Culture, Self.* London: Sage.

Shaw, J. (1991) An investigation into parents' conceptual development in the context of dialogue with a community teacher. Unpublished PhD, Newcastle University.

Stirrup, J., Evans, J., & Davies, B. (2017) Learning one's place and position through play: Social class and educational opportunity in early years education. *International Journal of Early Years Education,* 25(4), 343–360.

Sturrock, G., & Else, P. (1998) *The Playground as Therapeutic Space: Playwork as Healing – The Colorado Paper.* Available at: https://ipaewni.files.wordpress.com/2016/05/colorado-paper.pdf (accessed 29 April 2020).

Wood, E. (2010) Developing integrated pedagogical approaches to play and learning. In P. Broadhead, J. Howard, & E. Wood (eds) *Play and Learning in the Early Years.* London: Sage, pp. 9–27.

Wyness, M. (2012) *Childhood and Society,* 2nd edition. Basingstoke: Palgrave Macmillan.

4

PLAY IN THE GREAT OUTDOORS

Su Wall and Kay Owen

CONTENTS

Children's declining use of outdoor environments is well documented and this chapter considers how we reached this current position. It also considers ways in which outdoor environments can be used, and questions whether it is now time for professionals, parents and the wider community to create more outdoor opportunities for children. It is proposed that the outdoor environment is crucial for children's physical and mental health, and indeed for their holistic development, as it provides them with space, freedom, knowledge and fun, whilst also enabling an important connection with the natural world.

 THIS CHAPTER WILL...

- Explore historic and contemporary theories underpinning outdoor practices
- Explain how the outdoors promotes holistic development
- Consider the role of the outdoors as a learning environment within the current statutory framework and curricula
- Explore the concept of Forest Schools
- Discuss barriers to outdoor play.

KEY TERMS

emotional wellbeing, Forest School, mental health, nature connection, outdoor learning environment

INTRODUCTION

Many early childhood pioneers advocated outdoor learning, recognising that access to external environments promotes holistic development. Modern theorists agree that outdoor play – whether this be in a private space such as a garden, or in a shared community or public space – benefits both physical and **mental health**. Hystad, Payette, Nolwenn and Boileau (2019), for instance, highlight the links between access to green space and health and wellbeing. Playing outdoors enables children to reap the psychological benefits associated with **nature connection** (Richardson & McEwan, 2018), whilst also promoting physical activity. In doing so, it helps tackle some of the contemporary health issues associated with a sedentary lifestyle. Bento and Dias (2017) propose that the outdoors offers an exciting and rewarding learning environment that can enhance brain development and encourage movement, sensory experience and healthy life patterns – all of which are clearly beneficial to young children. However, despite these many recognised benefits, increasing globalisation, urban growth and technology have served to curtail opportunities for outdoor play (Bento & Dias, 2017). The subsequent reduction in physical activity and access to natural sunlight necessarily impact the development of healthy children. Let us consider each of these factors in more detail.

THE HISTORY OF OUTDOOR PLAY

Taking children outside to learn is certainly not a new concept, indeed it was advocated by many early childhood pioneers, such as Frobel (1782–1852), Montessori (1870–1952) and the Macmillian sisters (1859–1917, 1860–1931).

Friedrich Froebel (1782–1852)

Froebel (or Fröbel), one of the most influential pioneers of his time, viewed play as being central to children's learning and development. Smedley and Hoskins (2020) explain that Froebel advocated utilising nature's resources to enhance children's learning and development, including their health and **emotional wellbeing**. Froebel recognised that outdoor spaces are less pressurised than structured indoor learning environments. Indoors, adults generally decide what resources are to be made available and prescribe how they should be used. In contrast, outdoor play allows for greater freedom of expression (Dinkel et al., 2019). Froebel's kindergarten philosophy also included studying plants so that children could begin to understand natural phenomena and the interconnections between all living things. This both stimulates children's interest and helps them to grow up in harmony with nature.

Maria Montessori (1870–1952)

Montessori was an influential pioneer who is still recognised for her creative influence regarding the use of the outdoors in early years education. In her first book, *The Montessori Method* (1912), she explained her belief that children need to connect with nature and learn to care for living things. This will help children to:

- understand the cycles of life
- appreciate that living things may be dependent upon their care
- learn patience
- become inspired to live a natural life.

Like Froebel, Montessori created an environment that would encourage children to live in harmony with nature and allow them to learn through their senses. Children have an innate curiosity about the world and Montessori believed that being outdoors provides endless opportunities for children to experiment (what happens if I drop a pebble in a puddle?). The natural beauty and wonder of the world will also boost aesthetic appreciation and creativity. Schools that use Montessori's methods today continue to advocate regular use of the outdoors.

Margaret (1859–1917) and Rachel (1860–1931) McMillan

The McMillan sisters established the first open-air nursery in 1914. Their pedagogy emphasised the fundamentals of outdoor learning, with children having access to fresh air, exercise and a healthy lifestyle. Recognising that they were working with children from very poor and disadvantaged backgrounds, they also provided free school meals for the children. The McMillan sisters encouraged children in the nurseries to care for animals and plants outdoors, seeing this as a way to instil values of caring for themselves and for others (McMillan, 1904). Waller (2014) suggests that this outdoor environment-based pedagogy led to dramatic improvements in both the children's health and holistic development.

WHY TAKE EARLY YEARS GROUPS OUTDOORS?
1. It is developmentally appropriate and skill-enhancing

Children in the early years are coming to terms with their own identity and physical capabilities. They are learning about social relations and the world around them. They therefore need the time, space and opportunity to explore and utilise their developing skills in a varied and interesting physical environment. White (2010) suggests that outdoor environments are particularly successful in supporting skill development as they are both enabling and motivational. An outdoor environment allows children to move freely, explore the world using their senses and experience natural seasonal phenomena such as changes in the landscape and weather. Furthermore, the outdoor environment is remarkably adaptable, providing the space and opportunity for tailored and appropriate play and learning activities (Minn & Lee, 2016).

2. It improves physical health

Children who spend time in the natural environment are generally healthier and better physically developed (Fjortoft, 2004). Walking on uneven terrain, for instance, improves balance and coordination, whilst open and gross-motor play areas encourage young children to engage in moderate or vigorous physical activity (Dinkel et al., 2019). For infants and toddlers, this increased physical activity benefits healthy muscular, skeletal, cardiac and respiratory development, improves metabolic health and decreases adiposity (Wiseman, Harris & Downes, 2019). Exercise and improvements in physical health have been shown to have further knock-on effects. Amado-Alonso and colleagues (2019), for instance, demonstrated that children who participate in organised physical activity show greater emotional wellbeing, better intrapersonal and interpersonal skills, greater adaptability and improved mood states. Furthermore, given that patterns of activity established in early childhood are carried into adolescence and beyond (Poitras et al., 2017), regular physical activity in the outdoors is uniquely placed to impact on an individual's long-term health outcomes.

3. It improves emotional health

In light of increasing concerns over children's mental health and wellbeing, the DfE (2018) recognised a need to support children's resilience and emotional health. Outdoor creative and imaginative play builds skills and cultivates confidence, which in turn provide children with the assurance they need to share feelings and express emotions (Dowling, 2010). The contribution of nature connectedness to the individual's sense of wellbeing, and the subsequent benefits that it can bring, are also increasingly being recognised. For example, Sobko, Jia and Brown's (2018) study of preschoolers discovered that an awareness and enjoyment of nature reduces distress, emotional problems, hyperactivity, behavioural and peer difficulties, and improves prosocial behaviours.

 **TIME TO CONSIDER**

The World Health Organization suggests that in order to:

reach a state of complete physical, mental and social well-being, an individual or group must be able to identify and to realise aspirations, to satisfy needs, and to change or cope with the environment. Health is a positive concept emphasising social and personal resources, as well as physical capacities. (WHO, 1986: 1)

To what extent do you think outdoor play contributes to children achieving these aims?

OUTDOOR PLAY REPORTS

Some of the key documents from the past decade pertaining to outdoor play are summarised in Table 4.1. The Early Years Foundation Stage (EYFS) (DfE, 2017) (see Chapter 9) fully endorses outdoor play, emphasising its positive impact on children's wellbeing and development. The DfE (2017) stipulates that providers have a statutory duty to provide children with daily access to an outdoor play space. Practitioners and teachers are also encouraged to provide 'free flow', with children able to move between indoor and enabling outdoor environments.

Table 4.1 Key documents on play and their message

Key document	Key messages
Learning Outside the Classroom Manifesto (DfES, 2006)	Every young person, whatever their age, ability or circumstances, should experience the world beyond the classroom as an essential part of learning and personal development. Learning outside the classroom is about raising achievement through an organised, powerful approach to learning.
The Rose Report (2009)	A well-planned and vibrant curriculum including practical activities will promote understanding of the wider world. There is a need to develop stronger links between the Early Years Foundation Stage statutory framework (EYFS) and the National Curriculum. This should include active play-based learning both inside and outdoors.
The Nutbrown Report (2012)	Play is fundamental to children's wellbeing and development. There should be opportunities to play outdoors as well as indoors.
Learning through Landscapes (2020)	Children and young people need to connect with nature, become more active, learn outdoors and have fun.
Play England (2012)	Children should have access to outdoor space to play freely, experience nature, explore their environment and be with their friends.

What is an enabling outdoor environment?

It is one that:

- is safe, rich and allows children to explore freely whilst developing holistically
- recognises children learn best by following their interests and needs through play
- implements a child-centred approach
- comprises a varied, open play space, accessible for all children to explore and investigate
- allows opportunities for risky and challenging play (Tovey, 2010)

- offers some protection from the excesses of nature (e.g. a canopy for shade)
- feels emotionally safe and secure, enabling free expression and thus personal, social and emotional development (DfE, 2017).

Understanding and valuing outdoor learning

The Education Reform Act 1988 introduced the first National Curriculum (also 1988) with a focus on rigorous accountability, not only in terms of *what* was taught but also in *how* it was taught (see Chapters 1 and 9). Many felt that this eroded teachers' professionalism and transformed their role from one of autonomy to compliance (Sharp, Ward & Hankin, 2009). This has been further compounded by current assessment formats and the additional pressure of league tables that together have served to create a largely data-driven curriculum. Furthermore, the National Curriculum (DfE, 2014) makes no mention of the outdoor environment and shows no recognition of the wider learning that can occur there. Instead, the focus on core subjects such as maths and phonics carries an implicit assumption that priorities lie with formal indoor classrooms and the knowledge that can be acquired there. As such, it appears at odds with the NHS (2019) physical guidelines, which state that children aged 5–18 years should have 60 minutes of physical activity every day, ranging from moderate to vigorous exercise.

However, whilst accepting that the National Curriculum is overcrowded, Rose (2009) argues that schools remain in control of their pedagogy and daily timetabling. Indeed, the DfE (2014) regards the National Curriculum as just one element of the education system, leaving time and space during a typical school day for activities beyond the core curriculum. The absence of outdoor opportunities may therefore be attributable not simply to government directives, but also to factors at a more local level. A small-scale study with teachers of Reception, Year 1 and Year 2 (Wall, 2019) found that, whilst all of those interviewed agreed that the outdoor environment provided many opportunities to enhance children's development, on a day-to-day basis they experienced:

- a lack of funding for additional supervisory staff
- a lack of space, particularly for spontaneous use
- insufficient time to undertake the required additional planning
- a lack of confidence in their own ability to deliver lessons outdoors.

In essence, this meant that, whilst they remained committed to the principles of creative planning and creative teaching approaches, they encountered too many pressures and barriers to regularly capacitate outdoor play and learning.

As a result, the outdoor environment is predominantly used for playtime and lunchtime. However, issues with timetabling for intervention groups, a requirement to complete academic work prior to going outside and difficulties in managing classroom work, have meant that even these times are increasingly restricted. Furthermore, a DfE (2012) survey concluded that 25 per cent of schools do not improve pupils' fitness levels during PE because of low teacher expectations and excessive time being given over to briefings/instructions.

In combination, these factors render schooling a largely sedentary experience for the majority of children.

 **TIME TO CONSIDER**

Do you feel there is a need for more outdoor learning and outdoor play in schools?

Can you make any suggestions as to how the barriers teachers experience could be overcome?

BARRIERS TO OUTDOOR PLAY
Parental fear

Opportunities for children to play outside their home, explore the neighbourhood or even walk to nursery or school are being increasingly curtailed due to social changes (see Chapter 1). Many children are cocooned in a car or kept inside the home, becoming increasingly disengaged from the natural environment (Ridgers, Knowles & Sayers, 2012). Waite (2010) suggests that these restrictions on children's freedoms derive from parental fear (often heightened by media reports and social networking) regarding children's safety. Certainly, modern parents are far more anxious than their predecessors – seeing the safety risks rather than the opportunities in situations. This fear has led them to severely limit any form of risk-taking (Brussoni, Ishikawa & Han, 2018). Simmons (2020) explains that the current levels of surveillance experienced by parents have created self-doubt, meaning that many lack confidence in their own judgement and ability to parent. The resultant 'better safe than sorry' philosophy impels parents to keep children in relatively hazard-free environments, with enormous costs in terms of their experience of childhood.

Not only does parental fear lead to adult-imposed limitations, children's awareness of it serves to define their own attitude towards outdoor physical activity (Noonan, Boddy, Fairclough & Knowles, 2016).

Health and safety

Parental fear and social change have both helped fuel a culture of liability and blame (Rickinson et al., 2004). This in turn has necessitated an extensive consideration of potential health and safety issues and, ultimately, the removal of risk and challenge from the curriculum as teachers and practitioners fear accidents and litigation (Tovey, 2010). The Health and Safety Executive (HSE) (2006) recognised that, in some cases, schools and settings have been over-zealous, implementing unnecessary health and safety audits and policies.

Linked to this are concerns about the weather, with adults often appearing fearful about the threats posed to children from becoming too hot, too cold or wet. Indeed, bad weather is one of the most frequently cited reasons for not allowing outdoor play (Safefood, 2017).

Risky play

Tovey (2010) believes that the outdoors offers rich potential for challenge and risky play, granting children the space, freedom and opportunity to explore their own limits. Cunningham (2006) agrees, suggesting that the absence of risk and challenge is actually detrimental to healthy development. Furthermore, it deprives children of the opportunity to demonstrate their competency (Tovey, 2016) and limits practitioner/teacher expectations of their abilities. Children need to experience risk within a safe and controlled environment in order to understand their capabilities and develop the resilience that comes from experiencing and overcoming difficulties (Tremblay et al., 2015). Children must never knowingly be put in danger; however, successfully navigating risk and challenge provides children with a valuable life skill that they will need in order to meet the inescapable challenges of adulthood. Children are curious and have a desire to explore. It is inevitable that some accidents will occur, but with suitable planning, support and supervision, these should be minor and infrequent (Harper, 2017). Challenge commensurate with the child's ability and confidence will facilitate learning, personal development and self-reliance. Risk and challenge in an outdoor environment thus appear to teach critical life skills.

 **TIME TO CONSIDER**

To what extent do you agree that children need to participate in risky play?

Why do you think children's engagement with risky play outdoors is diminishing?

Is there a point at which an adult's desire to protect actually becomes potentially damaging to children?

Space and resources

Learning through Landscapes (2009) identified the vital role that the outdoors plays in learning and development. School grounds, parks and playgrounds can provide safe and diverse opportunities for healthy exercise, play and learning – all vital to the development of healthy, happy adults. Unfortunately, many green spaces are disappearing, particularly in urban and disadvantaged communities (Qiu & Zhu, 2017), and children with a disability find it particularly difficult to access suitable play provision (Lynch, Moore, Edwards & Horgan, 2019). There has also been a dramatic increase in school playing fields being labelled as unnecessary and sold (DfE 2020), partially because the DfE (2015) only recognises their use within PE and not the broader curriculum. In 2016, some 160 acres of school playing fields across 65 local authorities were identified as surplus to requirements. Since 2010, across these authorities, more than £100 million has been raised from the sale of school fields.

Currently, schools face a lack of funding, with many struggling to balance the books and cover ongoing costs and basics. Items such as outdoor play equipment are therefore often regarded as an expensive luxury outside budgetary priorities. However, as Tovey (2007) argues, what children really need is a space where they can create their own play using their imagination. This does not require expensive, fixed, permanent equipment.

Practitioners' confidence and training

We have already noted that many practitioners and teachers lack confidence in their ability to teach outdoors. Doubts about personal competency make individuals fearful and lead to an avoidance of the event or activity (Bandura, 1986; Maynard & Waters, 2007). Leaders, teachers and practitioners who have not been trained to plan, manage and capacitate outdoor play are, understandably, likely to simply avoid it and remain indoors (White, 2010). It is therefore critical that practitioners and teachers are made aware of the effectiveness of using the outdoors during their initial training, and given opportunities to develop competencies (Waite, 2010). Once in post, they require training and experience, supported by mentors, colleagues and local authorities, to help develop their confidence and competency in outdoor environments (O'Donnell, Morris & Wilson, 2006).

Parental attitudes and pressures

Hesketh, Lakshman and van Sluijs' (2017) systematic review demonstrates the importance of parents in determining barriers and facilitators to physical activity. Obviously, very young children have limited autonomy and are reliant on their carers to take them to shared or public spaces, or to play outdoors with them. Children's play behaviours are therefore substantially shaped by parental behaviours and attitudes (Sleddens et al., 2017). Unsurprisingly, parents who value physical activity, who encourage their child to participate or who act as role models by participating themselves, are more likely to have active children. On the other hand, parents who use the addition or reduction of screen time to reward and punish their children, unwittingly promote its value to the extent that their children will prefer sedentary activities and spend significantly less time engaged in active outdoor play (Wiseman, Harris & Downes, 2019).

Whilst it may appear tempting to blame parents for not ensuring their children engage in a variety of outdoor activities, it must be remembered that the decline in outdoor play has coincided with an increase in feminisation of the workforce, an increase in employment with unsociable hours and the shift in social attitudes detailed earlier. A parent under pressure (be that time-based or emotional) is more likely to put their child in a buggy or car. Parents working long hours may be too tired to facilitate outdoor activities, whilst those on low incomes may find the cost of joining clubs and providing specialist equipment prohibitively high. Each of these factors is likely to be exacerbated for lone parents or those caring for a child with additional needs. Parental behaviours may therefore be driven by circumstance as much as ideology.

 SPECIAL STUDY: FOREST SCHOOL

The history of Forest School

Over the last 20 years, Forest Schooling has grown across the UK as a form of alternate education, wherein children have access to forests and woods on a regular basis (Bilton, 2010). The **Forest School** concept originated in Scandinavia in the 1950s, where the outdoor learning environment was utilised all year round. In the 1990s, a group of nursery nurses from Bridgewater College in Somerset visited a preschool provision in Denmark and observed the outdoor, child-led, play-based pedagogy. They were so inspired that the pedagogy was introduced to the UK and has become an integral part of many early years settings and schools today (Constable, 2017).

What is Forest School?

Knight (2013) identifies Forest School as a learner-centred approach where the ever-changing landscape of the natural world is explored throughout the seasons. The Forest School Community (FSC, 2012) has published a set of principles outlining the fundamentals of the Forest School ethos (see Table 4.2).

Bilton (2010), however, notes that UK children generally access Forest School sporadically as it is rarely fully embedded in the curriculum. Some have questioned whether

Table 4.2 Forest School principles

Principles	Ethos
Principle 1	Forest School involves frequent, regular sessions in a woodland or natural environment and not simply a one-off visit. It is important that sessions are planned and adapted according to need.
Principle 2	A key aim of Forest School is to encourage and enable the child to develop a relationship with the natural world.
Principle 3	Forest School aims to promote the development of the whole child and augment resilience, confidence, independence and creativity.
Principle 4	Learners are given the opportunity and support to take risks that are both personally and environmentally appropriate.
Principle 5	The Forest School practitioners who run sessions should be fully qualified and ensure that they continuously maintain and develop their professional practice.
Principle 6	Learner-centred processes should be utilised in order to create a community for development and learning.

Source: Forest School Community (2012)

this diminishes the value of sessions and their ability to impact children's learning and development.

One of the fundamental principles of Forest School is the promotion of holistic development, specifically:

- resilience
- confidence
- independence gained from creative learning
- appropriate risk-taking within a supportive environment. (FSA, 2015)

We have already discussed the growth of risk-free, indoor environments (Savery, 2017) and considered how risky play can help children develop their sense of autonomy and self-efficacy. Forest Schools allow children to take supported risks, encouraging them to grow in confidence and recognise their own abilities and limitations (Tremblay et al., 2015). In doing so, Forest Schools help children to develop skills that they will most certainly need in later life.

EMOTIONAL WELLBEING

Emotional intelligence is the ability to recognise one's own feelings and those of others (see Chapter 6). Goleman (1995) suggests that it comprises:

- self-awareness
- self-regulation
- self-motivation
- empathy
- social skills.

Rather than being stable, these can all vary according to what we are working on and who we are working with (Mayer, Salovey & Caruso, 2004). It therefore follows that the provision of appropriate tasks and positive personal experiences will help boost key aspects of emotional wellbeing. Forest School provides opportunities for children, supported by practitioners, to complete group and individual tasks. These are largely determined by the children and strongly play-based, but with realistic targets attached (Knight, 2017). Children are therefore able to explore and learn at their own pace. As children also need to listen to and respect the decisions made by their peers, it helps develop cooperation, empathy and problem-solving skills (Constable, 2017). Practitioners report that intergroup conflict is rare and that children's involvement in the process, together with the support they receive, serves to minimise frustration and boredom.

Forest School practitioners also attempt to build a relationship, based on mutual trust and respect, with each individual child. Practitioners will engage fully with the child, use the child's name and ask individualised questions in order to build trust and confidence (Knight, 2017). By focusing on the individual, practitioners can raise children's confidence, encourage them to recognise their emotions and emotional responses, and begin to express these through play (Harris, 2018).

THE ENVIRONMENT

In addition to providing an appropriate emotional environment, it is important that the physical environment and its management meet certain criteria:

- The site will be large enough for group activities and to allow for rotation to prevent over-use and damage to the natural environment (Waite, 2010).
- The Forest School area is calm and less noisy than the typical nursery or school, thus producing an unhurried and relaxing learning environment (Harris, 2018).
- Boundaries, such as how far away from the practitioner feels safe and secure, are negotiated with the children and set at the beginning of any Forest School session.
- The voice of the child is heard and respected. As there is no right or wrong way of exploring the natural environment, children's decisions and choices can be regarded as being of equal value (Constable, 2017).

It must be noted that the rapid increase in the Forest School 'brand' has led to some variations in quality. Sackville-Ford and Davenport (2019) warn that the concept has been highjacked by some unscrupulous marketers and that adults must ensure they are treating the children in their charge to an authentic Forest School experience and not some pale imitation.

CASE STUDY 4.1

A group of children from an inner-city nursery visited a Forest School nursery that I (SW) was involved with. The city children came from a variety of cultural backgrounds but mainly lived in extended family groups and in properties with no gardens and limited access to open space. Their nursery, being situated in the centre of a busy city, had no grassed areas to play on either. Practitioners at the Forest School nursery were committed to the ideal of widening access to the outdoors and were therefore used to welcoming visitors from urban communities.

Two of the visiting children walked to the large, open, green space at the Forest School and suddenly stopped in amazement. They hesitantly touched the grass and, with the encouragement of a Forest School practitioner, began to tentatively stroke and feel it. Quickly, shoes and socks were taken off and the two children jumped and ran through the grass, shrieking with laughter. The Forest School practitioner spoke gently and introduced the new word 'grass', which the children then repeated.

One child had shown a reluctance to participate in creative activities or get dirty at his own nursery. During the session, the children were given the opportunity to use mud as an alternative to playdough. As he watched the others investigate the mud, the child became interested and started to join in. Initially, he was reserved and cautious but eventually became very happy and engaged. The child quietly said 'mud'.

The outdoor environment had therefore created opportunities for these children to:

- explore new textures using their senses
- engage freely in child-initiated play
- develop their vocabulary
- experience large, open spaces.

Reflective questions

- How do you think the children would have felt in experiencing mud or grass for the first time?
- Do you think Forest School offers different things for different children? Which group(s) do you think are most likely to benefit from the Forest School experience?

FINAL REFLECTION

Playing outside enhances children's physical and mental wellbeing, resilience and connectedness with nature (Roberts, 2017). The outdoors can be adapted to suit children of all ages, and activities tailored to meet the individual needs of the child/ children and, where necessary, curriculum. If they are provided with the correct clothing, children can also enjoy the outdoors throughout the year, regardless of the British weather! However, in order to ensure effective use of outdoor environments, support is still needed for practitioners and teachers to develop their knowledge and confidence (Knight, 2017). There is also a need to ensure that outdoor play spaces are available and accessible for all children, regardless of ethnicity, socio-economic status, or disability. Indeed, we would assert that the time is ripe for all those involved in environmental planning, curricular design or the care and welfare of children, to recognise that outdoor space is intrinsic to happy and healthy childhoods and is a fundamental right of all children.

KEY POINTS

- Outdoor play can make a major contribution, not just to children's physical development, but also to their holistic growth and wellbeing.
- The availability of outdoor play spaces has decreased substantially over the last two decades.
- Children raised in densely populated urban areas often have limited access to either private or public green spaces and playgrounds.
- Many early years practitioners feel that they lack the training and skills to utilise outdoor spaces, or encounter barriers that prevent regular outdoor play.

QUESTIONS TO CONSIDER

1 How far would you agree that The Great Outdoors offers unique play and learning opportunities that cannot be replicated elsewhere? What would you consider to be its most important contribution?
2 Reflect on the community where you live. Is there adequate provision for children to play outdoors? What could be done to improve it? You could perhaps design an outdoor area that addresses the points raised in this chapter.
3 Given that society has been aware of the importance of children spending time outdoors since Froebel, why do you think this remains low priority and under-resourced?
4 Chapter 1 noted that, prior to the Industrial Revolution, children spent extensive periods outdoors. Should we be concerned that children are becoming ever more separated from nature?

FURTHER READING

Bilton, H. (2017) *Taking the First Steps Outside: Under Threes Learning and Developing in the Natural Environment.* Oxon: Routledge. (An engaging book, full of beautiful photographs and practical advice about taking very young children outdoors.)

Forest School Association at www.forestschoolassociation.org – this official website provides information about the history and principles underpinning Forest School, as well as showing locations and highlighting training opportunities.

Holloway, S.L., & Pimlott-Wilson, H. (2018) Reconceptualising play: Balancing childcare, extra-curricular activities and free play in contemporary childhoods. *Transactions of the Institute of British Geographers*, 43(3), 420–434. (An interesting and wide-reaching consideration of factors influencing outdoor play.)

Learning through Landscapes at www.ltl.org.uk – this is the official website for the Learning through Landscapes charity, which is devoted to helping 'children and young people to connect with nature, become more active, learn outdoors and have fun'.

REFERENCES

Amado-Alonso, D., León-del-Barco, B., Mendo-Lázaro, S., Sánchez-Miguel, P.A., & Iglesias Gallego, D. (2019) Emotional intelligence and the practice of organized physical-sport activity in children. *Sustainability*, 11(6), 1615.

Bandura, A. (1986) *Social Foundations of Thought and Action: A Social Cognitive Theory*. Englewood Cliffs, NJ: Prentice Hall.

Bento, G., & Dias, G. (2017) The importance of outdoor play for young children's healthy development. *Porto Biomedical Journal*, 2(5), 157–160.

Bilton, H. (2010) *Outdoor Learning in the Early Years*. London: Routledge.

Brussoni, M., Ishikawa, T., & Han, C. (2018) Go play outside! Effects of a risk-reframing tool on mothers' tolerance for, and parenting practices associated with, children's risky play: Study protocol for a randomized controlled trial. *Trials*, 19(1), 173.

Constable, K. (2017) *The Outdoor Classroom Ages 3–7: Using Ideas from Forest Schools to Enrich Learning*. Oxon: Routledge.

Cunningham, H. (2006) *The Invention of Childhood*. London: BBC Books.

DfE (2012) *Beyond 2012: Outstanding Physical Education for All*. London: DfE

DfE (2014) *The National Curriculum*. London: DfE.

DfE (2015) *Disposal or Change of the Use of Playing Fields and School Land*. London: DfE.

DfE (2017) *The Early Years Foundation Stage*. London: DfE.

DfE (2018) *Mental Health and Wellbeing Provision in Schools*. London DfE

DfE (2020) *Decisions on the Disposal of School Land*. London DfE

Department for Education and Skills (DfES) (2006) *Learning Outside the Classroom Manifesto*. London: DfES.

Dinkel, D., Snyder, K., Patterson, T., Warehime, S., Kuhn, D., & Wisneski, D. (2019) An exploration of infant and toddler unstructured outdoor play. *European Early Childhood Education Research Journal*, 27(2), 257–271.

Dowling, M. (2010) *Young Children's Personal, Social and Emotional Development.* London: Sage.

Fjortoft, I. (2004) Landscape as playscape: The effects of natural environments on children's play and motor development. *Children, Youth and Environment*, 14(2), 21–44.

Forest School Association (FSA) (2015) *GB Forest School Trainers Network and the FSA.* Available at: www.forestschoolassociation.org/gb-forest-school-trainers-network-and-the-fsa.

Forest School Community (FSC) (2012) *The Forest School Principles.* Available at: www.forestschoolassociation.org/full-principles-and-criteria-for-good-practice/ (accessed 5 May 2020).

Goleman, D. (1995) *Emotional Intelligence.* London: Bantam Books.

Harper, N.J. (2017) Outdoor risky play and healthy child development in the shadows of the risk society: A forest and nature school perspective. *Child & Youth Services*, 38(4), 318–334.

Harris, F. (2018) Outdoor learning spaces: The case of forest school. *Area*, 50(2), 222–231.

Health & Safety Executive (HSE) (2006) *Health and Safety Executive Report.* London: HSE.

Hesketh, K.R., Lakshman, R., & van Sluijs, E.M.F. (2017) Barriers and facilitators to young children's physical activity and sedentary behaviour: A systematic review and synthesis of qualitative literature. *Obesity Reviews*, 18(9), 987–1017.

Hystad, P., Payette, Y., Nolwenn, N., & Boileau, C. (2019) Green space associations with mental health and cognitive function: Results from the Quebec CARTaGENE cohort. *Environmental Epidemiology*, 3(1), e040.

Knight, S. (2013) *Forest Schools and Outdoor Learning in the Early Years.* London: Sage.

Knight, S. (2017) *Forest School in Practice for all Ages.* London: Sage.

Learning through Landscapes (2009) *Play Out: A Guide to Developing Your Early Years Outdoors.* Exeter: Southgate Publishers.

Learning Through Landscapes (2020) *A Shared Vision and Values for Outdoor Play in the Early Years.* Available at: www.ltl.org.uk/publications/.

Lynch, H., Moore, A., Edwards, C., & Horgan, L. (2019) Advancing play participation for all: The challenge of addressing play diversity and inclusion in community parks and playgrounds. *British Journal of Occupational Therapy*, 83(2), 107–117.

Mayer, J. D., Salovey, P., & Caruso, D.R. (2004) Emotional intelligence: Theory, findings and implications. *Psychological Inquiry*, 15, 197–215.

Maynard, T., & Waters, J. (2007) Learning in the outdoor environment: A missed opportunity? *Early Years*, 27(3), 255–265.

McMillan, M. (1904) *Education Through the Imagination.* London: Swan Sonnenschein.

Minn, B., & Lee, J. (2016) Children's neighbourhood place as a psychological and behavioural domain. *Journal of Environmental Psychology,* 26, 51–71.

Montessori, M. (1912) *The Montessori Method* (trans. A.E. George). New York: Frederick A. Stokes Company. Available at: https://digital.library.upenn.edu/women/montessori/method/method.html (accessed 5 November 2020).

NHS (2019) *Physical Activity Guidelines for Children and Young People.* Updated 8/10/19. Available at: https://www.nhs.uk/live-well/exercise/physical-activity-guidelines-children-and-young-people/.

Noonan, R.J., Boddy, L.M., Fairclough, S.J., & Knowles, Z.R. (2016) Write, draw, show, and tell: A child-centred dual methodology to explore perceptions of out-of-school physical activity. *BMC Public Health,* 6(1), e008693.

Nutbrown, C. (2012) *The Nutbrown Report: Foundations for Quality.* London: DfE.

O'Donnell, L., Morris, M., & Wilson, R. (2006) *Education Outside the Classroom: An Assessment of Activity and Practice in Schools and Local Authorities.* London: DfES.

Play England (2012) *Design for Play: A Guide to Creating Successful Play Spaces,* London: DCSF and Play England.

Poitras, V.J., Gray, C.E., Janssen, X., Aubert, S., Carson, V., Faulkner, G., et al. (2017) Systematic review of the relationships between sedentary behaviour and health indicators in the early years (0–4 years). *BMC Public Health,* 17(5), 868.

Qiu, L., & Zhu, X. (2017) Impacts of housing and community environments on children's independent mobility: A systematic literature review. *International Journal of Contemporary Architecture: The New ARCH,* 4(2), 50–61.

Richardson, M., & McEwan, K. (2018) 30 days wild and the relationships between engagement with nature's beauty, nature connectedness and well-being. *Frontiers of Psychology,* 9. DOI: 10.3389/fpsyg.2018.01500.

Rickinson, M., Dillon, J., Teamey, K., Moris, M., Choi, M.Y., Sanders, D., et al. (2004) *A Review of Research on Outdoor Learning.* Slough: National Foundation for Educational Research (NFER), Kings College.

Ridgers, N., Knowles, Z.R., & Sayers, J. (2012) Encouraging play in the natural environment: A child-focused case study of forest school. *Children's Geographies,* 10(1), 49–65.

Roberts, A. (2017) *Forest Schools and Mental Wellbeing.* London: British Library.

Rose, J. (2009) *Independent Review of the Primary Curriculum.* Nottingham: DCSF.

Sackwille-Ford, M. & Davenport, H. (2019) *Critical Issues with Forest Schools.* Los Angeles: Sage.

Safefood (2017) *Let's Take on Childhood Obesity: Evaluation of a 3-year Public Health Campaign.* Cork: Safefood.

Savery, A. (2017) Does engagement in forest school influence perceptions of risk, held by children, their parents and their school staff? *International Journal of Primary Elementary and Early Years Education*, 45(5), 519–531.

Sharp, J., Ward, S., & Hankin, L. (2009) *Education Studies: An Issues Based Approach.* Exeter: Learning Matters.

Simmons, H. (2020) *Surveillance of Modern Motherhood: Experiences of Universal Parenting Courses.* London: Palgrave Macmillan.

Sleddens, E.F.C., Gubbels, J.S., Kremers, S.P.J., van der Plas, E., & Thijs, C. (2017) Bidirectional associations between activity-related parenting practices, and child physical activity, sedentary screen-based behavior and body mass index: A longitudinal analysis. *International Journal of Behavioral Nutrition and Physical Activity*, 14(1): 89.

Smedley, S., & Hoskins, K. (2020) Finding a place for Froebel's theories: Early years practitioners' understanding and enactment of learning through play. *Early Child Development and Care*, 190(8), 1202–1214.

Sobko, T., Jia, Z., & Brown, G. (2018) Measuring connectedness to nature in preschool children in an urban setting and its relation to psychological functioning. *PLoS ONE*, 13(11).

The Education Reform Act (1988) Available at: www.legislation.gov.uk/ukpga/1988/40/contents (accessed 29 February 2020).

Tovey, H. (2007) *Playing Outdoors: Spaces and Places, Risk and Challenge.* Maidenhead, Berks: McGraw-Hill Education (UK).

Tovey, H. (2010) Playing on the edge: Perceptions of risk and danger in outdoor play. In P. Broadhead, J. Howard and E. Wood (2010) *Play and Learning in the Early Years*. London: Sage

Tovey, H. (2016) *Bringing the Froebel Approach to Your Practice.* London: Routledge.

Tremblay, M., Gray, C., Babock, S., Barnes, J., Bradstreet, C., Carr, D., & Brussoni, M. (2015) Position statement on active outdoor play. *International Journal of Environmental Research and Public Health*, 12(6), 6475–6505.

Waite, S. (2010) Losing our way? The downward path for outdoor learning for children aged 2–11yrs. *Journal of Adventure Education and Outdoor Learning*, 10(2), 111–126.

Wall, S. (2019) An analysis of the views of Reception and Key Stage 1 teachers on the use of the outdoor as a learning environment and what factors influence the practice for outdoor learning. Unpublished Master's thesis, University of Derby.

Waller, T. (2014) Voices in the park: Researching the participation of young children in outdoor play in early years settings. *Management in Education* 28(4), 161–166.

White, J. (2010) *Outdoor Provision in the Early Years.* London: Sage.

Wiseman, N., Harris, N., & Downes, M. (2019) Preschool children's preferences for sedentary activity relate to parents' restrictive rules around active outdoor play. *BMC Public Health*, 19, 946.

World Health Organization (WHO) (1986). Intersectoral action for health: The role of intersectoral cooperation in national strategies for Health for All. Geneva : World Health Organization. Available at: www.who.int/iris/handle/10665/41545 (accessed 20 June 2020).

5

DIGITAL PLAY IN EARLY CHILDHOOD

Alistair Turvill

CONTENTS

Unlike other domains of play, 'digital play' is an emerging and nascent area of research, with the earliest instances of this term appearing in the literature as recently as 2003 (Edwards, 2019). This is partly because widespread access to digital technology is still a relatively recent phenomenon; however, digital play is a dynamic and rapidly expanding area. This chapter will introduce you to some of the major issues and debates in this exciting new field.

 THIS CHAPTER WILL...

- Consider what 'digital play' is, and how it differs from other forms of play
- Look at the factors that have enabled the modern proliferation of digital play
- Review the role of caregivers in guiding and mediating digital play
- Examine the role of commercial companies in driving and shaping digital play
- Discuss the opportunities and threats associated with digital play.

KEY TERMS

commercial influence, digital play, extrinsic rewards, impacts on development, mediation strategies, persuasive design, sedentary behaviour, technology

INTRODUCTION
Why do we need to think about digital play?

The portable, digital technology revolution of the last decade has provided most individuals and families in developed countries with greater access to powerful devices and platforms (Taylor & Silver, 2019). Modern advancements in technology offer rich visual, auditory and cognitive stimulation, novel and often predictable **extrinsic rewards**, low barriers to entry and, frequently, a narrower demand of input and/or effort from the individual (compared with non-digital activities). The ability to provide seductive and engaging experiences, in an accessible and portable format, has created a new and different offering in the domain of play. Obviously, this has also occasioned some differences in the nature and content of play behaviours. While there *is* huge variety in the behaviours observed within digital play, it is the emergence of phenomena such as an increase in **sedentary behaviour**, reduced social engagement and the potential development of compulsive behaviours, which sets digital play apart in the minds of some (Palmer, 2015). These differences, and the inevitability of the continued development and expansion of digital play, make it a phenomenon that requires adult consideration and understanding.

How did we get here?

Digital play is a domain of technological play, and whilst it *is* a contemporary phenomenon, the presence of technologies in the play lives of children is not purely a modern occurrence. Donahue (2015) shows that, throughout history, the toy industry has sought to create novel products for children by drawing on the emerging mechanical or analogue technologies of their day, for example clockwork motors, steam-driven components or small-scale radio transmitters. However, in 1947, John Bardeen, Walter Brattain and William Shockley changed the world forever with their 'research on semiconductors, and their discovery of the transistor effect'. The significance and impact of their discovery led to them being awarded the 1956 Noble Prize for Physics (Nobel Prize Organisation, 2020). Although it would take until the mid-1970s for the first commercially produced personal computers to become available (Ceruzzi, 2010), it is this transistor technology that is regarded as marking the birth of the modern, digital era (Riordan, Hoddeson & Herring, 1999).

Today, digital technologies are a constant and accepted part of life, omnipresent in many societies. This is especially so for the younger generations, whose experiences and activities are increasingly oriented around digital devices and platforms (Ofcom, 2020). Indeed, some differentiate younger from older generations with terms such as **digital natives** or **digital migrants** (Zevenbergen, 2007). The widespread emergence of smartphone, tablet and touch-screen technologies, heralded by the launch of the first Apple iPhone in 2007 (Goggin, 2009), is regarded as pivotal in ushering in this revolution. For the first time, advanced computational power was available in a truly portable and accessible format. What's more, whereas earlier devices had made higher physical and cognitive demands on us, the intuitive nature of the touchscreen medium significantly lowered barriers to engagement, enabling younger children to engage with these devices (Kucirkova, 2014). The relevance of this for early years children, practitioners and parents is clear – as access to an increasing variety of ever more powerful devices and platforms continues to expand, digital play behaviours and the influence of the digital play industry will continue to escalate. There is a responsibility for the early years sector and, indeed, wider society to understand and contribute to the shaping and development of this new behaviour and industry.

TIME TO CONSIDER

Take a moment to think about the range of digital activities that are undertaken by children, and make a list of as many as you can think of.

How many would you consider to be play? What makes some actions play and others not?

SPOTLIGHT ON RESEARCH

Play taxonomy categories are presented in Table 5.1, including an example of traditional play for each. Take some time to look over the 16 examples and consider how well you think this framework could accommodate forms of digital play. Try to think of digital versions of the actions described by Hughes (2002). Finally, compare your own efforts with that of academic researchers. Using the internet, search and recover a copy of the following open-source journal article:

Marsh, J., Plowman, L., Yamada-Rice, D., Bishop, J., & Scott, F. (2016) Digital play: A new classification. *Early Years*, 36(3), 242–253 (https://core.ac.uk/download/pdf/42620951.pdf):

- How similar are your own examples to those of the authors?
- Do you think this framework is suitable for understanding and categorising forms of digital play?
- Does it miss or overlook any important areas?

Passive or sedentary play

One notable omission to the taxonomy in Table 5.1 is the absence of *passive* play examples, such as Parten's (1932) concept of *onlooker play* – whereby a child gains enjoyment vicariously from the observation of another's play. Parten's (1932) theory suggested that this is particularly common in younger children, and so may also be relevant when considering digital play in the early years. There is huge variety within digital play behaviour, some involving significant amounts of physical (Althoff, White & Horvitz, 2016) or social engagement (Ralph, 2018), whilst others require much greater individual play and sedentariness. Some activities within digital play, for example viewing YouTube clips of other people playing games (Marsh, 2016a), or unboxing items (Marsh, 2016b), might be considered to be somewhat passive. The

Table 5.1 Play categories with examples of traditional play

Category	Traditional play	Digital play
Creative play	Play which encourages children to make, explore and create	
Object play	Children engaging in object play will examine and explore an object through touch and sight	
Symbolic play	Play behaviour where an object is used to represent something it is not	
Social play	Play involving the use of rule-based social interactions and events	
Locomotor play	Play involving physical movement	
Socio-dramatic play	Play that reflects children's real-life experiences or scenarios, e.g. going to the dentist	
Fantasy play	Play involving children taking on traits or identities which don't occur in real life, e.g. flying or being an animal	
Deep play	Play simulating risky events or experiences, often including aspects of fighting and/or surviving	
Dramatic play	Play concerning the dramatisation of events that the child has not directly participated in, e.g. playing for Manchester United	
Imaginative play	Play that occurs within the imagination and mind of a child	
Rough and tumble play	Energetic, physical play, without violence	
Recapitulative play	Play centred around legends, human history and ritual, perhaps including outdoor activities such as fire building or other bushcrafts	
Exploratory play	Play requiring children to explore spaces or objects to discover or understand more	
Role play	Play where a specific role or identity is adopted	
Mastery play	Play represented by efforts to control aspects of the environment, e.g. building a den outside	
Communication play	Play using language, for example nursery rhymes or stories	

Source: Hughes (2002)

opportunity for long periods of perceived or actual passivity is seen as being a key differentiator between some forms of digital and non-digital play. Gottschalk (2019) cites the divide between *active* and *passive* digital engagement as a key factor which determines the potential for either positive or developmental neutral/negative outcomes. This is challenged by Mustola, Koivula, Turja and Laakso (2018), however, who argue that we must progress beyond binary constructs such as *active* and *passive*, towards a more nuanced understanding of digital play. The authors challenge the perceived dichotomy of either receiving (passive) or producing (active) information due to the unknown extent of 'imagination, feelings, and thinking, for instance, and it is impossible to fully know and understand what is occurring in the mind of an individual receiving media information' (2018: 242). The authors conclude that it is reductive to frame some activities as passive when this cannot be evidenced. It is also necessary to consider Gottschalk's (2019: 29) point that 'not all media is created equal', and significant differences in outcomes emerge from events that may on the surface appear similar, for example watching a video. Findings from research demonstrate that the content of the video itself matters greatly, with exposure to appropriate educational content showing greater outcomes than non-educational content (Huber et al., 2018; Kostyrka-Allchorne, Cooper & Simpson, 2017), highlighting the erroneous conflation of sedentary and passive behaviours.

The revolutionary nature of digital technologies has enabled new dimensions of play. The ability to offer highly engaging, immersive and stimulating experiences, whilst also demanding a significantly lower or narrower input, or effort from the individual, enables greater sedentariness than might normally occur in traditional forms of play. This potential for prolonged periods of increased sedentariness differentiates some digital play behaviours from these other, more traditional forms of play, and is a key concern for some regarding digital play. Further, as already noted, some resist the notion that this sedentary behaviour should be categorised alongside these more traditional, active forms of play, due to the opportunity for potential detriment to the child in cases of excessive use. This links back to our earlier consideration regarding debates about what *is* or *is not* 'play', and, whilst it is right to exchange perspectives and explore arguments equally, it is important not to take a reductive approach to the activities considered, and to note the depth and variability in these events which might superficially appear the same.

WHY IS DIGITAL PLAY DIFFERENT?

As outlined above, factors such as increased sedentariness and solo play are identified as being defining and potentially problematic facets of digital play. We may ask, why is this the case? How do some forms of digital devices enable this? Modern digital devices create rich, engaging and exaggerated stimuli. When coupled with deliberate design features, they can effectively capture and hold human attention, in ways that natural, non-digital stimuli cannot. This ability is at the heart of the differences between digital play and more traditional forms of play.

Insights from psychology

Devices utilise the 'spotlight' nature of the human attention (McMains & Somers, 2004), and adopt **persuasive design** features to increase the likelihood of sustained engagement. Persuasive design exploits our **spotlight attention** system, by manipulating features which we are already disposed to be drawn towards. Examples of factors that can increase salience include: colour and contrast (Milosavljevic &

Cerf, 2008), orientation and direction (Treisman & Gormican, 1988), size (Huang & Pashler, 2005), unpredictability and/or novelty (Sun, Lim & Peng, 2013), and motion (Abrams & Christ, 2003), to name a few. The ability of digital devices to elicit more vivid, bright and/or contrasting colours than we might normally encounter in the physical world, as well as dynamic and/or novel movement and stimuli, mean that they are able to 'grab' attention via **unconscious processing** systems that direct and focus our conscious attention.

Persuasive design also incorporates the use of extrinsic rewards such as points or stickers to create more positive experiences and greater engagement. The deliberate design of commercial products which manipulate these aspects of the human attention and reward systems, is at the heart of what is referred to as the **attention economy**. This encompasses everything from apps (educational, e.g. Kaligo, or non-educational, e.g. Candy Crush) to games consoles or tablets, to social media platforms (e.g. Facebook, Instagram) and beyond. To generate income, businesses in the attention economy rely on users spending time on the platform in question, maximising the opportunity for advertising and upselling.

It should be said that the ability to capture and hold attention is not intrinsically problematic. Indeed, it is a credit to human research that we are able to understand the complex underlying systems that guide our experience of the world. Instead, it appears to be *how* this knowledge is applied which is important.

As touched on above, variations in the content, nature and framing of information received via digital mediums greatly influence the consequences and outcomes of digital exposure. Within early childhood especially, the responsibility for managing factors such as suitability of content and provision of appropriate support, fall upon a child's primary caregivers. Therefore, to understand how exposure and behaviour can differ between children, it is necessary to understand the differences in the approaches taken by caregivers. This will be considered in the next section.

MEDIATION

The role of parents and caregivers is particularly important when it comes to digital play in the early years. In this formative period, children depend on adults in their lives to provide opportunity, guidance and support. The balance between these factors will determine the potential for more or less positive outcomes in play activities (Hammond et al., 2012). The digital domain presents children with a different set of opportunities and threats from those they will encounter in the real world, requiring caregivers to make decisions about how much oversight, exposure and access they feel it is appropriate to provide. In Table 5.2, Livingstone and Helsper (2008) present a structured overview of how these approaches can vary, with five key forms described.

Table 5.2 Five key forms of mediation in digital play

Co-use	This is a shared activity between child and caregiver, for instance 'collaboratively surfing the web to track down pleasant content for mutual enjoyment'. The authors note that 'the adoption of this strategy was predicted by both positive and negative perceived effects of online behaviour, indicating that parents intend their collaborative surfing to reduce risks, such as computer addiction, while also enhancing positive experiences to share with their child'.
Active mediation	Purposeful discussion about safe use of the internet, social media or technology; tends to be less common as children grow up.
Restrictive mediation of access	Access rules, such as when and how long a child is allowed to go online.
Restrictive mediation of content	Specific content rules wherein parents declare what the child is permitted to do, visit or download.
Supervision	'Supervision was the most common type of guidance for younger children. Parents combine housekeeping activities with supervision, thereby granting the children some personal responsibility for their internet activities. Unsurprisingly, the prevalence of supervision coincides with having the computer within sight in the living room and having fewer computers at home, which actually are proxies for supervision. Perceived negative effects of internet usage predicted supervision, indicating that concerns about the internet rather than learning expectations prompt supervision.'

Source: Nikken & Jansz (2014)

 TIME TO CONSIDER

Do you have any experience with any of these strategies (either in applying them to others or experiencing them first hand)?

Consider how caregivers might modify the **mediation strategies** they adopt as their children get older.

 CASE STUDY 5.1

Oliver is 6 years old and has his own tablet. He enjoys playing 'Minecraft' whenever his parents let him, and he is allowed up to an hour a day on this game once he comes home from school. When he is playing, Oliver's parents will see him fascinated with what is on the screen, and he will often remain in the same spot for an extended period of time whilst enthralled by the game. Sometimes it can take his parents repeated efforts to get his attention when he is playing and he can be reluctant to stop when his allotted time is up.

Although playing on his tablet is one of his favourite things to do, Oliver also loves to play football in the garden, watch cartoons on TV and play with his toy cars. Oliver's 7-year-old sister, Amelia, also loves to play with digital devices; she will often borrow her mother's phone and use the camera function to take pictures of the family pets. Sometimes she will edit her pictures afterwards and share them with the whole family. Unlike Oliver's tablet use, Amelia's parents don't put clear and consistent limits on how long she is allowed to use the camera, although, when her mother asks for her phone back, Amelia often gets upset.

Reflective questions

- What do you perceive the key differences to be between Oliver and Amelia's digital play?
- Is it right that their parents take different approaches to these two actions? Why?
- Compare and contrast the opportunities and threats that you perceive to be associated with each of these two forms of digital play. Consider why you have identified the particular factors for each and what information or experience has led you to these conclusions.

THE POTENTIAL FOR IMPACT IN DIGITAL PLAY

The approaches described in the previous section modify the balance of potential opportunity and threat presented to children.

One effort to categorise the possible modalities of threat has been made by Livingstone, Haddon and Görzig (2012), who identify the categories of *conduct, contact* and *content*. This framework purports that children can be exposed to risk by:

- the *conduct* of themselves or others (for example, bullying or other abusive behaviours) – this relates specifically to peer-to-peer engagements, rather than exchanges with adults
- the threat posed by nefarious adults, either through actions such as stalking or harassment, sexual grooming or ideological persuasion; this is labelled as *contact* by Livingstone et al. (2012)
- the risk posed by exposure to inappropriate content such as violence or pornography; this is contained under the category of *content*.

Occurrences within each of these categories can be further labelled as *aggressive, sexual, values*-based or *commercial*. Opportunity for exposure to these factors is intermediated by the actions of caregivers. While risk can never be entirely mitigated, choices regarding the degree of oversight exercised, the limitations put on access, or the structure and guidance provided, increases or decreases the chance of events occurring.

The ways in which events can impact a child are varied and unique; however, they can be reduced down to two key factors:

1   The threat posed by exposure to harmful behaviour or content
2   The threat posed by the displacement of other, important, non-digital activities.

This is reminiscent of the work of Anderson et al. (2001) who differentiated theories of media impact (TV) in childhood as being either 'content-based', i.e. the nature of the content, for instance violent or sexual, is what causes negative or positive affect; or 'content-independent', where the consumption of media content and its displacement of other important activities are what cause change, rather than the specific nature of the media.

Threat 1: Exposure to harmful behaviour or content

The role of parents and caregivers

The ability of caregivers to intercede in the digital play lives of children in their care, is dependent primarily on their own knowledge and support. The ability to mediate the risk of exposure to inappropriate content may depend on their understanding of the potential for harm and their awareness of how to use parent locks on software or hardware devices (Livingstone et al., 2015). Evidence shows that it is often parents themselves who expose children to inappropriate content. A study by Tomopoulos et al. (2014) reported that children aged 2 and under were frequently exposed to inappropriate background content by their parents, in the false belief that the children were too young to understand and wouldn't be affected. Here we can see that it is not only knowledge of technology that plays a role in the mediation of risk, but also knowledge of children and development itself.

Commercial influence and interests

To engage in any form of digital play, it is necessary for a child to adopt the use of at least one (and often more) commercial product(s). While this is not exclusive to digital play, it is a defining and central feature of this domain. As we have already touched upon (Donahue, 2015), the presence of commercial interests in the play lives of children is not a new event. However, whilst traditional toy companies would profit from the sale of a physical object, the digital domain provides significantly greater opportunities for commercial entities to target children for financial gain. The economic success of the digital games industry is a testament to this, with its estimated value being greater than that of the film and music industries combined (Entertainment Retailers Association, 2019).

A commercial company's persistent need for sales, growth and profit can drive the pursuit of ever more accessible and engaging experiences to entice and capture the market's attention. As previously mentioned, one way to achieve this is through the use of persuasive design features intended to exploit features of human cognitive processing. These ensure longer periods of engagement and a greater likelihood of repeat use.

Companies may also profit from the gathering of personal or behavioural data for commercial interests, often begotten via user 'agreement' to a set of terms and conditions. In many instances, these are prohibitively complex (Elshout et al., 2016), meaning that adults struggle to read and understand them, never mind children. While the purchase of a traditional toy would typically be a single, discrete event, the interactive nature of the digital environment allows the exchange between company and consumer to continue. This can take the form of upgraded or additional features, the gathering of users' behavioural or personal information, or the introduction of gambling features such as 'loot boxes' which may or may not provide children with new additions to their game.

Protecting children from commercial exploitation

Efforts to address these and other commercial threats posed to children by the digital gaming industry are ongoing:

- The UK Children's Commissioner's (2017) report *Growing Up Digital* advocates shortening and simplifying terms and conditions so that meaningful informed consent can take place.
- The introduction of a new 'Children's Digital Ombudsman' to promote the rights and protection of children in the industry is proposed.
- Curbing the threat posed by facilitating gambling in the form of 'loot boxes' has recently been recommended in the UK by the Digital, Culture Media and Sport Select Committee (2019).
- The upholding of children's rights within digital gaming is being considered by UNICEF (2019).

Threat 2: Displacement of other, important, non-digital activities

Earlier, we considered some of the potential threats posed by digital activity. Livingstone et al.'s (2012) theory does not include the possibility of digital activities displacing other, non-digital events. However, typical child development is fostered by a broad and varied range of physical, cognitive, social and emotional experiences. Whilst the specific balance and proportion of these components is variable and unique to all of us, a reduction in 'real-world' activities due to increased digital engagement, has the potential to skew developmental trajectories and outcomes (RCPCH, 2019).

Physical activity

Findings from Howie and colleagues (2017) report that children aged 3–5 who regularly engage in digital play on a tablet, show significantly poorer physical development, specifically neck posture, posture variation and overall less movement (even when compared to TV viewing), than 3–5-year-olds who do not, or rarely, engage in digital play. Here, we see that it is not the device or game that is directly problematic, but rather the sedentary behaviour that it enables (and the tendency for greater physical movement it displaces (Cadoret et al., 2018)). However, evidence also suggests that reducing the time children spend engaging in digital play does not necessarily result in an increase in physical activity (Kardefelt-Winther, 2017). We should not therefore assume a direct causal relationship between an increase in digital play and an increase in sedentariness. As discussed in Chapters 1 and 4, factors such as parental anxiety and loss of outdoor play spaces are hypothesised to also be significant in reducing physical activity. In contrast to this, there is clear evidence demonstrating that digital play can displace and disrupt sleep in young children, but, further to this, that the potential positive gains that children may yield from digital play are also mediated by children's sleep quality and duration (Nathanson & Beyens, 2018).

Reading

It is not just 'displacement' but also 'replacement' that we see as a consequence of digital expansion. Baron's (2015) research into the impact of reading on-screen instead of paper, showed differences between digital and non-digital activities that on the surface may appear similar. Findings show that digital readers are more likely to skim-read and jump around within the content, commit less attention to the overall task, and, in later testing, show significantly lower recall and understanding of the content. In an echo of the seminal work of McLuhan (1994), we see that it is not only the message (the specific content encountered) which is critical in shaping experience, but also the medium (the format of information) in which the message is framed and delivered.

Summary

In summary, there is potential for threat or harm to occur to young children during digital play, primarily due to:

- exposure to inappropriate content
- the nefarious actions of specific individuals (either adult or child)
- the actions of corporate entities in pursuit of commercial gain.

However, the threats posed by some of these can be mitigated by the mediation of caregivers, and, going forwards, by greater governance of the commercial entities that profit from digital play.

While there has been significant consideration of the potential negative impacts of digital exposure on child development and wellbeing, the evidence in support of this is lacking in quality. In a 2017 study from Przybylski and Weinstein, looking at a representative sample of over 120,000 English children, there was no evidence found linking harmful outcomes and moderate use of digital devices. It should be noted that these findings are not applicable in the case of excessive digital gaming and play, with the most recent update to the International Classification of Diseases (WHO, 2018) being the first to include 'gaming disorder' as a formal medical diagnosis, where individuals display compulsive and/or addictive tendencies relating to gaming, which have a significantly negative impact on their wider lives.

Opportunities

The emergence and proliferation of digital technologies has been accompanied, in many cases, by significant increases in urbanisation, and the loss of important outdoor play spaces (see Chapter 1). As discussed by Harlow and Smith (Chapter 7), it may be argued that these losses amount to an infringement on the rights of children to have access to appropriate play opportunities. These changes are accompanied by increased parental anxiety about risk and safety, leading to a greater tendency towards favouring indoor play, often of a less physical nature (Boyd, Lee & Holt, 2013). The rich opportunities presented by various forms of digital play are a significant contributor towards compensating for some of these losses. The combination of increased digital play opportunities, paralleled with reduced traditional play options, has created an environment where digital play becomes the preferred form of play available for some children and caregivers. The potential opportunities offered to children by digital play are varied and are dependent on factors such as the nature of the activity, appropriateness for the age, and the functionality of the hardware or software.

Creativity

The breadth of content, structure, nature and demands of digital play can allow numerous opportunities for creativity to be incorporated. Indeed, evidence shows that increasing opportunity for play and creativity is one of parents' key motivations when downloading apps for their children to use (Marsh et al., 2015). Robson's (2014) 'Analysing Children's Creative Thinking' (ACCT) framework breaks creative behaviour down into the categories of:

- exploration and engagement
- involvement and enjoyment
- persistence.

Within each of these categories, the actions are further segmented into subtypes, which are then used to observe, label and analyse aspects of children's creative behaviour. Solely focusing on the use of different applications (apps) in tablet technology, Marsh et al. (2018) looked at a sample of 2000 UK-based families with at least one child aged 0–5. The researchers observed and recorded the children's behaviour when using a range of apps on tablet devices, and sought to apply Robson's (2014) ACCT framework to the data. Findings reported repeated instances of creativity in the behaviour observed in children, but significant variation in the frequency and type. This was partly determined by the features and limitations of the apps themselves, and also by the child's individual preferences and abilities. Key features more likely to promote creativity within apps are also identified, including clear aims, appropriate scaffolding using pictures and sounds, and repetition of information regarding navigation or function of the app.

Learning and development

Parents cite 'supporting learning' as their key motivation when enabling children's app use on tablet devices (Marsh et al., 2015). While learning and development should not be the primary goal of play (Besio, 2016), a multitude of game-based apps are aimed at supporting learning and education in early childhood. Earlier discussions in this chapter regarding persuasive design within digital products are also relevant here, with the same methods able to promote increased engagement and reward for users. In cases where the focus is primarily on educational topics such as reading or arithmetic, there is evidence that greater understanding and retention of information are possible. One example evaluated by Aunio and Mononen (2018) is 'Lola's World', an app aimed at improving children's mathematical abilities. The study focused on children who were considered 'low-performing' in maths, and aimed to establish whether use of this app significantly improved ability when compared to control groups. While children did improve, the children playing the maths game improved no more than the children in the control groups (however, methodological and sample limitations do challenge the robustness of these findings). Here we see the importance of evaluation when it comes to educational apps – with over 200,000 education apps listed on the Apple store alone in 2018 (Pendlebury, 2018), the potential for wasted time and lost opportunity is clear. However, it should be noted that, in most cases, empirical research is not carried out on products to establish the veracity of claims made (Hirsh-Pasek et al., 2015; Kucirkova, 2014).

In an attempt to address this problem, Hirsh-Pasek et al. (2015) focus on transferring understanding from existing research on learning to the principals of educational app design. They highlight the importance of four 'key pillars':

1   active involvement of the user in the materials
2   providing engaging content (e.g. using characters or narrative)
3   creating meaning and links with existing knowledge or experience
4   social interaction (either with other users or characters within the game).

These principles can be a helpful resource for guiding caregivers' app selections, with examples that do not aim or claim to satisfy these criteria best avoided. However, caution should still be exercised when using these as selection criteria, as even these factors will not *guarantee* a positive impact or outcomes from the use of educational apps.

Further efforts to demystify the world of educational apps can be seen in the recent Hungry Little Minds programme from the UK Government (Gov.uk, 2020), with a list of recommended apps selected by experts for caregivers to use with children. However, there is still a dearth of empirical research to support positive claims regarding these recommended apps, and, in cases where there is some preliminary research (e.g. Kaligo), findings suggest that outcomes may be inconsistent, and mixed at best (Bonneton-Botté et al., 2020). The threats posed by displacement which have already been outlined, reinforce the need to ensure that digital activities, especially those claiming to promote development, are efficacious, otherwise their impact may be more negative than positive.

Despite the challenges in identifying which apps reliably provide positive developmental outcomes, some evidence is available. Pitchford, Kamchedzera, Hubber and Chigeda (2018) discovered that children with special educational needs and/or disabilities showed significant improvement in mathematical ability following the use of interactive apps. Similarly, some apps aimed at promoting physical development are supported by research (Axford, Joosten & Harris, 2018). Bonneton-Botté et al. (2020) reported significant benefits for children of moderate initial ability, but not for children of higher or lower ability. This finding shows that outcomes will vary based on the individual, meaning we cannot expect apps to provide uniform benefit to all users. In order to achieve wider benefits, appropriate scaffolding in the form of caregiver co-viewing is necessary (Strouse, Troseth, O'Doherty & Saylor, 2018).

ASSOCIATED ISSUES

This chapter has highlighted some key features of digital play. However, it has only been possible to consider a small portion of this vast and expanding topic. As noted previously, this is still a nascent area of investigation, and accelerating rates of technological development, coupled with changes to social and behavioural norms, promise to continue driving change and offering novelty for a long time to come. Currently, the zeitgeist primarily surrounds tablet technology, the expanse of commercial apps available, and the associated opportunities and threats. However, it is inevitable that even this will be displaced by new mediums and technologies in years to come. These, in turn, will offer a raft of new opportunities and threats which families and society will need to accommodate and adjust to.

When reflecting on the role and impact of digital play, it is essential that we do not adopt a 'one-size-fits-all' approach. The potential benefits or risks will differ between individuals according to their abilities, preferences and opportunities.

Socio-economic inequalities

Although beyond the scope of the current chapter's discussions, it should be noted that socio-economic inequalities are an important mediating factor in outcomes, with significant differences in access, skills and opportunities for children reported within UK households (Zhang & Livingstone, 2019). Most recently, these digital inequalities in the UK have been highlighted by the 2020 coronavirus pandemic, with significant disparity in access to resources for some families (Holmes & Burgess, 2020).

Guidelines

Also beyond the scope of this chapter but an important adjunct to digital play, is the provision of guidelines for caregivers regarding the types of play that are or are not appropriate (UNICEF, 2019), or the duration or nature of digital gaming that is suitable for certain children. In this domain, there are numerous different authorities offering advice; however, in many cases these conflict or disagree, with some advocating strict limits on screen-based activities, and others rejecting arbitrary limits and emphasising the importance of the type of activities which are undertaken. (See Straker et al., 2018, for a review of this debate.)

FINAL REFLECTION

In summary, digital play offers young children both rich, varied opportunities for enjoyment and growth, and significant risk of harm or distress. Particularly in early childhood, it is the child's immediate caregivers who will determine which of these events is most likely to occur. Caregiver mediation strategies are a critical component in shaping the digital environment and play experiences of children; it is also important to note that the wider public, political and professional communities play an important role too in guiding future aspects of digital play in early childhood.

KEY POINTS

- Digital play is a hugely varied and dynamic topic area, with the promise of increased variety and new examples in the near future.
- Caregivers have a great role and responsibility in the mediation and facilitation of digital play opportunities.
- Significant commercial interests are present in this area of play, which creates the need to consider the appropriate protection of children and their data.

QUESTIONS TO CONSIDER

1   What is best practice when it comes to early childhood and digital activities?
    A significant growth in digital engagement by children of all ages has created a demand for guidance to advise caregivers on how to best support their children in the digital domain. In response to this, a number of bodies have provided documents, three of which are listed below:

- American Paediatric Association (2016) Media and young minds. https://pediatrics.aappublications.org/content/138/5/e20162591.
- Royal Paediatric Society (2019) The health impacts of screen time: A guide for clinicians and parents. www.rcpch.ac.uk/sites/default/files/2018–12/rcpch_screen_time_guide_-_final.pdf.

- World Health Organization (2019) Guidelines on physical activity, sedentary behaviour and sleep for children under 5 years of age. https://apps.who.int/iris/handle/10665/311664.

Recover at least two of these, then compare and contrast the advice given. Do they differ in significant ways?

Consider the reasoning for any discrepancies you identify. Which of these differing perspectives do you think is the 'best' option, and why?

2. Read and reflect on this source and consider the key findings from the authors: Straker, L., Zabatiero, J., Danby, S., Thorpe, K., & Edwards, S. (2018) Conflicting guidelines on young children's screen time and use of digital technology create policy and practice dilemmas. *The Journal of Pediatrics*, 202, 300–303.

   a. Do you agree with the main conclusions?
   b. Which of the guidelines reviewed do you think are most helpful for caregivers?
   c. What aspects do you think are most problematic and in need of further development?

3. As outlined in the chapter, digital play is a dynamic and expanding area within human, technological and commercial development. Consider the ways future forms of digital play may be reimagined. What new threats and/or opportunities might these offer?

FURTHER READING

Donohue, C. (ed.) (2019) *Exploring Key Issues in Early Childhood and Technology: Evolving Perspectives and Innovative Approaches*. London: Routledge. (This source provides a detailed academic discussion on a broad range of contemporary topics from a range of different experts in the field.)

Mantilla, A., & Edwards, S. (2019) Digital technology use by and with young children: A systematic review for the Statement on Young Children and Digital Technologies. *Australasian Journal of Early Childhood*, 39(3), 76–83. (This systematic review aims to 'advise adults on appropriate digital technology use "by and with" young children aged birth to eight years. Four themes are canvassed in this review: (1) healthy practices; (2) relationships; (3) pedagogy; and (4) digital play'. It provides a valuable and detailed insight into the current literature regarding technology and early childhood on a range of different topics.)

Marsh, J., Plowman, L., Yamada-Rice, D., Bishop, J.C., Lahmar, J., Scott, F., Davenport, A., Davis, S., French, K., Piras, M., Thornhill, S., Robinson, P., & Winter, P. (2015) *Exploring Play and Creativity in Pre-Schoolers' Use of Apps: Final Project Report*. Available at: www.techandplay.org (accessed 5 May 2020).

(This website hosts the named report and considers technology in very early childhood and the role that apps play in the emergence of creativity. It provides tailored, accessible, evidence-based information for a range of groups, including parents, practitioners and even app developers.)

REFERENCES

Abrams, R.A., & Christ, S.E. (2003) Motion onset captures attention. *Psychological Science*, 14(5), 427–432.

Althoff, T., White, R.W., & Horvitz, E. (2016) Influence of Pokémon Go on physical activity: Study and implications. *Journal of Medical Internet Research*, 18(12), e315.

Anderson, D.R., Huston, A.C., Schmitt, K.L., Linebarger, D.L., Wright, J.C., & Larson, R. (2001) Early childhood television viewing and adolescent behavior: The recontact study. *Monographs of the Society for Research in Child Development*, 66(1), i–147.

Aunio, P., & Mononen, R. (2018) The effects of educational computer games on low-performing children's early numeracy skills: An intervention study in a preschool setting. *European Journal of Special Needs Education*, 33(5), 677–691.

Axford, C., Joosten, A.V., & Harris, C. (2018) IPad applications that required a range of motor skills promoted motor coordination in children commencing primary school. *Australian Occupational Therapy Journal*, 65(2), 146–155.

Baron, N.S. (2015) *Words Onscreen: The Fate of Reading in a Digital World*. New York: Oxford University Press.

Besio, S. (2016) The need for play for the sake of play. In *Play Development in Children with Disabilities*. Warsaw: Sciendo Migration, pp. 9–52.

Bonneton-Botté, N., Fleury, S., Girard, N., Le Magadou, M., Cherbonnier, A., Renault, M., … & Jamet, E. (2020) Can tablet apps support the learning of handwriting? An investigation of learning outcomes in kindergarten classrooms. *Computers & Education*, 151, 103831.

Boyd, K.A., Lee, H., & Holt, N.L. (2013). Family member's perceptions of change in children's active free play: An intergenerational study. *Sports and Exercise Psychology* 45(1),

Cadoret, G., Bigras, N., Lemay, L., Lehrer, J., & Lemire, J. (2018) Relationship between screen-time and motor proficiency in children: A longitudinal study. *Early Child Development and Care*, 188(2), 231–239.

Ceruzzi, P.E. (2010) 'Ready or not, computers are coming to the people': Inventing the PC. *OAH Magazine of History*, 24(3), 25–28.

Digital, Culture Media and Sport (DCMS) Select Committee (2019) *Immersive and Addictive Technologies.* Available at: https://publications.parliament.uk/pa/cm201719/cmselect/cmcumeds/1846/184602.htm (accessed 6 June 2020).

Donahue, M.Z. (2015) *From Wind-Up Dolls to Handheld Computers, Toys Follow Evolution of Tech.* Available at: https://insider.si.edu/2015/12/from-wind-up-dolls-to-handheld-computers-toys-follow-evolution-of-tech (accessed 22 February 2020).

Edwards, S. (2019) Digital play. In C. Donohue (ed.) *Exploring Key Issues in Early Childhood and Technology.* New York: Routledge.

Elshout, M., Elsen, M., Leenheer, J., Loos, M., & Luzak, J. (2016) Study on Consumers' Attitudes towards Terms and Conditions (T&Cs) Final Report. *Report for the European Commission, Consumers, Health, Agriculture and Food Executive Agency (Chafea) on behalf of Directorate-General for Justice and Consumers.* Brussels: European Commission. Available at: https://ec.europa.eu/info/sites/info/files/terms_and_conditions_final_report_en.pdf (accessed 5 November 2020).

Entertainment Retailers Association (2018) Streaming drives entertainment sales 9.4% higher in 2018 to sixth consecutive year of growth but physical remains crucial to deliver megahits. Press release. Available at https://eraltd.org/news-events/press-releases/2019/streaming-drives-entertainment-sales-94-higher-in-2018-to-sixth-consecutive-year-of-growth/.

Goggin, G. (2009) Adapting the mobile phone: The iPhone and its consumption. *Continuum*, 23(2), 231–244.

Gottschalk, F. (2019) Impacts of technology use on children: Exploring literature on the brain, cognition and well-being. *OECD Education Working Paper No. 195.* Available at: www.oecd.org/officialdocuments/publicdisplaydocumentpdf/?cote=EDU/WKP%282019%293&docLanguage=En (accessed 8 May 2020).

Gov.uk (2020) *Early Years Apps Approved to Help Families Kick Start Learning at Home.* Available at: www.gov.uk/government/news/early-years-apps-approved-to-help-families-kick-start-learning-at-home (accessed 6 June 2020).

Hammond, S.I., Müller, U., Carpendale, J.I., Bibok, M.B., & Liebermann-Finestone, D.P. (2012) The effects of parental scaffolding on preschoolers' executive function. *Developmental Psychology*, 48(1), 271–281.

Hirsh-Pasek, K., Zosh, J.M., Golinkoff, R.M., Gray, J.H., Robb, M.B., & Kaufman, J. (2015) Putting education in 'educational' apps: Lessons from the science of learning. *Psychological Science in the Public Interest*, 16(1), 3–34.

Holmes, H., & Burgess, G. (2020) *Coronavirus has Highlighted the UK's Digital Divide.* Cambridge Centre for Housing & Planning Research. Available at: www.cchpr.landecon.cam.ac.uk/Research/Start-Year/2017/building_better_opportunities_new_horizons/digital_divide (accessed 1 July 2020).

Howie, E.K., Coenen, P., Campbell, A.C., Ranelli, S., & Straker, L.M. (2017) Head, trunk and arm posture amplitude and variation, muscle activity, sedentariness and physical activity of 3 to 5 year-old children during tablet computer use compared to television watching and toy play. *Applied Ergonomics*, 65, 41–50.

Huang, L., & Pashler, H. (2005) Attention capacity and task difficulty in visual search. *Cognition*, 94(3), B101–B111.

Huber, B., Yeates, M., Meyer, D., Fleckhammer, L., & Kaufman, J. (2018) The effects of screen media content on young children's executive functioning. *Journal of Experimental Child Psychology*, 170, 72–85.

Hughes, B. (2002) *A Playworker's Taxonomy of Play Types*, 2nd edition. London: PLAYLINK.

Kardefelt-Winther, D. (2017) How does the time children spend using digital technology impact their mental well-being, social relationships and physical activity? An evidence-focused literature review. *Innocenti Discussion Paper 2017-02*. Florence, Italy: UNICEF Office of Research – Innocenti. Available at: www.unicef-irc.org/publications/pdf/Children-digital-technology-wellbeing.pdf (accessed 16 June 2020).

Kostyrka-Allchorne, K., Cooper, N.R., & Simpson, A. (2017) The relationship between television exposure and children's cognition and behaviour: A systematic review. *Developmental Review*, 44, 19–58.

Kucirkova, N. (2014) iPads in early education: Separating assumptions and evidence. *Frontiers in Psychology*, 5, 715.

Livingstone, S., Haddon, L. and Görzig, A. (eds) (2012) *Children, Risk and Safety Online: Research and Policy Challenges in Comparative Perspective*. Bristol: The Policy Press.

Livingstone, S., Mascheroni, G., Dreier, M., Chaudron, S., & Lagae, K. (2015) *How Parents of Young Children Manage Digital Devices at Home: The Role of Income, Education and Parental Style*. London: EU Kids Online, LSE. Available at: http://eprints.lse.ac.uk/63378/1/__lse.ac.uk_storage_LIBRARY_Secondary_libfile_shared_repository_Content_EU%20Kids%20Online_EU_Kids_Online_How%20parents%20manage%20digital%20devices_2016.pdf (accessed 12 July 2020).

Mantilla, A., & Edwards, S. (2019) Digital technology use by and with young children: A systematic review for the Statement on Young Children and Digital Technologies. *Australasian Journal of Early Childhood*, 39(3), 76–83.

Marsh, J.A. (2016a) The digital literacy skills and competences of children of pre-school age. *Media Education: Studi, Ricerche, Buone Pratiche*, 7(2), 197–214.

Marsh, J.A. (2016b) 'Unboxing' videos: Co-construction of the child as cyberflâneur. *Discourse: Studies in the Cultural Politics of Education*, 37(3), 369–380.

Marsh, J., Plowman, L., Yamada-Rice, D., Bishop, J.C., Lahmar, J., Scott, F., Davenport, A., Davis, S., French, K., Piras, M., Thornhill, S., Robinson, P., & Winter, P. (2015) *Exploring Play and Creativity in Pre-Schoolers' Use of Apps: Final Project Report*. Available at: www.techandplay.org (accessed 5 May 2020).

Marsh, J., Plowman, L., Yamada-Rice, D., Bishop, J., & Scott, F. (2016) Digital play: A new classification. *Early Years*, 36(3), 242–253.

Marsh, J., Plowman, L., Yamada-Rice, D., Bishop, J., Lahmar, J., & Scott, F. (2018) Play and creativity in young children's use of apps. *British Journal of Educational Technology*, 49(5), 870–882.

McLuhan, M. (1994 [1964]) *Understanding Media: The Extensions of Man*. Cambridge, MA: MIT Press. Available at: https://web.mit.edu/allanmc/www/mcluhan.mediummessage.pdf (accessed 4 June 2020).

McMains, S.A., & Somers, D.C. (2004) Multiple spotlights of attentional selection in human visual cortex. *Neuron*, 42(4), 677–686.

Milosavljevic, M., & Cerf, M. (2008) First attention then intention: Insights from computational neuroscience of vision. *International Journal of Advertising*, 27(3), 381–398.

Mustola, M., Koivula, M., Turja, L., & Laakso, M.L. (2018) Reconsidering passivity and activity in children's digital play. *New Media & Society*, 20(1), 237–254.

Nathanson, A.I., & Beyens, I. (2018) The role of sleep in the relation between young children's mobile media use and effortful control. *British Journal of Developmental Psychology*, 36(1), 1–21.

Nikken, P., & Jansz, J. (2014) Developing scales to measure parental mediation of young children's internet use. *Learning, Media and Technology*, 39(2), 250–266.

Nobel Prize Organisation (2020) *The Nobel Prize in Physics 1956*. Available at: www.nobelprize.org/prizes/physics/1956/summary (accessed 22 April 2020).

Ofcom (2020) *Children and Parents: Media Use and Attitudes Report 2019*. Available at: https://www.ofcom.org.uk/research-and-data/media-literacy-research/childrens/children-and-parents-media-use-and-attitudes-report-2019 (accessed March 2020)

Palmer, S. (2015) *Toxic Childhood: How the Modern World is Damaging our Children and What We Can Do About It*. London: Orion.

Parten, M.B. (1932) Social participation among pre-school children. *Journal of Abnormal and Social Psychology*, 27, 243–326.

Pendlebury, T. (2018) All the 2018 education apps Apple announced. *CNET*. Available at: www.cnet.com/pictures/all-the-2018-education-apps-apple-announced (accessed 16 June 2020).

Pitchford, N.J., Kamchedzera, E., Hubber, P.J., & Chigeda, A.L. (2018) Interactive apps promote learning of basic mathematics in children with special educational needs and disabilities. *Frontiers in Psychology*, 9, 262.

Przybylski, A.K., & Weinstein, N. (2017) A large-scale test of the Goldilocks hypothesis: Quantifying the relations between digital-screen use and the mental well-being of adolescents. *Psychological Science*, 28(2), 204–215.

Ralph, R. (2018) Media and technology in preschool classrooms: Manifesting prosocial sharing behaviours when using iPads. *Technology, Knowledge and Learning*, 23(2), 199–221.

Riordan, M., Hoddeson, L., & Herring, C. (1999) The invention of the transistor. *Reviews of Modern Physics*, 71(2), S336–S345.

Robson, S. (2014) The analysing children's creative thinking framework: development of an observation-led approach to identifying and analysing young children's creative thinking. *British Educational Research Journal* 40(1), 121–134.

Royal College of Paediatrics and Child Health (RCPCH) (2019) *The Health Impacts of Screen Time: A Guide for Clinicians and Parents*. Available at: www.rcpch.ac.uk/sites/default/files/2018–12/rcpch_screen_time_guide_-_final.pdf (accessed 5 April 2020).

Straker, L., Zabatiero, J., Danby, S., Thorpe, K., & Edwards, S. (2018) Conflicting guidelines on young children's screen time and use of digital technology create policy and practice dilemmas. *The Journal of Pediatrics*, 202, 300–303.

Strouse, G.A., Troseth, G.L., O'Doherty, K.D., & Saylor, M.M. (2018) Co-viewing supports toddlers' word learning from contingent and noncontingent video. *Journal of Experimental Child Psychology*, 166, 310–326.

Sun, Y., Lim, K.H., & Peng, J.Z. (2013) Solving the distinctiveness–blindness debate: A unified model for understanding banner processing. *Journal of the Association for Information Systems*, 14(2), 49–71.

Taylor, K., & Silver, L. (2019) Smartphone ownership is growing rapidly around the world, but not always equally. *Pew Research Center*, 5. Available at: www.pewresearch.org/global/wp-content/uploads/sites/2/2019/02/Pew-Research-Center_Global-Technology-Use-2018_2019-02-05.pdf (accessed 1 July 2020).

Tomopoulos, S., Brockmeyer Cates, C., Dreyer, B.P., Fierman, A.H., Berkule, S.B., & Mendelsohn, A.L. (2014) Children under the age of two are more likely to watch inappropriate background media than older children. *Acta Paediatrica*, 103(5), 546–552.

Treisman, A., & Gormican, S. (1988) Feature analysis in early vision: Evidence from search asymmetries. *Psychological Review*, 95(1), 15–48.

UK Children's Commissioner (2017) *Growing Up Digital*. Available at: www.childrenscommissioner.gov.uk/wp-content/uploads/2017/06/Growing-Up-Digital-Taskforce-Report-January-2017_0.pdf (accessed 15 June 2020).

UNICEF (2019) *Child Rights and Online Gaming: Opportunities & Challenges for Children and the Industry*. Available at: www.unicef-irc.org/files/upload/documents/UNICEF_CRBDigitalWorldSeriesOnline_Gaming.pdf (accessed 5 June 2020).

World Health Organization (WHO) (2018) *International Classification of Diseases (ICD): ICD-11*. Available at: www.who.int/classifications/icd/en (accessed 5 November 2020).

Zevenbergen, R. (2007) Digital natives come to preschool: Implications for early childhood practice. *Contemporary Issues in Early Childhood*, 8(1), 19–29.

Zhang, D., & Livingstone, S. (2019) *Inequalities in How Parents Support their Children's Development with Digital Technologies. Parenting for a Digital Future: Survey Report 4*. Available at: www.lse.ac.uk/media-and-communications/assets/documents/research/preparing-for-a-digital-future/P4DF-Report-4.pdf (accessed 1 June 2020).

6

PLAY AND GENDER

Kay Owen and Jenny Hallam

CONTENTS

This chapter explores how children develop their gender identity and discusses the extent to which this influences or is influenced by play. We consider some of the important milestones in gender development and the changes in play behaviours that accompany them.

THIS CHAPTER WILL...

- Outline key milestones in gender development
- Discuss research regarding differences in boys' and girls' play behaviours
- Investigate whether adults have a role in gender-typing play
- Discuss the relationship between play and emergent gender identity
- Consider some possible implications of gender-typed toys and play.

KEY TERMS

gender/gender identity, gender-typed behaviour, sex, stereotypes

INTRODUCTION

Imagine that a family member or close friend calls to tell you that their baby has been safely delivered. Probably the first question you ask is whether they have had a boy or a girl. You may even have attended a 'gender reveal' party where friends and family gather to learn whether the coming child is male or female. Knowing a person's sex would therefore appear to be regarded as extremely important. Some would argue that it subsequently does much to shape expectations and behaviour towards the child, not just by those who are involved in the baby's upbringing but also by society at large. The suggestion is that society holds expectations regarding suitable male and female behaviours and that this even spills over into the conscious or unconscious management of children's play. Visit any toy store or watch a group of young children playing and you will probably notice a difference in what girls and boys play with and how they play. The question is whether the differences you observe in the playground are innate or learnt. Are toy manufacturers responding to demand or creating demand? This chapter will help you to formulate your own opinion by considering a variety of theories and research findings.

Throughout the chapter, you will notice that, over the years, gender research has come in and out of fashion (see Chapter 1). You should therefore critically consider the likelihood that older findings still hold true.

DEFINING SEX AND GENDER

Before we move on, it is important to explore some definitions. The American Psychological Association (2015) offers the following distinctions:

Sex: the biological aspects of being male or female such as genitalia. It is connected to chromosomes, hormones and physical manifestations.

Gender: the psychological, behavioural, social, and cultural aspects of being male or female (i.e., masculinity or femininity). It refers to the attitudes, feelings, and behaviours that a culture associates with each biological sex.

Gender identity: a person's awareness of their identification as male or female and its implications.

Gender typing: the process of acquiring the values and behaviours considered appropriate for that sex.

Gender role stereotypes: ideas about what males and females are traditionally supposed to be like. Behaviour that is compatible with cultural expectations is referred to as *gender-normative*; behaviours that are viewed as incompatible with these expectations constitute *gender non-conformity*.

As sex differences are easily explained, this chapter will largely focus on gender development and the emergence of gender identity.

Let's begin our investigation, as we did in the Introduction, with the birth of a new baby.

 **TIME TO CONSIDER**

Type 'nursery ideas for baby girls' and then 'nursery ideas for baby boys' into your search engine. What do you notice about the images that appear? What do they suggest about social expectations regarding gender-typed personality and behaviour? Try repeating the exercise to look at clothes for baby boys and girls.

KEY MILESTONES IN GENDER DEVELOPMENT
Gender recognition

As soon as they can visually track objects and focus their attention on what they see, babies begin to develop notions of similarity and difference. This gradually extends into an ability to categorise and recognise that certain things are the same or belong together. One of the earliest categories to emerge is gender. Over the years, research has suggested that infants recognise the visual differences between male and female (Owen & Barnes, 2019):

- 6–9-month-old infants can distinguish male and female based on hairstyle (Intons-Peterson, 1988) and voice (Martin, Ruble & Skrybalo, 2002).
- 1-year-olds can tell the difference between photographs of men and women (Leinbach & Fagot, 1993).
- 2–3-year-olds use words such as 'boy' or 'girl' in their speech and can correctly identify their own gender (Thompson, 1975).
- 3-year-olds consistently designate particular colours, clothing and hairstyles as belonging to boys or girls (Picariello, Greenberg & Pillemer, 1990).
- 3-year-olds reliably separate given names into 'girl's names' or 'boy's names' (Bauer & Coyne, 2006).

Although recognition of difference is initially based on physical aspects such as height, facial hair and bone structure, young children believe that girls can grow up to be daddies and boys can grow up to be mummies if they want to. By the time they are about 5, children recognise that gender is fixed.

Development of gender identity

Fagot, Lienbach & O'Boyle (1992) found that 2–3-year-olds who could correctly identify people in photos as being boys and girls were more aware of gender stereotypes. Awareness and acceptance of stereotypical ideas develop throughout the early years, and young children believe that boys and girls must behave according to their gender roles. Two-year-olds are therefore surprised by instances of gender non-conformity, such as men putting on lipstick (Poulin-Dubois et al., 2002). They will also reject other children who violate gender stereotypes; a boy who plays with girl's toys will probably find himself being rejected by both boys and girls. Between 3 and 4 years old, three-quarters of girls exhibit what is termed 'gender appearance rigidity', often demanding to wear pink dresses and/or tutus, regardless of whether they are suited to the activity or weather conditions. This is particularly prevalent in girls who realise their gender is fixed for life (Halim et al., 2014). By the time they are 4–5 years old, children are aligning themselves with others of their gender. They report positive same-gender and negative other-gender attitudes, with both being based largely on gender stereotypes (Halim et al., 2016).

Recognition of sex differences therefore appears to stem from the observation of physical difference, whereas recognition of appropriate gendered behaviours is influenced by social norms. Let us consider some potential sources of cultural information.

Parents and siblings

From the very beginning, the way parents talk to and about their babies varies according to their sex. For instance, baby girls are described as cuddly and cute and are held closely. Boys are more likely to be commended for the strength of their grip or kick and are held less frequently by their parents. Mothers talk more and use more supportive speech towards girls (Leaper, Anderson & Sanders, 1998), and both mothers and fathers use more emotion words with daughters than with sons (Kuebli & Fivush, 1992). In early play, reactions such as fear and uncertainty are condoned amongst girls, whereas boys are expected to be bolder. Parents generally give children gender-typical chores, such as cooking and cleaning for daughters and washing the car for sons (Leaper, 2002). Children also learn from observing their parents and siblings. Children who have a working mum or a stay-at-home dad are less aware of gender stereotypes than those who come from traditional families (Turner & Gervai, 1995). Children with same-sex siblings are more likely to engage in gender-typed activity than those who have opposite-sex siblings. Finally, parents comment more on their daughter's appearance, sending out messages that it's important for girls to look good.

School and nursery

In Western cultures, teachers value stereotypically feminine behaviours such as sitting quietly and getting on with things. Assertiveness and aggression are not encouraged, so boys can suffer more criticism in the classroom than girls (Huston, 1983). However, research has also shown that boys dominate the classroom. Teachers are more likely to select boys to answer questions and boys receive more praise than girls when they give the correct answer (Sadker & Sadker, 1994). Bian, Leslie and Cimpian (2017) discovered that, at age 5, children thought both girls and boys could be 'really, really smart' (children's version of adult brilliance), but, by age 6, girls were less likely than boys to believe members of their gender were 'really, really smart'. Subsequently, girls began to avoid activities for 'really, really smart' children. These findings suggest that gendered notions of brilliance are acquired early and have an immediate effect on children's interests.

The media

Sexism in children's books and TV programmes has lessened in recent years. However, male characters are still usually leaders who make important decisions and respond to emergencies, whereas female characters are more passive and look after the house or work in the caring professions (Signorielli & Leers, 1992). Research has shown that children who watch a lot of TV are more likely to prefer gender-specific activities, have highly stereotyped views of men and women (Signorella, Bigler & Liben, 1993) and believe people think that boys are better (Halim, Ruble & Tamis-LeMonda, 2012).

 SPOTLIGHT ON RESEARCH

Golden, J.C., & Jacoby, J.W. (2018) Playing princess: Preschool girls' interpretations of gender stereotypes in Disney princess media. *Sex Roles*, 79, 299–313.

The princesses portrayed in Disney films provide clear and consistent messages regarding gender norms and roles. Golden and Jacoby examined how preschool girls interpret these messages through their pretend play and in their discussions. They recruited 31 3- to 5-year-old girls from a range of racial/ethnic and socio-economic backgrounds. The participants all attended one of two preschools in rural New England. Data collection involved a variety of methods, including pretend play observations, semi-structured interviews and parent questionnaires. Participants held stereotypical beliefs about the princesses and demonstrated highly gendered behaviours when pretending to be the princesses. Data was analysed using thematic analysis and identified four themes that defined the participants' princess play: beauty, a focus on clothing and accessories, princess body movements, and an exclusion of boys.

Reflective question

The authors conclude: 'Based on the outcomes of our study, parents and educators might reconsider the type and amount of media they provide for their children, acknowledging the effects of these images on their children's behaviours and understandings of gender' (Golden & Jacoby, 2018: 311). Do you agree that this is necessary?

It would appear, therefore, that from birth onwards, sex and gender have an impact on some of the ways in which children are treated, how they are expected to behave and how they view themselves.

THE EMERGENCE OF GENDERED PLAY BEHAVIOURS

In this section, we shall consider research evidence regarding how emergent gender identity is manifested in play. This links to some of the developmental milestones discussed in Chapter 1 and Chapter 2.

Considerable research has been conducted in this area, with numerous studies show-ing clear indications of gender conformism in children's play and in their toy selec-tion (see Table 6.1; Kollmayer et al., 2018). As with gender identity and stereotypes, we need to consider whether these differences in play behaviours are part of an innate bias, or the result of the child's environment. Given that parents are gener-ally the primary influence during early childhood, we shall begin by considering the influence of attitudes and behaviours within the home.

Play with parents

Research has consistently discovered that parents tend to rate same-gender-typed and gender-neutral toys as more desirable for their children than cross-gender-typed

Table 6.1   Toy choices and play behaviours by age group

Age in years	Toy choices and play behaviours
0–3	Gender-typed toy/play preferences emerge.
	At 14–22 months, boys prefer to play with trucks, hammers and cars, and girls prefer to play with dolls and soft toys (Smith & Daglish, 1977).
	At 18 months, children show greater involvement when playing with same-sex type toys than when playing with cross-sex toys (Caldera, Huston & O'Brien, 1989).
	A significant proportion of 18–24-month-old infants refuse to play with cross-sex toys, even when there is nothing else for them to play with (Caldera, Huston & O'Brien, 1989).
	Infants who show greater interest in a toy truck than in a doll at 6–9 months old, show significantly greater male-typical toy and activity preferences at age 4 (Lauer, Ilksoy & Lourenco, 2018).
	Between 2 and 2½ years old, 25% of children can sort photos into 'boys' and 'girls' piles and identify boys' and girls' toys (Campbell, Shirely & Caygill, 2002).
	2½–3½-year-olds ascribe activities such as cooking, sewing and giving kisses to girl dolls, and playing with trucks, fighting and climbing to boy dolls (Kuhn et al., 1978).
3–6	Children are more aware of the types of toys, activities and achievements considered appropriate for boys and girls (Serbin, Powliishta & Gulko, 1993).
	However, girls show more non-stereotypical responses than boys (Signorella, Bigler & Liben, 1993).
	When offered a choice between a doll and a train, girls are more inclined to choose the doll and boys to choose the train. If the doll is pink, this increases the girl's enthusiasm and the boy's avoidance (Wong & Hines, 2015). Once acquired, gender-typical colour preferences seem to influence toy preferences.
7–11	Children are more likely to accept girls engaging in cross-sex activities than boys. Boys judge other boys who engage in cross-sex activities particularly harshly.
	As they get older, children increasingly realise that gender discrimination is unfair (Killen, Pisacane, Lee-Kim & Ardila-Rey, 2001).

toys (Kollmayer et al., 2018). They respond more positively when they see their child playing with sexually stereotyped toys (Caldera, Huston & O'Brien, 1989), and choose gender-stereotypic toys when interacting with their children (Eisenberg, Wolchick, Hernandez & Pasternack, 1985). It is therefore no surprise that most parents also buy gender-traditional toys for their children (Etaugh & Liss, 1992). This means that girls are provided with more dolls and toys directed towards domestic activities, whilst boys receive more educational toys and items focused outside the home (Parsons & Howe, 2006). A parent's apparent approval does much to shape play, even amongst pre-verbal children. Toddlers continue or halt play according to parental response (Bandura, 1992; Feinman et al., 1992). Young children therefore have both the materials and the motivation to engage in gender-typed play.

During the toddler period, fathers initiate more play than mothers (Clark-Stewart, 1977) and whilst they encourage symbolic play, the themes fathers use differ stereotypically with boys and girls (Farver & Wimbarti, 1995). Indeed, parents show a general tendency to endorse gender-conformist play behaviours (Beresin & Sutton-Smith, 2010), particularly when playing with sons (Lynch, 2015). Parents' own levels of gender conformism predict children's attitudes (Dawson, Pike & Bird, 2015; Halpern & Perry-Jenkins, 2016). So, if dad refuses to play with the baby doll, his sons are also likely to refuse. Research suggests that play is less stereotypic and less dichotomised amongst children of lesbian and gay parents (Goldberg, Kashy & Smith, 2012). These children have less stereotypic attitudes towards gender, but still gender-type themselves in a gender-conformist fashion (Sumontha, Farr & Patterson, 2017).

During playful interactions with their children, fathers tend to engage in more physically rousing play (roughhousing, throwing infants in the air and run-and-chase games) than do mothers (Hughes, 2009). Instead, mothers' play tends to involve a teaching component and is more verbal than that of fathers. They spend more time naming objects, labelling and pointing than they do in physically active play (Hughes, 2009).

Parents are more likely to encourage daughters than sons to engage in pretend play (Gleason, 2005), with mothers being more likely than fathers to join in (Lindsey & Mize, 2001). Girls are therefore significantly more likely to participate in pretend play than boys (Gmitrova, Podhajecka & Gmitrov, 2009). Girls are also inclined to focus on family-related themes in their play (Anggard, 2011). Parents are more likely to condone risk-taking amongst boys (Rosen & Peterson, 1990), so boys engage in more play behaviours that are highly correlated with injury.

Thus, whilst the timing and intensity of gender-typing in children's play is probably mediated by a range of environmental factors (Fromberg & Bergen, 2006), parental attitudes certainly appear to play a role (Eisenberg et al., 1985).

TIME TO CONSIDER

Make a list of toys you would consider to be gender-neutral.

Given that modern Western society expects fathers to help care for their children and men to be able to cook, should baby dolls and toy kitchens be considered gender-neutral?

Choosing playmates

Who and what children play with changes according to their gender awareness (see Table 6.2). Leinbach and Fagot (1986) found that 2-year-old boys who could provide accurate gender labels for people in photographs rarely played with dolls, but boys who were unable to provide gender labels played with dolls as much as girls. Similarly, children who could accurately gender-label headshot photos were more likely to have same-sex playmates than those who could not (Fagot, Leinbach & Hagan, 1986).

Once children reach school age, they usually maintain gender group boundaries. Girls who attempt to join a boy's playgroup are generally ignored, whilst boys who

Table 6.2   Attitude towards toys and playmates by age group

Age in years	Attitude towards toys and playmates
0–3	2-year-old girls prefer to play with other girls and 3-year-old boys prefer to play with other boys (La Freniere, Strayer & Gauthier, 1984).
	Preference for same-sex playmates is known as gender segregation and has been observed in several different cultures.
3–6	Young children believe that it is wrong to exclude other children from playing with toys such as trucks or dolls based on their gender, but they do it anyway (Killen et al., 2001).
	4-year-olds report greater interest in gender-typed and neutral toys than in cross-gender-typed toys. However, when observed, girls in particular play with both neutral and cross-gender toys (Dinella, Weisgram & Fulcher, 2017).
	5-year-olds prefer social robots (such as ASIMO) to be gender-matched to them, but 9–12-year-olds show no preference (Sandygulova & O'Hare, 2018).
	Gender segregation intensifies
	4–5-years-olds reject playmates of the other sex (Ramsey, 1995).
	6½-year-olds spend 10 times more time with same-sex friends than with opposite-sex friends (Maccoby, 1998).
7–11	*Gender preferences are even more pronounced*
	Children who have cross-sex friendships are likely to be rejected by their peers (Kovacs, Parker & Hoffman, 1993).
	Gender-stereotyped preferences increase steadily throughout childhood, especially amongst boys, but decrease by age 12 (Kanka, Wagner, Buchmann & Spiel, 2019).

attempt to join in with girls' play are ridiculed by both males and females (Fagot & Leinbach, 1989). When children cluster into same-sex groupings, girls are usually more socially skilled than boys (Serbin, Moller, Powlishta & Gulko, 1991). As dramatic play increases during the preschool years, boys are more likely to focus on dangerous or heroic themes, whilst girls engage in more family-focused play (Anggard, 2011). However, we cannot be certain of the direction of influence here. Socially skilled children generally choose to play with other socially skilled children (Fabes et al., 2012) and having same-sex playmates may foster gender awareness and gender-typing (Ayres, Khan & Leve, 2006) It is therefore possible that segregated play is determined by factors other than personal toy or activity preferences. We shall therefore briefly consider some of the main non-physical differences between boys and girls, and the theoretical explanations as to their basis.

SEX DIFFERENCES: ARE MALES AND FEMALES REALLY DIFFERENT?

Maccoby and Jacklin (1974) conducted a review of sex difference research and concluded that there are only four small and reliable differences between men and women: verbal ability; visual/spatial abilities; mathematical ability; and aggression. At first glance, these appear to support well-known gender stereotypes within Western society.

Verbal ability

Girls acquire language earlier and have greater verbal abilities than boys (Schaadt, Hesse & Friederici, 2015). This advantage continues into adulthood and women are better than men at maths tasks that require some level of verbal reasoning (Gallagher, Levin & Cahalan, 2002).

However, research has shown that parents talk more to baby girls during play (Bornstein et al., 1999), and the amount of time parents spend talking to their child is a strong predictor of their later verbal ability. So verbal skills may be the result of increased interaction (Fivush, Brotman, Buckner & Goodman, 2000), or perhaps parents talk more to baby girls because they show a talent in this area.

Visual/spatial abilities

Whilst there are some differences according to the task, boys generally outperform girls in visual/spatial abilities. This can be detected in 4-year-olds and continues throughout the life span (Halpern, 2012).

Spatial ability has been linked to computer game usage and, as such, children's visual/spatial capabilities have increased in recent years (Subrahmanyam, Kraut, Greenfield & Gross, 2001). Boys, however, tend to play computer games more than girls and traditional 'boys' toys' such as construction sets support the development of visual/spatial skills.

Mathematical ability

For over two decades, boys have performed slightly better than girls in most tests of mathematical ability. When considering those who achieve highly in maths and science, males outnumber females by over 2 to 1 (Reilly, Neumann & Andrews, 2015).

Aggression

Boys are more physically and verbally aggressive than girls (Ostrov & Keating, 2004). These differences occur across socio-economic groups and cultures, are observable in children as young as 2 and increase throughout childhood (Knight, Fabes & Higgins, 1996). Girls engage in more relational aggression than boys, excluding other girls from the social group or talking about them (Crick, Casas & Ku, 1999).

More recent research has suggested that the following areas should be added to the list of sex differences proposed by Maccoby and Jacklin (1974):

- Boys are more active than girls.
- Girls are more timid than boys and less likely to take risks.
- From conception, boys are more vulnerable and more prone to atypicalities such as autism.
- From toddlerhood, boys are more likely to display anger, whilst girls show greater emotional sensitivity.
- Girls are more compliant to requests made by authority figures such as parents and teachers.
- Boys have slightly higher levels of self-esteem, particularly as they get older.

 **TIME TO CONSIDER**

What are currently the most popular toys for girls, and what are the most popular toys for boys? Looking through the lists, do you notice any correlation between the toys and the differences noted above? Do you think that manufacturers are responding to girls' and boys' innate abilities, or are the toys responsible for gender-typing children?

ARE THERE OTHER EXPLANATIONS FOR THE DIFFERENCES BETWEEN THE SEXES?

Before making our minds up, we should consider some theories that have been pro-posed to explain gender development and gender differences. These tend to either emphasise biological differences or social influence. We'll look at the evolutionary and biological explanations first.

Evolutionary theory

Evolutionary theory is based on the assumption that sex differences can be explained by our evolutionary past. It is suggested that men needed strong visual/spatial skills in order to be good hunter-gatherers (Geary, 2004). Furthermore, men had to com-pete to attract a mate and so those who were aggressive, assertive and competitive were more likely to successfully reproduce. Through the process of natural selection, visual/spatial ability, aggression, assertiveness and competitiveness became more pronounced in men.

Women, on the other hand, have to put far more investment into raising children because they carry the child for 9 months. In order to successfully raise children, women need to be kind, gentle and nurturing. They also need strong relationships with other women who can help with childcare.

Biological theories

Biological research indicates that there are small but consistent physical and struc-tural differences between male and female brains (Cahill, 2005). These differences are believed to originate in the developing foetal brain and are affected by sex hormones. For example, the area of the brain associated with spatial ability is rich in sex hormone receptors, and so exposure to high levels of male hormones during foetal develop-ment may lead to this area of the brain becoming highly specialised (Cahill, 2005).

Further research has demonstrated that being exposed to the 'wrong' hormones in the womb influences gender (Berenbaum, 2017). This applies to female foetuses who are exposed to high levels of testosterone in the womb and children who have a con-genital adrenal hyperplasia (CAH). This leads to girls having an XX genetic endow-ment, but male genitalia. Money and Ehrhaart (1972) studied a group of girls born with CAH who had undergone 'corrective' surgery at a young age and were raised as girls. It was reported that these girls were tomboys with a strong preference for boy's toys and activities. They also outperformed women in spatial ability tasks. This sug-gests that hormones have an important role to play in deciding gender.

Social learning theory

For social learning theorists such as Bandura, children learn about their gender role in two different ways:

- *Direct tuition*: Children receive rewards for acting in gender-appropriate ways and are punished or discouraged when they step outside of their gender stereotype.
- *Observational learning*: Children learn about their gender role from observing same-sex role models.

This links to our previous points regarding the encouragement children receive from their parents and peers to behave in a gender-conformist manner.

Developmental psychologists have reached two major conclusions:

1 Males and females are more psychologically similar than they are different.
2 Most gender role stereotypes are cultural myths that have no basis in 'fact'.

In this chapter, we have established that girls and boys differ in how they play and what they play with. Our final question is whether this is of any importance in terms of their learning and development.

DOES IT REALLY MAKE ANY DIFFERENCE WHAT CHILDREN PLAY WITH?

Yes, it develops specific skill sets. We have established that parents tend to select gender-stereotypic toys when interacting with their children. The toys, in turn, then shape the nature of the communication. Masculine toys generally evoke less conversation, less teaching and less physical contact (Caldera, Huston & O'Brien, 1989). Stereotypically female toys elicit higher levels of verbal and social interaction and more complex thematic play (Cherney et al., 2003). Consider playing with a train and some track as opposed to a doll and a tea set and the differences are clearly apparent. Girls' play is therefore liable to encourage social skills and empathy in the way we discussed in Chapter 2. It also encourages language, interaction and physical proximity. Boys' play encourages greater spatial awareness, self-reliance and risk-taking. Physical proximity is generally only achieved during play-fighting or relatively aggressive games.

Yes, it promotes sexual stereotypes. Murnen, Greenfield, Younger and Boyd (2016) analysed popular dolls and action figures and discovered that female characters were far more likely than male characters to be depicted with traditional feminine stereotyped cues (e.g. decorative clothing) and sexually submissive, hyper-feminine cues (e.g. revealing clothing). Male characters were far more likely to be portrayed with traditional masculine characteristics like functional clothing and the body-in-motion, and they were often depicted with hyper-masculine accessories such as possessing a weapon.

Yes, it shapes aspirations. The types of toys children are provided with does much to influence their perceptions of both their present and future self (Auster & Mansbach, 2012; Halim, Rubel & Tamis-LeMonda, 2013). For instance, girls who played with Barbies in a randomised trial, regarded females as having far fewer career options than those who played with less stereotypical toys (Sherman & Zubriggen, 2014). Similarly, children who engaged with Disney princess media and products, showed more female gender-stereotypical behaviour one year later than those who had not played with the toys (Coyne et al., 2016).

 CASE STUDY 6.1

As a mother of two boys aged 4 and 7, I have reflected upon my sons' toy preferences and how their play has changed as they have got older. When my sons were very young (between the ages of 0–3 years) they were both very happy to play with a range of toys and their gender was never an issue. Their playroom was a wonderful mix of construction toys, dolls, pushchairs and a play kitchen that we used for creative role play. These toys were seamlessly incorporated into our spontaneous play. Once, for example, we were role playing being builders on a construction site. My son brought over his doll and set up a childcare area so the baby was safe whilst we worked. We then split our time between building and caring for the baby. When my elder son entered school at 4 years old, things started to change. He would tell me that girls were stupid (even though some of his closest friends were girls) and started to make a distinction between boys' toys and girls' toys. This perception shaped his toy preferences and his toy box was suddenly filled with action figures. He also started to reprimand his younger brother for playing with dolls and other 'girl toys'. I was quite shocked and wondered why this change had happened. I noted that other boys who had a sister demonstrated a very different attitude towards toys and challenged the notion of 'toys for boys' and 'toys for girls'. However, when I watched toy adverts, I could see very clear and consistent messages about the types of toys that boys should play with. When shopping for toys, there was a clear separation of boys' and girls' toys. It appeared that these messages were having a powerful effect in setting expectations surrounding play. Transgression from societal norms was seen as wrong. As my elder son has got older, I have noticed that he once again considers that 'toys are toys'. I have heard him telling his younger brother that if you like a toy then it's OK to play with it because toys are for everyone. However, he is still personally unwilling to play with toys marketed at girls.

Source: Jenny Hallam, chapter co-author

FINAL REFLECTION

Whilst a child's sex is identifiable from the time they are in utero, their notions of gender identity emerge progressively throughout the first years of life. 'Influential others' such as peers, parents and teachers all affect the timing and intensity of this gender identification process and the incidence of gender-conformist play. This clearly has implications for children's future development. As adults caring for children, we need to consider whether there is a need to balance provision in order that children develop their own innate abilities rather than only developing those which are gender conformist.

KEY POINTS

....

- From early infancy, children can distinguish between male and female based on physical characteristics.
- By the time they are 3 years old, children have clear notions of their own gender identity and the associated gender typing.
- Regardless of whether they agree or disagree, young children state a preference for gender-typed toys and same-sex playmates and ostracise those who do not conform.
- Gender typing in appearance, gender segregation and play behaviours is particularly marked between the ages of 3 and 4 years old (Halim, Ruble, Tamis-LeMonda & Shrout, 2013).
- Gender-conformist toys and play serve to establish gender-typed behaviours and abilities.

QUESTIONS TO CONSIDER

....

1   Think back over the factors we have considered. To what extent do you think that play in early childhood has a role in shaping children's gender identity and establishing the sex differences noted in the chapter?
2   How many explanations can you think of for the finding that young children generally have same-sex playmates? Which of these factors do you think is the most important?
3   To what extent do you think adults should intervene in order to make play more gender neutral?
4   Do you think toy manufacturers should reduce the gender segregation of toys?

FURTHER READING

Kollmayer, M., Schultes, M.-T., Schober, B.,Hodosi, T., & Spiel, C. (2018) Parents' judgements about the desirability of toys for their children: Associations with gender role attitudes, gender-typing of toys, and demographics. *Sex Roles*, 79, 329–341. (An informative article covering the relationships between several different aspects.)

Let Toys Be Toys campaign: www.lettoysbetoys.org.uk (The campaign is asking the toy and publishing industries to stop limiting children's interests by promoting some toys and books as only suitable for girls, and others only for boys. The website contains information and ideas.)

REFERENCES

American Psychological Association. (2015) *APA Dictionary of Psychology*, 2nd edition. Washington, DC: APA.

Anggard, E. (2011) Children's gendered and non-gendered play in natural spaces. *Children, Youth and Environments*, 21(2), 5–33.

Auster, C.J., & Mansbach, C.S. (2012) The gender marketing of toys: An analysis of colour and type of toy on the Disney Store website. *Sex Roles*, 67(7–8), 375–388.

Ayres, M.M., Khan, A., & Leve, L.D. (2006) Gender, identity and play. In D. Bergen & D.P. Fromberg (eds) *Play from Birth to Twelve: Contexts, Perspectives and Meanings*, 3rd edition. New York: Routledge.

Bandura, A. (1992) Social cognitive theory of social referencing. In Feinman, S. (ed.) *Social Referencing and the Social Construction of Reality in Infancy*. Boston, MA: Springer, pp. 175–208. https://link.springer.com/chapter/10.1007/978-1-4899-2462-9_8

Bauer, P.J., & Coyne, M.J. (2006) When the name says it all: Preschoolers' recognition and use of the gendered nature of common proper names. *Social Development*, 6(3), 271–291.

Berenbaum, S.A. (2017) Beyond pink and blue: The complexity of early androgen effects on gender development. *Child Development Perspectives*, 12(1), 58–64.

Beresin, A.R., & Sutton-Smith, B. (2010) *The Grown-ups Giveth, the Grown-ups Taketh Away; Misunderstanding Gendered Play*. Jackson: University Press of Mississippi.

Bian, L., Leslie, S-J., & Cimpian, A. (2017) Gender stereotypes about intellectual ability emerge early and influence children's interests. *Science*, 355(6323), 389–391. DOI: 10.1126/science.aah6524

Bornstein, M., Haynes, O., Pascual, L., Painter, K., & Galperin, C. (1999) Play in two societies: Pervasiveness of process, specificity of structure. *Child Development*, 70, 317–331.

Cahill. L. (2006) Why sex matters for neuroscience. *Nature Reviews Neuroscience*, 7, 477–484.

Caldera, Y.M., Huston, A.C., & O'Brien, M. (1989) Social Interactions and play patterns of parents and toddlers with feminine, masculine and neutral toys. *Child Development*, 60(1), 70–76.

Cherney, I.D., Kelly-Vance, L., Glover, K.G., Ruane, A., & Ryall, B.O. (2003) The effect of stereotyped toys and gender on play assessment of children aged 18-47 months. *Educational Psychology*, 23(1), 95–106.

Clark-Stewart, K.A. (1977) *Child Care in the Family: A Review of Research and Some Propositions for Policy*. New York: Academic Press.

Coyne, S.M., Linder, J.R., Rasmussen, E.E., Nelson, D.A., & Victoria Birkbeck, V. (2016) Pretty as a princess: Longitudinal effects of engagement with Disney princesses on gender stereotypes, body esteem, and prosocial behavior in children. *Child Development*, 87(6), 1909–1925.

Crick, N.R., Casas, J.F., & Ku, H-C. (1999). Relational and physical forms of peer victimization in preschool. *Developmental Psychology*, 35(2), 376–385. https://psycnet.apa.org/doi/10.1037/0012-1649.35.2.376

Dawson, A., Pike, A., & Bird, L. (201). Associations between parental gendered attitudes and behaviours and children's gender development across middle childhood. *European Journal of Developmental Psychology*, 13(4), 452–471.

Dinella, L.M., Weisgram, E.S., & Fulcher, M. (2017) Children's gender-typed toy interests: Does propulsion matter? *Arch Sex Behaviours*, 46, 1295–1305. doi:10.1007/s10508-016-0901-5

Eisenberg, N., Wolchik, S.A., Hernandez, R., & Pasternack, J.F. (1985) Parental socialization of young children's play: A short-term longitudinal study. *Child Development*, 56(6), 1506–1513.

Etaugh, C., & Liss, M.B. (1992) Home, school and playroom: Training grounds for adult gender roles. *Sex Roles*, 26(3/4), 129–133.

Fabes, R.A., Hanish, L.D., Martin, C.L., Moss, A., & Reesing, A. (2012) The effects of young children's affiliations with prosocial peers on subsequent emotionality in peer interactions. *British Journal of Developmental Psychology*, 30(4), 569–585.

Fagot, B.I., & Leinbach, M.D. (1989) The young child's gender schema: Environmental input, internal organization. *Child Development*, 60(3), 663–672.

Fagot, B.I., Leinbach, M.D., & Hagan, R. (1986) Gender labelling and the adoption of sex-typed behaviours. *Developmental Psychology*, 22(4), 440–443.

Fagot, B.I., Leinbach, M.D., & O'Boyle, C. (1992) Gender labelling, gender stereotyping and parenting behaviours. *Developmental Psychology*, 28 (2), 225–230.

Farver, J.A.M., & Wimbarti, S. (1995) Indonesian children's play with their mothers and older siblings. *Child Development*, 66(5), 1493–1503.

Feinman, S., Roberts, D., Hsieh, K-F., Sawyer, D., & Swanson, D. (1992) A critical review of social referencing in infancy. In Feinman, S. (ed.) *Social Referencing and the Social Construction of Reality in Infancy*. Boston, MA: Springer.

Fivush, R., Brotman, M.A., Buckner, J.P., & Goodman, S.H. (2000) Gender differences in parent–child emotion narratives. *Sex Roles*, 42, 233–253. https://doi.org/10.1023/A:1007091207068

Fromberg, D.P., & Bergen, D. (2006) *Play from Birth to Twelve: Contexts, Perspectives and Meanings*, 2nd edition. New York, Routledge.

Gallagher, A., Levin, J., & Cahalan, C. (2002) Cognitive patterns of gender differences on mathematics admissions tests. *ETS Research Report Series*, 2, i–30

Geary, D.C. (2004) Mathematics and learning disabilities. *Journal of Learning Disabilities*, 37(1), 4–15.

Gleason, T.R. (2005) Mothers' and fathers' attitudes regarding pretend play in the context of imaginary companions and of child gender. *Merrill-Palmer Quarterly*, 51(4), 412–436.

Gmitrova, V., Podhajecka, M. & Gmitrov, J. (2009) Children's play preferences: Implications for the preschool education. *Early Childhood Development and Care*, 189(3), 339–351.

Goldberg, A.E., Kashy, D.A., & Smith, J.Z. (2012) Gender-typed play behaviour in early childhood: Adopted children with lesbian, gay and heterosexual parents. *Sex Roles*, 67(9), 503–515.

Golden, J.C., & Jacoby, J.W. (2018) Playing princess: Preschool girls' interpretations of gender stereotypes in Disney princess media. *Sex Roles*, 79, 299–313. https://doi.org/10.1007/s11199-017-0773-8

Halim, M.L.D., Ruble, D.N., Tamis-LeMonda, C.S. (2012) Four-year-olds beliefs about how others regard males and females. *British Journal of Developmental Psychology*, 31(1), 128–135. doi.org/10.1111/j.2044-835X.2012.02084.x

Halim, M.L.D., Ruble, D.N., Tamis-LeMonda, C.S., & Shrout, P.E. (2013) Rigidity in gender-typed behaviours in early childhood: A longitudinal study of ethnic minority children. *Child Development*, 84(4), 1269–1284. https://doi.org/10.1111/cdev.12057

Halim, M.L.D., Ruble, D.N., Tamis-LeMonda, C.S., Shrout, P.E., & Amoio, D.M. (2016) Gender attitudes in early childhood: Behavioural consequences and cognitive antecedents. *Child Development*, 88(3), 882–899.

Halim, M.L.D., Ruble, D.N., Tamis-LeMonda, C.S., Zosuls, K.M., Lurye, L.E., & Greulich, F.K. (2014) Pink frilly dresses and the avoidance of all things 'girly': Children's appearance rigidity and cognitive theories of gender development. *Developmental Psychology*, 50(4), 1091–1101.

Halpern, D.F. (2012) *Sex Differences in Cognitive Abilities*, 4th edition. New York: Psychology Press.

Halpern, H.P., & Perry-Jenkins, M. (2016) Parents' gender ideology and gendered behavior as predictors of children's gender-role attitudes: A longitudinal exploration. *Sex Roles*, 74(11–12), 527–542.

Hughes, F.P. (2009) *Children, Play and Development*, 4th edition. London: Sage.

Huston, A.C. (1983) Sex-typing. *Handbook of Child Psychology*, 4(4), 387–467.

Intons-Peterson, M.J., (1989) *Children's Concepts of Gender*. Mahwah, NJ: Lawrence Erlbaum Associates Inc.

Kanka, M.H., Wagner, P., Buchmann, M., & Spiel, C. (2019) Gender-stereotyped preferences in childhood and early adolescence: A comparison of cross-sectional and longitudinal data. *European Journal of Developmental Psychology*, 16(2), 198–214. DOI: 10.1080/17405629.2017.1365703

Killen, M., Pisacane, K., Lee-Kim, J., & Ardila-Rey, A. (2001) Fairness or stereotypes? Young children's priorities when evaluating group exclusion and inclusion. *Developmental Psychology*, 37(5), 587–596.

Knight, G.P., Fabes, R.A., & Higgins, D.A. (1996) Concerns about drawing causal inferences from meta-analyses: An example of the study of gender differences in aggression. *Psychological Bulletin*, 119(3), 410–421.

Kollmayer, M., Schultes, M.-T., Schober, B.,Hodosi, T., & Spiel, C. (2018) Parents' judgements about the desirability of toys for their children: Associations with gender role attitudes, gender-typing of toys, and demographics. *Sex Roles*, 79, 329–341.

Kovacs, D.M., Parker, J.G., & Hoffman, L.W. (1993) Behavioural, affective, and social correlates of involvement in cross-sex friendship in elementary school. *Child Development*, 67(5) 2269–286.

Kuebli, J., & Fivush, R. (1992) Gender differences in parent-child conversations about past emotions. *Sex Roles*, 27(11), 683–698.

Kuhn, D., Nash, L., & Brucken, L. (1978) Sex role concept of two- and three-year-olds. *Child Development*, 49(2), 445–451.

La Freniere, P., Strayer, F.F., & Gauthier, R. (1984) The emergence of same-sex affiliative preferences among preschool peers: A developmental/ethological perspective. *Child Development*, 55(5), 1958–1965.

Lauer, J.E., Ilksoy, S.D., & Lourenco, S.F. (2018) Developmental stability in gender-typed preferences between infancy and preschool age. *Developmental Psychology*, 54(4), 613–620. https://doi.org/10.1037/dev0000468

Leaper, C. (2002) Parenting boys and girls. In M. H. Bornstein (ed.) *Handbook of Parenting: Children and Parenting*. London: Lawrence Erlbaum Associates Publishers, pp. 189–225.

Leaper, C., Anderson, K.J., & Sanders, P. (1998) Moderators of gender effects on parents' talk to their children: A meta-analysis. *Developmental Psychology*, 34(1), 3–27. https://doi.org/10.1037/0012-1649.34.1.3

Leinbach, M.D., & Fagot, B.I. (1993) Categoriacal habituation to male and female faces: Gender schematic processing in infancy. *Infant Behaviour and Development* 16(3), 317–333.

Lindsey, E.W., & Mize, J. (2001) Interparental agreement, parent-child responsiveness and children's peer competence. *Family Relations*, 50(4), 348–354.

Lynch, M. (2015) Guys and dolls: A qualitative study of teachers' views of gendered play in kindergarten. *Early Child Development and Care*, 185(5), 679–693.

Maccoby, E. E. (1998) *The Two Sexes: The Implications of Childhood Divergence for Adult Relationships*. Cambridge, MA: Harvard University Press.

Maccoby, E. E., & Jacklin, C. N. (1974) *The Psychology of Sex Differences*. Stanford, CA: Stanford University Press.

Martin, C.L., Rubel, D.N., & Szkrybalo, J. (2002) Cognitive theories of early gender development. *Psychological Bulletin*, 128(6), 903–933.

Money, J., & Ehrhardt, A. A. (1972) *Man and Woman, Boy and Girl: Differentiation and Dimorphism of Gender Identity from Conception to Maturity*. New York: Johns Hopkins University Press.

Murnen, S.K., Greenfield, C., Younger, A., & Boyd, H. (2016) Boys act and girls appear: A content analysis of gender stereotypes associated with characters in children's popular culture. *Sex Roles*, 74(1–2), 78–91.

Ostrov, J.M., & Keating, C.F. (2004) Gender differences in preschool aggression during free play and structured interactions: An observational study. *Social Development*, 13(2), 255–277. https://doi.org/10.1111/j.1467-9507.2004.000266.x

Owen, K., & Barnes C. (2019) The development of categorisation in early childhood: A review, *Early Child Development and Care*, 191(6), 1–8. DOI: 10.1080/03004430.2019.1608193

Parsons, A., & Howe, N. (2006) Superhero toys and boys: Physically active and imaginative play. *Journal of Research in Childhood Education*, 20(4), 287–300.

Picariello, M.L., Greenberg, D.N., & Pillemer, D.B. (1990) Children's sex-related stereotyping of colours. *Child Development*, 61(5), 1453–1460.

Poulin-Dubois, D., Serbin, L.A., Colburne, K.A., Sen, M.G., & Eichstedt, J.A. (2002) Gender stereotyping in infancy: Visual preferences for and knowledge of gender-stereotyped toys in the second year. *International Journal of Behavioural Development*, 25(1), 7–15.

Ramsey, P.G. (1995) Changing social dynamics in early childhood classrooms. *Child Development*, 66(3), 764–773.

Reilly, D., Neumann, D. L., & Andrews, G. (2015) Sex differences in mathematics and science achievement: A meta-analysis of National Assessment of Educational Progress assessments. *Journal of Educational Psychology*, 107(3), 645–662. https://doi.org/10.1037/edu0000012

Rosen, B.N., & Peterson, L. (1990). Gender differences in children's outdoor play injuries: A review and an integration. *Clinical Psychology Review*, 10(2), 187–205. https://doi.org/10.1016/0272-7358(90)90057-H

Sadker, M., & Sadker, D. (1986) Sexism in the classroom: From grade school to graduate school. *Phi Delta Kappan*, 67(7), 513–515.

Sandygulova, A., & O'Hare, G.M.P. (2018) Age- and gender-based differences in children's interactions with a gender-matching robot. *International Journal of Social Robotics*, 10, 687–700. doi:10.1007/s12369-018-0472-9

Schaadt, G., Hesse, V., & Friederici, A.D. (2015) Sex hormones in early infancy seem to predict aspects of later language development. *Brain and Language*, 141, 70–76.

Serbin, L.A., Moller, L.C., Powlishta, K.K., & Gulko, J. (1991) The emergence of sex segregation in toddler playgroups, In C. Leaper (ed.) *The Development of Gender and Relationships*. San Francisco, CA: Jossey-Bass, pp. 7–18.

Serbin, L.A., Powlishta, K.K., Gulko, J., Martin, C.L., & Lockhead, M.E. (1993) The development of sex typing in middle childhood. *Monographs of the Society of Research in Child Development*, 58(2), 1–99.

Sherman, A.M., & Zubriggen, E.L. (2014) 'Boys can be anything': Effect of Barbie play on girls' career cognitions. *Sex Roles*, 70(5), 195–208.

Signorella, M.L., Bigler, R.S., & Liben, L.S. (1993) Developmental differences in children's gender schema about others: A meta-analytic review. *Developmental Review*, 13(2), 147–183.

Signorielli, N. & Lears, M. (1992). Children, television, and conceptions about chores: Attitudes and behaviors. Sex Roles, 27, 157–170.

Smith, P.K., & Daglish, L. (1977) Sex differences in parent and infant behaviour in the home. *Child Development*, 48(4), 1250–1254.

Subrahmanyam, K., Kraut, R., Greenfield P., & Gross, E. (2001) The impact of computer use on children's and adolescents' development. *Journal of Applied Developmental Psychology*, 22(1), 7–30.

Sumontha, J., Farr, R.H., & Patterson, C.J. (2017) Children's gender development: Associations with parental sexual orientation, division of labour and gender ideology. *Psychology of Sexual Orientation and Gender Diversity*, 4(4), 438–450. https://doi.org/10.1037/sgd0000242

Thompson, S. (1975) Gender labels and early sex role development. *Child Development*, 46, 339–347.

Turner, P. J., & Gervai, J. (1995) A multidimensional study of gender typing in preschool children and their parents: Personality, attitudes, preferences, behavior, and cultural differences. *Developmental Psychology*, 31(5), 759–772. https://doi.org/10.1037/0012-1649.31.5.759

Wong, W.I., & Hines, M. (2015) Effects of gender color-coding on toddlers' gender-typical toy play. *Archives of Sexual Behavior*, 44(5), 1233–1242.

7

WHAT ARE WE PLAYING AT?

Carol Fenton

CONTENTS

This chapter is about therapeutic play. Play is an essential element in the holistic development of children and Positive Play, play therapy and nurture group interventions help children to resolve inner conflicts by encouraging the development of self-control, self-respect and a management of emotions when difficulties are experienced in a child's life.

 THIS CHAPTER WILL...

- Discuss the importance of play in the wellbeing of the child
- Explain aspects of social and emotional development that may require play intervention for children at risk
- Explore some of the play-based interventions children may be engaged in to enhance their wellbeing
- Enable reflection on the role of a professional in supporting children.

KEY TERMS

behaviour, emotional, mental health, nurture groups, play therapy, Positive Play, social

INTRODUCTION

My interest in **Positive Play**, **play therapy** and **nurture groups** is grounded in my undergraduate study. I read with interest *Dibs: In Search of Self* (Axline, 1964). This book had a profound effect on me and I have referred to it on numerous occasions, both within my professional career as a teacher and headteacher and now as a lecturer of undergraduate students. Indeed, it is a book I recommend to any student interested in the social and emotional development of children. I have always been of the opinion that children's behaviour is a portrayal of their lived experience. As an educational care officer, I was asked to support a child demonstrating significant disaffected behaviour who had been excluded from a number of schools. The headteacher of the school was determined that this child would not be excluded again. The use of solution-focused therapy counselling, a person-centred approach advocated by Rogers (1957), proved to be the vital step this child needed. He was not excluded. My own teaching and leadership of a school recognised that this person-centred approach was crucial in supporting children with both short- and long-term emotional problems manifesting in adverse behaviour and negative mental health.

THE IMPORTANCE OF PLAY AND THE LINKS TO CHILDREN'S WELLBEING

The playing adult steps sideward into another reality; the playing child advances forward to new stages of mastery. (Erik H. Erikson, 1902–1994, 1995: 200)

In Chapter 1, Owen suggests that common play behaviours support physical development whilst also introducing activities and behaviours that will be useful in adult life. In considering the holistic development of the child, it is useful to consider the impact not just of physical growth, but also that of the child's mental and social development within the social and emotional developmental sphere.

The importance of role and imaginative play in the social and emotional development of the child cannot be underestimated. Meggit (2012) notes that children learn to understand a number of concepts through play, and in role play children copy the way they have observed others behave in certain situations. More broadly, Cattanach (2008) defines play as the vehicle in which the child begins to recognise moving beyond 'me' to develop a relationship with the wider world, and, importantly, Ruby (2018) acknowledges that wellbeing, in terms of social and emotional development for children, is a significant factor in the resultant state of mental health in adulthood.

It follows then that play enables the child to develop a stable state of emotional health, based on their ability to detach themselves from 'me' and move towards wider world relationships and adult life satisfaction. Consider, then, how this links to the importance of the child's wellbeing. Bethune (2018) notes that happiness is a state for which humans strive and it is very much an individual position. This is closely linked to wellbeing and, if children are taught the skills to lead a happy life, they are then equipped with the means to deal with the difficulties of life and an ability to look after themselves. The Children's Society in the Good Childhood Report (2020) identified that children's wellbeing can be determined by their subjective wellbeing (a self-assessment of how their lives are going) and their psychological wellbeing (a sense of meaning, purpose and engagement with life). When these two are aligned, children flourish. It is of course recognised that happiness involves both positive and negative emotions, the creation of strong social ties and the ability to contribute to the wider, social sphere (Bethune, 2018). Indeed, this is also the basis of resilience, a fundamental aspect of leading a happy life, as the two co-exist.

A necessary question raised, therefore, is whether happiness can be taught. Lucas (2007) puts forward the 'set point' theory, arguing that people will always return to a set point despite good or bad events in their lives. This theory was based on the belief that happiness levels seldom change around a biologically established set point. Lucas notes, however, that recent studies have identified that adaptation is not certain, as the extent to which people adapt is significantly individual. Bethune (2018) would agree, noting that the latest research demonstrates that raising the set point of happiness can be shaped by individual contributions; in effect, actions and choices. It follows then that play, the child's work, is perhaps one of the most significant vehicles in teaching children the concept of happiness, and hence, in turn, increasing their capacity to develop strong social ties and their ability to contribute to the wider social sphere that are fundamental aspects of a happy life.

 TIME TO CONSIDER

Can happiness be taught?

What do you consider to be the basis of happiness in life?

How can you measure it, and can you measure it?

ASPECTS OF SOCIAL AND EMOTIONAL DEVELOPMENT THAT MAY REQUIRE PLAY INTERVENTION FOR CHILDREN AT RISK

Wellbeing

The Children's Society (2020) noted that 10 per cent of young people suffer from low levels of wellbeing, whilst Green et al. (2005: xxl) professed that 'one in ten young people aged 5–16 had a clinically diagnosed mental disorder'. A mental disorder, as defined by ICD-10-CM (CDC, 2020), is determined as being a 'clinically recognisable set of symptoms or behaviour associated in most cases with considerable distress and substantial interference with personal function' (Green, 2005: x). The importance of children's subjective and psychological wellbeing has already been highlighted by the Children's Society as the underpinning aspect of their ability to flourish.

Self-esteem

Of course, linked to wellbeing is self-esteem. Howard, Burton, Levermore and Barrell (2017) note that, in the early years, the child begins to develop the concept of self-worth, an ability to determine how they think about themselves. This, according to Glazzard and Bligh (2018), includes the child's idea of their 'ideal self'. If there is a discrepancy between the 'ideal self' and the self-concept, this will result in low self-esteem. Howard and colleagues (2017) cite Young Minds (2017), in that an individual with low self-esteem will feel that they do not deserve love and support, whereas those with positive self-esteem, as a result of nurtured self-efficacy (an ability to overcome challenges), are the opposite. Dowling (2014) supports this, in that children will not develop an accurate idea of their own self-worth until about 6 years of age. Importantly, the interactions they have with others around them will provide them with the skills and ability to make these judgements about themselves. Glazzard and Bligh (2018) state that, even in challenging circumstances, children need to be taught the value of persevering with social relationships because their sense of self will be affected by their interactions, and the challenges in those relationships will support the development of social resilience.

Clearly, it can be deemed that the more positive relationships children engage in, the higher their self-esteem will be. Significantly, Howard and colleagues (2017) recognise that everyone exists in relation to others and that relationships provide the messages that determine self-worth, reflected back through the eyes and minds of others.

Resilience

Further studies (e.g. DfE, 2014) have suggested that a child absorbs *risk* factors which make them vulnerable, and *protective* factors that make them resilient. This is a fine balance – if the protective factors can be accessed and applied, they counterbalance the risk factors and promote resilience. The word resilience comes from the Latin word 'resilire', meaning to recoil or leap back. In this sense, it is the ability of the child to bounce back from adversity (Glazzard and Bligh, 2018). A less resilient child, one with a low self-concept and self-esteem, will take longer to recover from negative experiences. Howard et al. (2017) agree, noting that other aspects such as attachment and familial warmth, are essential for the child to cope in adversity. Indeed, Bowlby (1997) stated that a warm, intimate and consistent relationship with a primary caregiver is essential for a child's mental health. These are the factors that contribute to an individual's secure self-esteem and self-concept.

The role of adults in building resilience

It has been recognised by Ruby (2018) that recently schools have started to acknowledge the critical role they can perform to support the emotional wellbeing and mental health of children. Despite this, however, school staff have to rely on informal identification with no universal screening. Notwithstanding this, The Pursuit of Happiness Report (CentreForum Commission, 2014: 36) and the House of Commons Health Committee (2014) recommended training be accessed by educational staff, in child development, mental health and psychological resilience, to aid in the identification of vulnerable children. Likewise, the findings of the Children and Young People's Mental Health and Well-Being Taskforce, Future in Mind (DoH, 2015), noted that it was imperative that children and young people are taught to improve their resilience skills, that the workforce be developed and that early intervention enable improvement to access for services as part of the culture of the setting's core business. Glazzard and Bligh (2018) support this, drawing on the range of protective factors that help children become resilient. They believe that, within school, it is the teacher's responsibility to support and encourage the development of the child's positive sense of self. They can do this by demonstrating mutual respect, empathy and a sense of being valued, as some children are unable to demonstrate these characteristics intuitively. With this in mind, there is evidence that schools that embed the development of social and emotional skills in children, achieve an 11 per cent gain in improvement of behaviour and subsequent gain in attainment (Durlack et al., 2011). Likewise, Hughes and Schlösser (2014) note that emotionally challenged children may experience difficulties with peer relationships and academic progress, often continuing into their adult lives.

Whilst this may seem incongruent to mention, as this chapter is focused on social and emotional development and not attainment, it must be noted that educational attainment will always be the basis for the child's future economic status. Indeed, two of the Every Child Matters outcomes (HM Treasury, 2003) noted that children should make a positive contribution to society and not engage in anti-social behaviour, and not be disadvantaged from achieving economic wellbeing and reaching their full potential.

TIME TO CONSIDER

Review the UNCRC (at www.unicef.org.uk/what-we-do/un-convention-child-rights) and consider how the child is entitled to special care and assistance and a right to a voice. How could you ensure this for the children in your care?

CASE STUDY 7.1

The prologue of *Dibs: In Search of Self* (Axline, 1964) tells the reader that Dibs initially 'would not talk. He would not play. Judged mentally defective, he was oblivious to both other children and his teacher'. It explains the struggles and difficulties he faced, stating 'Dibs experienced profoundly the complex process of growing up'. The book then explains how psychotherapy enabled him to find greater happiness and security through a recognition that 'the stabilising centre he searched for with such intensity was deep down inside [him]self'.

Reflective questions

- You will notice that the excerpt states that Dibs 'would not' talk or play rather than that he could not. Why do you think a child may select not to do these things?
- What do you think the author means by 'Dibs experienced profoundly the complex process of growing up'? Do you think most children have this experience?

PLAY-BASED INTERVENTIONS CHILDREN MAY ENGAGE IN TO SUPPORT THEIR WELLBEING

Howard and colleagues (2017) acknowledge that the identification of children deemed to be in need of intervention sits within both the medical and psychological model and will also take account of sociological factors. Notwithstanding this, the humanistic approach developed by Carl Rogers will always be adopted. His idea that the fundamental conditions of empathy, unconditional positive regard and congruence are the foundation of the therapeutic relationship underpin all approaches to therapy (Rogers, 1957). Bennathan and Boxall (1998) advocated the use of play to help children express their fears, and provide encouragement to enable them to move on from any trauma they may have suffered. It is also recognised by Glazzard and Bligh (2018) that there are numerous factors that may affect a child's wellbeing detrimentally, so it is essential that the holistic development of the child is valued and a safe nurturing environment is provided.

Pugh (2015) notes that policy in the past ten years has been adapted to reflect the challenges for young children and adolescents in developing resilience and psychological wellbeing, and Child and Adolescent Mental Health Services (CAMHS) provide a network of support which includes, at tier two, play therapy (Howard et al., 2017). Likewise, the House of Commons Health Committee (2014: 98) commissioned CAMHS to invest in 'early intervention providing timely support before mental health problems become entrenched'.

 SPECIAL STUDY: POSITIVE PLAY

The Positive Play support programme was established by Derbyshire County Council over 20 years ago and is a 'unique early intervention programme designed to raise the self-esteem and emotional wellbeing of shy, timid, disaffected and challenging children and young people'.

The Positive Play support centre has a suite of rooms including a rainbow room, an enchanted forest, a sensory magic room, an office and a courtyard. It also has a comprehensive library for the use of schools and practitioners who are supported by the Positive Play team.

One-to-one sessions are delivered in a sensory environment using the natural medium of play. The structured sessions are tailored to meet individual needs, assisting in developing listening and communication skills, addressing anger management issues and helping children and young people to deal with the consequences of their actions. It is designed to equip children and young people with the necessary resilience, social and life skills to manage the issues that confront them, enabling them to access the curriculum and achieve their potential.

Aims and objectives

- To allow young people a space to express and communicate feelings and difficulties in their lives, through a variety of media, in constructive rather than aggressive ways and in a safe, non-threatening environment
- To help young people feel good about themselves and raise self-esteem by providing activities that look at their strengths, and by valuing what they do and making it special
- To provide a non-authoritarian, supportive, reliable, safe, unconditional relationship within schools and other settings
- To provide some of the early experiences that may have been missed but which are necessary for formal education and social interaction
- To help young people acquire the complex range of life skills needed to achieve their full potential.

Source: www.derbyshire.gov.uk/education/schools/attendance-behaviour-welfare/support/positive-play/positive-play-support-programme.aspx

Reflective question

Positive Play offers experiences, positivity and individualised support. Devise a case study for a child accessing Positive Play. What do you imagine their life experience was like prior to joining the programme? What sort of behaviours might they be demonstrating? How do you think involvement in Positive Play might impact them?

PLAY THERAPY

A decidedly effective method of helping children with problems has been detailed by Axline (1996). Play therapy is based on the fact that play is a child's acceptable instrument of self-expression. Play therapy can take the form of directive (adult led) or non-directive (child led) play. Adults can talk through their dilemmas as they have the cognition level to articulate them, but children need to be given the opportunity to play out their feelings. Hall (2019, citing Terr, 1990 and Ogawa, 2004) says that children who have experienced trauma may present as sad, hopeless, angry and vulnerable. They may attempt to withdraw mentally and emotionally from the traumatic experience. She goes on to note that children may fluctuate between passivity and rage, sometimes turning their anger on themselves. Cattanach (2008), too, notes that many children have their quality of life impacted by past trauma to a degree that they need restorative help, as a disregard of their human rights will result in an erosion of their sense of self. Individuals need permission to completely accept themselves (Axline, 1996), to be accepted by others whilst allowing for an assimilation of their own personality. In addition, the compelling necessity to strive for self-realisation allows the individual to take responsibility and direction for the freedom of passage in their life. This of course needs to be nurtured, and for some children these conditions are sadly lacking. See Figures 7.1 and 7.2 for examples of the play therapy process.

Hall (2019) acknowledges the broader role of the play therapist in working with children who have suffered grief and trauma, involving caregivers in discussions to better equip them to provide the support and love required to find a way through for the child.

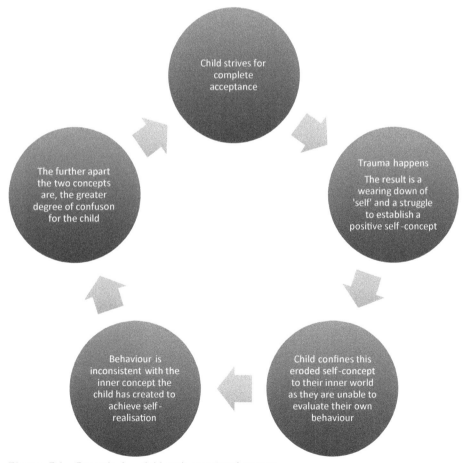

Figure 7.1   Example 1 – child with emotional trauma

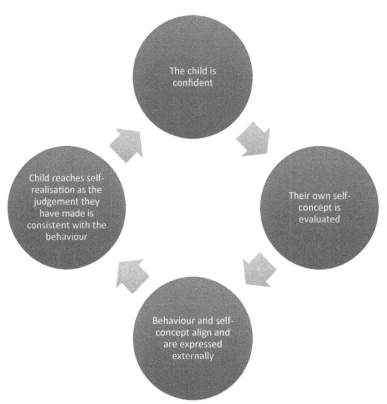

Figure 7.2 Example 2 – child without emotional trauma

Sometimes traumatic experiences overcome the child's capability to cope, and Cattanach (2008) explains that a narrative of events which makes sense of their experience will give the child a strong sense of self and the skill to co-construct events with the play therapist.

The concept of attachment in play therapy is explored by Ryan and Wilson (1996). They note that the responsiveness to individual needs helps a child to discover and safely interact in unfamiliar situations, without feeling overwhelming anxiety. In this way, there is a close link between the child's exploratory system and attachment system, and the discovery of the child's sense of identity. Engel (1995, cited in Cattanach, 2008) notes that every story a child tells can be used to develop an understanding of the storyteller as it contributes to a self-portrait which conveys a dimension of who the child is. This narrative approach to play therapy is based on social construction theory and narrative therapy. Within this approach:

- The child plays and the adult listens with empathy – whether working with small toys or objects, drawing a picture or making marks in clay, the child has control of their world and it is an enriching experience for them.

- The adult asks questions to clarify the child's intentions and to help the child to make sense of their own lives and learn empathy, whilst adults develop an understanding of the child's world and their place in it.
- The quality of the adult listener determines the interchanges of the play.
- Adults must value play for the child and the life-enhancing process of the relationship.
- Play is given meaning as it happens by the collaborative partnership.
- Frameworks are constructed that allow the child to sequence, order, predict and make sense of feelings.
- The development of identity is based on the stories the child tells about themselves – identity can be explored and shifted. (Cattanach, 2008: 21–25)

Ryan and Wilson (1996) note that, because of an emotionally abused child's earlier troubled relationships with adults, creating a trusting environment can be difficult. A pivotal aspect of play therapy is the re-establishment of the child's voice and autonomy, and this is achieved with an acceptance of the therapist that the child chooses the activity. The child does not have to deal with experiences that are painful in a passive, powerless way.

Some of the principles of play therapy are as follows:

- By being able to take an *active* stance within their own thoughts, the child turns a *passive* stance into a self-determining one.
- In non-directive play therapy, the least coercive of approaches, the child is given authentic choices in terms of both activities and medium.
- Rather than interpreting the child's behaviour, the therapist is reflective and allows the child to assimilate their mental activity in a non-threatening environment.
- The therapist helps the child to deal with their problems on a symbolic level, bringing into awareness unconscious experiences.
- Therapeutic interpretation and developmental assessment are an essential part of the therapist's role. (Ryan & Wilson, 1996)

NURTURE GROUPS

Inner London during the late 1960s was a cause for concern. Significant numbers of children entering school were displaying extreme behavioural issues and were either being excluded from school or placed in special schools to manage their behaviour. In the late 1960s, Marjorie Boxall, an educational psychologist working in London, recognised that these were not solutions to the problems being experienced by such children. She determined that the adverse circumstances some children were growing up in were severe enough to limit the nurturing process that is essential from birth (Boxall, 2002). The subsequent introduction of nurture groups into schools, supported by the development of *The Boxall Profile Handbook for Teachers* (Bennathan & Boxall, 1998), which gives a clear explanation and an assessment tool for children identified as requiring a nurture group placement, has now become established practice.

Cooper and Whitebread (2007) explain that the growth in nurture group provision for children with emotional, behavioural and learning problems, has been ever-increasing in the past ten years. Nurture groups' principles and practice are based on attachment theory (Bishop, 2008), essentially a reiteration of the importance of early nurturing detailed by Boxall. This critical period in childhood for babies to form bonds with primary caregivers facilitates the capacity for the child to develop trusting relationships based on reliability and, thus, predictability. It has been recognised that a significant number of children for whom attendance in a nurture group is beneficial, find it difficult to trust adults because of the adverse experiences they have encountered. They have the opportunity in the group to build trusting relationships with adults (Bennathan & Boxall, 1998). Cunningham, Hartwell and Kreppner (2019) also specify the important element of the attachment experiences offered in an educational setting. For the child's internal working model, detailed by Bowlby, to be positive, a secure attachment has to exist for them to see themselves as worthwhile.

The groups, Bishop (2008) notes, allow the intervention of schools to intercede proactively to meet individual needs, whilst Vincent (2017) acknowledges that the nurture group approach is a valuable way in which to support negative aspects of children's behaviour. Whilst research has found that children are able to respond appropriately in social contexts (Cunningham et al., 2019), it has also been recognised that there is a need for practitioners to enable the children to transfer the social skills learned into the broader context. Indeed, as early as 1972 and the publication of the James Report, the Department for Education and Skills recognised that in-service training was necessary for all teachers (Lucas, 2019). Bennathan and Boxall (1998) had already identified that, for nurture groups to be successful, teachers require sufficient understanding of the holistic developmental factors that contribute to the wellbeing of children, and this has to be underpinned by the school ethos.

On a typical school day, the following will occur:

- Class registration
- A collection of the children and a group session in a sitting area
- A sharing of news
- A discussion about the activities and a carefully controlled conversation about what to choose

- An art or craft activity
- A snack, and the social skills associated with this
- Formal work
- Individual activities. (Bennathan and Boxall, 1998)

Bishop (2008) acknowledges that, as a result of nurture group provision, there is no requirement for children to fit into the constraints of a mainstream classroom where they will invariably suffer a stressful day filled with anxiety, confusion and failure. These children often present as disorientated, unfocused and impatient, with very little understanding of themselves and indeed the world in which they live. The defensive state these children exist in serves as protection from perceived threat. By recognising when a child is unable to deal with the challenges of school life, schools can meet the needs of these susceptible children.

 SPOTLIGHT ON RESEARCH

Taylor, D.D., Meaney-Walen, K.K., Nelson, K.M., & Gunger, A. (2019) Investigating group Adlerian play therapy for children with disruptive behavior: A single-case research design. *International Journal of Play Therapy*, 28(3), 168–182.

Objective

The research sought to investigate the impact of Adlerian group play therapy on children's disruptive classroom behaviours.

Method

The research used a qualitative single case design (SCD) to examine the effects of Group Adlerian Play Therapy (GAdPT) with children identified by the teacher as having disruptive classroom behaviour in a charter school in a southeastern state of the USA. To qualify, the children had to:

a. be aged 5–10
b. be identified by the teacher as having a disruptive behaviour (inattention, aggression, rudeness or disobedience)
c. score in the borderline or clinical range on the teacher report form (TRF)
d. have parental consent.

Three children met these criteria.

Data analysis

Two instruments were used for data collection: the teacher report form (TRF) and the direct observation form (DOF) used for collecting observational data. Data was plotted at three data points in three phases. The median baseline point was used as the comparison score for intervention and follow-up phases. Analysis of the average number of data points above or below the median baseline score provided estimates of the treatment effect.

Results

Each participant's outcomes remained independent as the change across phases was compared to the baseline phase. For two of the participants, the baseline improved before the start of the intervention which limited the validity of the intervention being the change factor. For all three participants, the follow-up phase revealed a very significant treatment effect. For two of the participants, there were lasting positive changes that were maintained after the intervention.

Conclusion

The authors concluded that because SCD was used within this study, sweeping statements could not be made about the effectiveness of GAdPT. The mixed results with the three children, although positive, indicated that further research was required.

Note

Future single case studies could:

- create a manipulation of independent variables and repeated measures in an alternative to studies of large groups
- measure the causal relationship between interventions and outcomes.
  (Lobo, Moeyaert, Cunha & Babik, 2017)

 TIME TO CONSIDER

Access a Boxall profile and consider how this might apply to a child you have worked with.

What would you consider to be adequate training to support disaffected children?

FINAL REFLECTION

Socially, attitudes towards children's mental health have changed significantly in the last ten years. Previously, it would have been unusual to claim a child in the early years was suffering from adverse mental health, but acceptable to discuss a child who has suffered emotional abuse. Research to highlight the prevalence of mental illness in children focuses on the emotional aspects of development, and consideration must be given to how these aspects link and the subsequent detriment to the holistic development of the child. This must continue for society to adequately support the growing pervasiveness of mental illness in our youngest children. It is the responsibility of all who care for and educate children to gain the skills to identify and intervene to arrest the cycle of damage.

KEY POINTS

- Play is closely linked to a child's social, emotional development and wellbeing.
- Positive self-esteem is the basis of stable wellbeing in a child.
- Play-based intervention attempts to allow the child to reach a state of emotional equilibrium.

QUESTIONS TO CONSIDER

1   What are your views on introducing children to the language of mental health?
2   What do you consider the differences, if any, to be in Positive Play, play therapy and nurture groups?
3   What do you consider to be the benefits of these interventions?
4   How effective would you consider the Boxall profile to be in assessing the immediate needs of a child with emotional difficulties?
5   Considering the age of the seminal texts, what could this indicate about these interventions?

FURTHER READING

www.nurtureuk.org provides full information about the purpose and running of nurture groups.

www.playtherapy.org.uk is an information resource with extensive detail about play therapy and therapeutic play.

www.publichealthscotland.scot is the Public Health Scotland website, which is informative and provides useful links and videos.

The Scottish Government has been particularly responsive to the need to support children who have faced adverse childhood experiences (ACEs) – see www.gov. scot/publications/adverse-childhood-experiences-aces.

REFERENCES

Axline, V.M. (1964) *Dibs: In Search of Self.* New York: Penguin.

Axline, V.M. (1996) *Play Therapy.* London: Longman.

Bennathan, M., & Boxall, M. (1998) *The Boxall Profile: A Guide to Effective Intervention of Pupils with Emotional and Behavioural Difficulties; Handbook for Teachers.* East Sutton: Association of Workers for Children with Emotional and Behavioural Difficulties.

Bethune, A. (2018) *Well-being in the Primary Classroom.* London: Bloomsbury Education.

Bishop, S. (2008) *Running a Nurture Group.* London: Sage.

Bowlby, J. (1997) *Attachment and Loss, Vol. 1: Attachment.* London: Pimlico.

Boxall, M. (2002) *Nurture Groups in Schools: Principles and Practice.* London: Paul Chapman.

Cattanach, A. (2008) *Narrative Approaches in Play with Children.* London: Jessica Kingsley.

CentreForum Commission (2014) *The Pursuit of Happiness: A New Ambition for our Mental Health.* Available at: http://repository.tavistockandportman.ac.uk/1478/1/Jenkins%20the-pursuit-of-happiness.pdf (accessed 6 November 2020).

Centers for Disease Control and Prevention (CDC) (2005) *International Classification of Diseases, Tenth Revision, Clinical Modification (ICD-10-CM).* Available at: www.cdc.gov/nchs/icd/icd10cm.htm (accessed 7 November 2020).

Cooper, P., & Whitebread, D. (2007) The effectiveness of nurture groups on student progress: Evidence from a national research study. *Emotional and Behavioural Difficulties,* 12(3), 171–190.

Cunningham, L., Hartwell, B.K., & Kreppner, K. (2019) Exploring the impact of nurture groups on children's social skills: A mixed-methods approach. *Educational Psychology in Practice,* 35(4), 368–383.

Department for Education (DfE) (2014) *Mental Health and Behaviour in Schools.* Updated 2018. Available at: www.gov.uk/government/publications/mental-health-and-behaviour-in-schools-2 (accessed 7 November 2020).

Department for Education and Skills (DfES) (1972) *Teacher Education and Training Report (The James Report).* London: Her Majesty's Stationery Office.

Department of Health (DoH) (2015) *Future in Mind: Promoting and Improving Our Children and Young People's Mental Health and Wellbeing.* London: DoH.

Dowling, M. (2014) *Young Children's Personal, Social and Emotional Development,* 4th edition. London: Sage.

Durlack, J.A., Weissberg, R.P., Dymnicki, A.B., Taylor, R.D. and Schellinger, K.B. (2011) The impact of enhancing students' social and emotional learning: A meta-analysis of school based universal interventions. *Child Development,* 82(1), 405–432.

Engel S. (1995) *The Stories Children Tell: Making Sense of the Narratives of Childhood.* New York: Henry Holt and Company.

Erikson, E. H. (1995) *Childhood and Society*. London, Vintage Books.

Glazzard, J., & Bligh, C. (2018) *Meeting the Mental Health Needs of Children 4–11*. St Albans: Critical Publishing.

Green, H., McGinnity, A., Meltzer, H., Ford, T., & Goodman, R. (2005) *Mental Health of Children and Young People in Great Britain 2004*. Basingstoke: Palgrave Macmillan.

Hall, J.G. (2019) Child-centred play therapy as a means of healing children exposed to domestic violence. *International Journal of Play Therapy*, 28(2), 98–106.

HM Treasury (2003) *Every Child Matters*. London: TSO. Available at: www.gov.uk/government/publications/every-child-matters (accessed 7 November 2020).

House of Commons Health Committee (2014) *Children and Adolescents' Mental Health and CAMHS: Third Report of Session 2014–15*. London: TSO.

Howard, C., Burton, M., Levermore, D., & Barrell, R. (2017) *Children's Mental Health and Emotional Well-Being in Primary Schools*. London: Sage.

Hughes, N., & Schlösser, A. (2014) The effectiveness of nurture groups: A systematic review. *Emotional and Behavioural Difficulties*, 19(4), 386–409.

Lobo, M.A., Moeyaert, M., Cunha, AB., & Babik, I. (2017) Single case design, analysis and quality assessment for intervention research. *Journal of Neurological Physical Therapy*, 41(3) 187–197.

Lucas, R.E. (2007) Adaptation and the set point model of subjective well-being: Does happiness change after major life events? *Current Directions in Psychological Science*, 16(2), 75–79.

Lucas, S. (2019) On the origins of nurture. *International Journal of Nurture in Education*, 5, 7–20.

Meggit, C. (2012) *Understanding Child Development*. London: Hodder.

Ogawa, Y. (2004) Childhood trauma and play therapy for traumatized children. *Journal of Professional Counselling Practice, Theory & Research*, 32(1), 19–29.

Pugh, K. (2015) *Model Specification for Child and Adolescent Mental Health Services: Targeted and Specialist Levels (Tiers 2/3)*. London: NHS England.

Rogers, C. (1957) The necessary and sufficient conditions for therapeutic change. *Journal of Consulting Psychology*, 21, 95–103.

Ruby, F.J.M. (2018) Social and emotional well-being of primary school pupils: Insights from the Boxall Childhood Project. *International Journal of Nurture in Education*, 4, 6–14.

Ryan, V., & Wilson, K. (1996) *Case Studies in Non-directive Play Therapy*. London: Bailliere Tindall.

Taylor, D.D., Meaney-Walen, K.K., Nelson, K.M., & Gunger, A. (2019) Investigating group Adlerian play therapy for children with disruptive behavior: A single-case research design. *International Journal of Play Therapy*, 28(3), 168–182.

Terr, L. (1990). *Too Scared To Cry*. New York: Harper and Row.

The Children's Society (2020) *The Good Childhood Report*. Available at: www. childrenssociety.org.uk/good-childhood (accessed 7 November 2020).

Vincent, K. (2017) 'It's small steps, but that leads to bigger changes': Evaluation of a nurture group intervention. *Emotional and Behavioural Difficulties*, 22(4), 303–316.

Young Minds (2017) Wise up: Prioritising Wellbeing in Schools. Available at: https://youngminds.org.uk/media/1428/wise-up-prioritising-wellbeing-in-schools.pdf (accessed 15 October 2018).

8

CHILDREN'S RIGHT TO PLAY

Julianne Harlow and Martin Smith

CONTENTS

This chapter is about the political context of play, specifically the right to play, as in Article 31 of the United Nations Convention on the Rights of the Child (UNCRC) (United Nations Children's Fund, UNICEF, 1989). The information it provides should enhance your knowledge and understanding of children's rights and the extent to which Article 31 is upheld by contemporary society. The chapter will also help you to identify some of the approaches and skills you may need to develop as an effective advocate for children's right to play.

 THIS CHAPTER WILL...

- Outline the development of Article 31
- Explain how progress for the right to play is scrutinised and identify some of the key messages that have arisen from scrutiny
- Explore the innovative approach that the Welsh Assembly Government has taken in embedding Article 31 into Welsh law
- Consider the political context of Article 31 and its interaction with other policies in the UK
- Consider some of the approaches and skills that those working with young children could use to advocate for their right to play.

KEY TERMS

advocacy, children's rights, inalienable rights, inherent rights, interdependent and interrelated rights, invisible rights, policy, unconditional rights, universal rights

INTRODUCTION

Chapter 2 has outlined substantial evidence on the value and significance of play for all aspects of a child's development. However, over time and to date, numerous policies within our local, national and global communities have impacted on children and their opportunities to play. Such policies have represented and continue to represent the ideologies, interests and concerns of those holding political power. A child's right to play is enshrined in Article 31 of the UNCRC (UNICEF, 1989). This demonstrates that play is recognised as a human rights issue, a political matter of global concern and a right worthy of protection. Despite the laudable goals that the UNCRC offers, infants and children in their early years are a politically powerless group, dependent on adults to advocate for or with them to protect their rights. This chapter will explain how the right to play has developed. It will offer some analysis of Article 31 as a basis to consider the approaches and skills that those working with children may need to develop to fulfil their role as advocates for children's right to play.

DEVELOPMENT OF THE RIGHT TO PLAY AGENDA: THE UNCRC

The right to play was coined in 1959 by the UN General Assembly in the Declaration of the Rights of the Child. This constituted the first acknowledgement by the international community of the value of play and recreation (UN Committee on the Rights of the Child (UNCRC), 2013). One of ten fundamental principles relating to the rights of children, integrated with, but placed at the end of, discourse on a child's entitlement to education and their best interests, is the seventh principle:

> The child shall have full opportunity for play and recreation, which should be directed to the same purposes as education; society and the public authorities shall endeavour to promote the enjoyment of this right.

In the above statement, the purposes of play were the same as the purposes of education which the UN Commission on Human Rights (UNCHR) (1959) stated 'will promote his general culture and enable him, on a basis of equal opportunity, to develop his abilities, his individual judgement, and his sense of moral and social responsibility, and to become a useful member of society'.

This, however, constituted a limited view of play, one that merely extended the right to an education and served to create useful societal members. Playing for fun, entertainment or diversion was, at this point in time, not expressly a right guaranteed or protected (González, 2016).

The 1970s has been identified as a period within the work of Save the Children movements as being characterised by a shift from 'charity' in the form of ad hoc humanitarian actions to that of 'rights' (Lindkvist, 2019). However, it wasn't until 1989 that the UNCRC, a global framework for children's rights, was adopted by the Assembly (UNICEF, 1989). For those who work with children and who champion their rights in their work, the process of the development of the UNCRC is a good example of the sustained efforts needed over a lengthy period of time to equip children as holders of their rights. The UNCRC is the world's most endorsed human rights convention, currently ratified by all nations other than the USA.

Overview and guiding principles of the UNCRC

The UNCRC comprises 54 articles that detail the civil, political, economic, social and cultural rights which children are deemed to need to enable them to maximise their developmental potential and live healthy and safe lives. Four of these articles: Article 2: Non-discrimination; Article 3: Best interests of the child; Article 6: Survival and development; and Article 12: Respect for the views of the child, have been described as guiding principles (CRAE, 2018) as they form the framework through which all the rights in the UNCRC should be implemented. Those working with children thus need a heightened awareness of the value of children's rights and an appreciation of the guiding principles, in the context of Article 31, as they seek to fulfil their advocacy role.

Article 31: The right to play

States Parties recognize the right of the child to rest and leisure, to engage in play and recreational activities appropriate to the age of the child and to participate freely in cultural life and the arts.

States Parties shall respect and promote the right of the child to participate fully in cultural and artistic life and shall encourage the provision of appropriate and equal opportunities for cultural, artistic, recreational and leisure activity.

The right to play has been recognised as a unique and innovative aspect of the UNCRC that conveys with it a sense of legitimacy and seriousness as an entitlement as opposed to an optional luxury (Davey & Lundy, 2011). The text of Article 31 represents a strengthening of the 1959 proclamation (UNCRC, 2013) and a broader, less restrictive view of play in which the right to play is separated from the right to education. At this point in time, Article 31 neither attempts to define play nor prescribe its purpose because 'children are just as entitled as adults to forms of play and recreation which appear purposeless to others' (UNICEF, 2007: 470).

The nature of children's rights

The nature of all rights within the UNCRC is that they are: **universal, inherent, inalienable, unconditional, indivisible, interdependent and interrelated** (UNICEF, 2020). Thus, the Office of the High Commissioner for Human Rights (1997) comments that Article 31 should be considered in combination with other relevant articles of the Convention, including the right to education. This is in the context of Article 31 contributing to the development of the child's abilities to their fullest potential. Whilst it is clear that the developmental benefits of play should be acknowledged and valued, it is important that society does not 'instrumentalise play' (Lester & Russell, 2008) by viewing it merely as a tool to achieve other benefits. Instrumentalisation serves to negate the inherent value of play (Holloway & Pimlott-Wilson, 2014; Voce, 2015; Whitebread, Basilio, Kuvalja & Verma, 2012), and yet Powell (2008) found instrumentalisation to be widespread across a range of policy areas, reflective of government priorities at the time.

The various elements of Article 31 – rest, leisure, play and recreational activities – are mutually linked and reinforcing (UNCRC, 2013). However, the confusion of play with these other elements frequently leads to a political ignoring of play in its own right and it being afforded a diminished role in policies and programmes involving recreation, leisure, sport or education (International Play Association (IPA), 2010). Consequently, Article 31 has been described as neglected (Davey & Lundy, 2011; Hodgkin & Newell, 2002), left behind and forgotten (Fronczek, 2009; IPA, 2013; Rico & Janot, 2019; Voce, 2015). A lack of research into children's experiences of play from a rights-based perspective, and a dearth of academic analysis on the substance and remit of Article 31, suggests that Article 31 has also been neglected in academic circles (Davey & Lundy, 2011). This is notwithstanding the fact that children view play as one of the most important aspects of their lives (IPA, 2010).

 TIME TO CONSIDER

Consider policy, guidance and emerging research relevant to children in the context of the coronavirus pandemic. How has children's right to play been impacted positively and negatively by the political response?

Upholding the UNCRC

The most powerful driver for the implementation of the UNCRC within a nation comes through giving direct force to it in domestic law (CRAE, 2016). Although the UNCRC was ratified by the UK Government in 1991, it has not been incorporated into law in England, Scotland or Northern Ireland. In these countries, therefore, there is no legal obligation to comply with Article 31. This supports criticism that the UNCRC 'lacks teeth' (Fortin, 2009: 60). Consequently, children who are more vulnerable to violations of their economic and social rights (Nolan, 2014) are unable to claim legal redress for any infringement of their convention rights. Starmer's (2019) renewed calls for the full incorporation of the UNCRC into UK legislation demonstrate that this continues to be an issue of political contention. Policies and guidance, however, do state regularly that their aims reflect the principles of the UNCRC. Examples of Article 31 being referred to in this way are evident in a number of policy documents in the devolved nations (Northern Ireland Executive, 2011; Scottish Government, 2013; Welsh Government, 2014).

Scrutiny of Article 31 by the Committee

Governments are regularly scrutinised by the Committee on the Rights of the Child (CRC), a body of independent experts which monitors the progress made in the realisation of children's rights. Each government is obliged to submit *regular reports* detailing how they are implementing the UNCRC. Scrutiny is further enhanced through a Universal Periodic Review (UPR) undertaken by the Human Rights Council. A recent example of reporting to the Committee in respect of Article 31 is the report submitted by the UK Government (UNCRC, 2015) which set out the funding and focus of play provision, strategy and policy across England, Northern Ireland, Scotland and Wales.

Scrutinising such reports enables the Committee to make specific recommendations to each government in the form of *concluding observations* (UNCRC, 2020). In its response to the fifth periodic report cited above, concern was expressed (UNCRC, 2016) over the withdrawal of the play strategy in England, the under-funding of play and leisure policies in Northern Ireland, Scotland and Wales, and the lack of sufficient play spaces and facilities, particularly for children with disabilities and those in marginalised and disadvantaged situations. Concluding observations and recommendations (UNCRC, 2016: sections 74 & 75) to the UK and its devolved governments included a need for the UK to:

- Strengthen its efforts to guarantee the right of the child to rest and leisure and to engage in play and recreational activities appropriate to the age of the child, including by adopting and implementing play and leisure policies with sufficient and sustainable resources
- Provide children, including those with disabilities and children in marginalised and disadvantaged situations, with safe, accessible, inclusive and smoking-free spaces for play and socialisation and public transport to access such spaces
- Fully involve children in planning, designing and monitoring the implementation of play policies and activities relevant to play and leisure, at community, local and national levels.

The UK's response to scrutiny

Unfortunately, recommendations made by the Committee, such as those above, have not always been adopted by the UK. As a consequence, important issues of concern regarding children's right to play are not addressed, and re-emerge over time. It had been hoped that the requirement for countries to produce regular reports detailing their progress in implementing children's rights would encourage the effective implementation of children's rights (Fortin, 2009). Although some of the Committee's concerns have been addressed, the UK Government has chosen the policies that suit it and ignored those that do not (Fortin, 2009). This point is supported by CRAE (2018) which reported that the UK Government supported only 28 per cent of the recommendations made by the Universal Periodic Review in respect of children's rights. This raises questions as to whether the rights afforded to children are valued equally, and the extent to which they are considered a political priority. The UK's stance is not unique. Social policies implemented by a number of countries have focused, to a large extent, on child survival and child protection rights. Subsequently and unjustifiably, rights such as the right to play have been left behind or forgotten (Rico & Janot, 2019).

General Comment No. 17

In addition to making concluding observations, the Committee also provides *general comments* which interpret and analyse specific articles of the UNCRC or deal with themes that emerge from the reports. General comments state what is expected of governments, as they seek to implement children's rights (Child Rights International Network (CRIN), 2018). The publication of General Comment No. 17 followed concerns that poor recognition was being given by states to Article 31.

These specific concerns included:

- a lack of investment in appropriate play provisions
- weak or non-existent protection of the right to play in law
- the lack of prominence of children in national and local-level planning initiatives
- difficulties experienced by particular groups of children in enjoying the right to play, including girls, children from poor backgrounds, children with disabilities, children from indigenous groups and children belonging to minority groups.

General Comment No. 17 (UNCRC, 2013) thus aimed to increase understanding of the importance of the right to play for children's wellbeing and development, to facilitate the application of the right and to emphasise the obligations of governments, the private sector and those working with children. The Committee highlighted that where investment had been made, this was generally in the provision of structured and organised activities, but that of equal importance was a need to create time and space for children to engage in spontaneous play, recreation and creativity.

Re-defining play

In a legal analysis of Article 31, the Committee (UNCRC, 2013: 3–4) defines children's play as follows:

> any behaviour, activity or process initiated, controlled and structured by children themselves; it takes place whenever and wherever opportunities arise. Caregivers may contribute to the creation of environments in which play takes place, but play itself is non-compulsory, driven by intrinsic motivation and undertaken for its own sake, rather than as a means to an end.

The subtext of Article 31 is that human creativity is the foundation for these activities and should therefore not be 'limited, censored or regulated' (González, 2016: 164). Whilst the concept and construct of play is contested, the importance of an agreed, shared definition of play cannot be overstated. Powell (2008) found that policy documents published under the Labour Government produced an inconsistent conceptualisation of play. Despite calls on Britain's political parties to support a manifesto for play (Play England, IPA England & The Playwork Foundation, 2019) ahead of the General Election, in England there is no current strategy for play. Absence of a play strategy has been recognised to negatively impact both local authority play facilities and staffed play provision (Bolt, 2018). Powell (2008) noted that constructions of play in policy form a discourse that controls where and how children may play, and that inconsistencies lead to gaps in the means to deliver opportunities for extensive, sustainable and equitable play. Agreeing the Committee's (UNCRC, 2013) definition of play would form a good foundation for policy makers and all those working with children, to reach a common consensus in the promotion and safeguarding of contexts, situations, settings and resources that uphold children's right to play.

SPECIAL STUDY: THE RATIFICATION OF ARTICLE 31 INTO WELSH LAW

General Comment No. 17 (UNCRC, 2013) specifically recommended that governments consider the introduction of legislation that addressed the principle of play sufficiency. However, governments rarely prioritise play on their national political agendas (UNICEF, 2007; Voce, 2015; Wood, 2017). One notable exception is the Welsh Government which has accepted the recommendation to incorporate at least some children's rights, principles and provisions into law. Wales thus became the first in the world to legislate on play (Russell & Lester, 2013; Towler, 2015) through the Children and Families (Wales) Measure 2010 (National Assembly for Wales, 2010) and subsequently introduced the Rights of Children and Young Persons (Wales) Measure 2011 (National Assembly for Wales, 2011). The latter requires that ministers have due regard to all aspects of the

UNCRC when developing new or amending existing policies and/or legislation. Fortin (2009) advocates that the UNCRC should be incorporated in its entirety or not at all. Wales, therefore, 'stands, potentially as a beacon to the rest of the world in its approach to supporting rights generally and children's right to play specifically' (Lester & Russell, 2013: 11). Both the legislative initiative and political process used by the Welsh Government were welcomed by the Committee (UNCRC, 2016). The play policy development timeline demonstrates a clearly focused, systematic and sustained process over 20 years that is still ongoing. Throughout this time, the process has been supported and informed by a series of eight national State of Play reviews (Play Wales, 2020a). These have provided information as to how various national policies and funding programmes have supported play provision at local level, and have identified common issues regarding children's play (Play Wales, 2020a).

In Wales, therefore, national government-level support for play in terms of policy and strategy is well defined and incontrovertible (Play Wales, 2020b). In the context of section 11 of the Children and Families (Wales) Measure, which embedded Article 31 into Welsh law, play sufficiency means having regard to both the quantity and quality of play opportunities. This means that local planning policy must support children's right to play, and it is unlawful for local authorities not to help secure sufficient play opportunities for children in their locality. Long (2017), however, found that simply providing more opportunities was neither an automatic indicator of satisfaction nor the only approach to increasing play sufficiency. Long (2017) suggested that parental fear, socio-economic conditions and the development of a play culture within communities are factors that influence children's opportunities and freedom to play more significantly.

Reflective question

In the local community in which you live or work, to what extent are play activities both appropriate to the age of the children you work with and supported by sufficient and sustainable resources? How safe, accessible and inclusive are play spaces for children with disabilities or those otherwise marginalised or disadvantaged through poverty?

Interaction of policy

Whilst the UNCRC aims to guide national and local governments in their political decision-making, the benefits of play are often overlooked by policy makers, leading to calls for play to be integrated across all aspects of children's policy (CCE, 2018). All national and local government policies, but in particular health, education, socio-economic and housing policies, have the potential to impact positively or negatively on children's play opportunities.

AUSTERITY, CHILD POVERTY AND PLAY

Inadequate resourcing of play is a concern (UNCRC, 2016). Opportunities for children to realise their right to play remain limited, with no advancement having been made in adequately resourcing play and leisure (CRAE, 2018). Funding allocated to play has been negatively impacted by welfare reform and austerity measures from 2010 onwards. The play strategy (DCSF, 2008) was withdrawn in 2012, resulting in the diversion of much of its £235 million budget. Recent austerity measures imposed by central government on local authorities have led to the closure of many services that supported play, particularly in the early years. For example, funding for Sure Start and children's centres has been cut significantly, particularly in more deprived local authorities, and an estimated 500 children's centres have been closed (IHE, 2020). Reforms to child and housing benefit, and local funding cuts have resulted in a number of issues for poorer families. These include less money and fewer play opportunities, together with difficulties in sourcing good quality, affordable holiday clubs (CCE, 2018). Where parents have been entitled to government help with meeting costs through tax-free childcare schemes, bureaucratic processes have been a barrier to many parents not taking up the opportunities (CCE, 2018).

Difficulties such as these compound the problems that children from poorer households experience when realising their right to play. The Institute for Health Equity (2020), for example, states that in 2016 the air in the closest play space for 14 per cent of children under 16 years of age in Greater London, exceeded the legal limit for nitrogen dioxide. Two thirds of these children were living in either the most or second-most deprived quintile. Safe play spaces matter to children. When a representative sample of children aged 6–17 years was asked what matters when helping kids be the best they can be, 13 per cent identified schools staying open in the evening, at weekends and during the holidays to provide a safe space for activities and play (CCE, 2020). The UK Government's decision to cut local authority public health grants in recent years has also resulted in disinvestment in health visiting services (Institute of Health Visiting (IHV), 2019). This has had a significant impact on health visitors' opportunities to work with families (Golberg, cited in IHV, 2019) and to discuss play, as mandated by policy (DoH, 2009). Consequently, concerns about the readiness of children for school have persisted (IHV, 2019).

The UK is facing a poverty crisis, with 30 per cent of children (4.2 million) living in poverty, 2 million of whom are aged under 5 (Child Poverty Action Group (CPAG), 2020). Child poverty is not an inevitability but largely a consequence of political and policy choices (IHE, 2020). Measures to respond to the coronavirus pandemic show that radical political action is possible but has not been mirrored in an urgent response to the rising levels of child poverty (CPAG, 2020). Indeed, the Government's slow reaction and subsequent U turn in respect of Marcus Rashford's recent campaign on tackling food poverty (Siddique, 2020) demonstrates a reluctance to pro-actively and willingly prioritise the needs and rights of children. After ten years of austerity, the emerging cost of the coronavirus epidemic does not bode well for public finances, child and family poverty or children's play opportunities. This is in the context of a pre-election manifesto that pledged to create a fair, just society and equality of opportunity (Conservative and Unionist Party, 2019) and yet failed to mention children's rights or play.

CASE STUDY 8.1

This case study reflects the increasing use of *poor doors* strategies by housing developers.

Aisha is 6 and lives with her parents and younger brother Rauf, a wheelchair user in a new housing development in South London. The housing development comprises a mix of social, shared ownership and private homes. Aisha's dad is a cleaner and her mum works part-time as a carer. The family was attracted to the new development by plans which showed gardens and shared play spaces alongside photographs which represented children at play. Marketing information provided by the developers included a play strategy that emphasised opportunities for all children in the housing development to play, with the purpose of creating a sense of community cohesion and togetherness. Shortly after moving in, Aisha's family was told that, apart from one small area containing some play equipment specifically for the use of children in social housing, the gardens and remaining play spaces were only for the use of those children and families in private accommodation. Notices stating these rules were placed at strategic points across the housing development, and hedges were planted where there should have been accessible paths to the play areas. This was upsetting for Aisha and Rauf as they had friends living in the private housing area who were in their class at school. Access to the local park was difficult as it was over a mile away and Rauf's wheelchair was too heavy for his mother to push.

Reflective questions

- What would you consider the emotional, social, cognitive and physical impacts of play segregation on children to be?
- Efforts to improve outcomes for children, families and their communities are often viewed in the context of *social value* and the role that our public institutions and private sector organisations have to play in supporting communities. Take some time to research and consider what *social value* means, along with its relevance for children's right to play.
- What could the local community do to improve the situation above?

SPOTLIGHT ON RESEARCH

Lambert, V., Coad, J., Hicks, P., & Glacken, M. (2014) Young children's perspectives of ideal physical design features for hospital-built environments. *Journal of Child Health Care*, 18(1), 57–71.

Objective

The research sought to explore young children's perspectives of hospital environments so that the physical places and social spaces of a proposed children's hospital would be responsive to their needs.

Method

A qualitative methodology, arts-based participatory approaches including semi-structured interviews, drawing, arts and crafts were used. Digital records and electronic field notes gathered during interactions and dialogue with children were thematically analysed.

Results

Fifty-five children aged 5–8 years, representing both genders, various ethnic groups and experiencing different health conditions, took part. Three emergent themes were identified: physical environment, access and space. Children valued a colourful, creative, comfortable interior environment from which they could easily access the external environment. Children talked about the effective, efficient and creative use of space for visual displays and play. They discussed the possibility of going on a nature walk and of having a garden to allow for free movement and outdoor access to play equipment. Children expressed the need for adequate age-appropriate play facilities and activities in waiting areas. They visualised shared play areas central to and surrounded by individual bedrooms. For some children with restricted movement, the ability to bring everything 'to the bedside' was emphasised. To personalise their space, children used artwork and objects such as teddies from home. Children talked about missing many of their toys and activities. Those requiring longer hospital stays identified the need for more space to store their 'stuff', including toys and books, together with the need for adaptable and moveable storage systems such as toy boxes.

Conclusion

The authors concluded that understanding and blending the perspectives of children and professionals can act as a catalyst for the creation of innovative environments that surpass the needs and expectations of all. In the context of this chapter, this study illustrates that children have their own perspectives on how their right to play may be achieved in a hospital setting.

Reflective question

How do you think this study upholds children's rights in respect of: Article 2 (non-discrimination), Article 3 (best interests of the child), Article 6 (life, survival and development), Article 12 (right to be heard), Article 24 (right to health) and Article 31 (right to play)? To what extent are the children in your setting consulted about play and recreation? Are their needs met and views realised?

ADVOCACY

Professionals working with young children need to have not only a deep understanding of the research base on the value of play but also to 'become savvy professional advocates' (Nicholson & Shimpi, 2015). UNICEF (2010: 3) states that:

> Advocacy is the deliberate process, based on demonstrated evidence, to directly and indirectly influence decision makers, stakeholders and relevant audiences to support and implement actions that contribute to the fulfilment of children's and women's rights.

This definition of advocacy means that advocacy practice should be planned, proactive and underpinned by research on play. Play advocates need to be able to influence all those who have the power to support the implementation of Article 31. This includes politicians working at all levels in society, those who fund or commission children's services, a range of charities and service providers in education, health and children's social care. Advocacy practice must crucially include families and children themselves. As policies that impact on play are developed across different levels of society, play advocates need to be aware of the wider policy agenda and its potential impact on play. They need to develop knowledge and skills across all spheres of influence (Figure 8.1) to advocate effectively for children's right to play.

A rights-based approach to play advocacy

The UNCRC is an important tool for advocacy (Freeman, 2007: 5) – all those who work with children should therefore use their knowledge of Article 31 to advocate for children's right to play. A rights-based approach to play advocacy will begin with an understanding of children's lives in the context of shortfalls in the realisation of their Article 31 rights. The key elements of this approach as applied to play include:

- Promotion of children's participation in play research and the planning and evaluation of play policy and facilities
- Targeting accountability for the shortfalls in progress being made in children's right to play on those with power
- Emphasising that the right to play applies to all children without exception or discrimination
- Efforts to ensure that national laws and policies are aligned with Article 31. (UNICEF, 2010)

As the ability to communicate knowledge in a convincing, confident and professional manner has been identified as important for play advocacy (Play Wales, 2015), it will be essential that all those working with young children, reflect critically on their knowledge and the approaches and advocacy skills they should use if children's right to play is to be realised (see Figure 8.1).

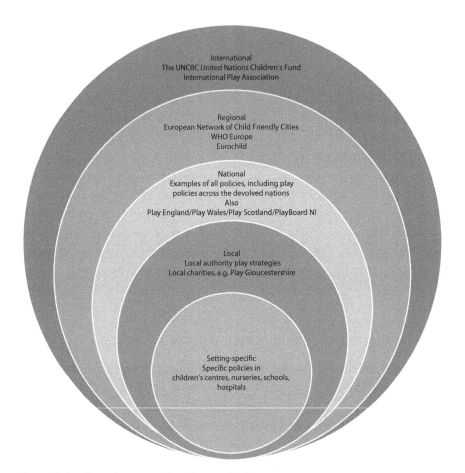

Figure 8.1   Play advocacy – the spheres of influence

FINAL REFLECTION

Our understanding of the right to play continues to evolve in line with changes in society, academic research, and scrutiny of Article 31 by the UN and other children's rights advocates. In the devolved nations of the UK, there are inconsistencies in the extent to which the right to play has been prioritised and transformed into reality. We have learned that the Welsh Assembly Government has led the way by embedding Article 31 into national legislation, and remains committed to the ongoing realisation of this right through its partnership with Play Wales. We have identified that those who work with young children are important advocates for children's right to play and should develop their knowledge and skills so that they can fulfil their advocacy role effectively.

KEY POINTS

- Society's understanding of the right to play has evolved over time and this evolution will continue.
- Scrutiny of Article 31 is essential so that governments can be held to account in their progress in equipping children with the right to play.
- All those who work with children must develop skills and opportunities to advocate for children's right to play across different spheres of influence.

QUESTIONS TO CONSIDER

1   In 1926, the ex-prime minister, David Lloyd George, said: 'The right to play is a child's first claim on the community. Play is nature's training for life. No community can infringe that right without doing deep and enduring harm to the minds and bodies of its citizens.' What does this statement say about the right to play in 1926? Was David Lloyd George right? What evidence can you find to support his views?
2   The Welsh Assembly Government has been described as a 'beacon' to the world in its approach to supporting children's right to play. Where do the governments of England, Scotland and Northern Ireland stand in their plans to embed Article 31 into their nation's laws?
3   Consider the community in which you live or work. What three things do you con-sider need to improve to help children realise their right to play? What can you do about these? Identify the policies and groups that could support a play advocacy role in your work setting.
4   Refer back to the case study of Aisha and Rauf. What would your advocacy role involve here? What spheres of influence (Figure 8.1) would your advocacy practice involve?

FURTHER READING

The International Play Association aims to protect, preserve and promote children's right to play. It has active groups across the world, including in the UK, that initiate a variety of projects promoting this right. You can discover more at ipaworld.org.

The KidsRights Index is the annual global index which ranks how countries adhere to, and are equipped to improve, children's rights. It is an example of a partnership initiative between the KidsRights Foundation, the Erasmus School of Economics and the International Institute of Social Studies. It may be accessed at www.kidsrightsindex.org.

REFERENCES

Bolt, S. (2018) *Play England's Response to 'Child's Play' Report by Children's Commissioner*. Available at: www.playengland.org.uk/play-englands-response-to-childs-play-report-by-childrens-commissioner (accessed 30 June 2020).

Child Poverty Action Group (CPAG) (2020) *Child Poverty Continues to Rise as Pandemic Response Falls Short for Families*. Available at: https://cpag.org.uk/news-blogs/news-listings/child-poverty-continues-rise-pandemic-response-falls-short-families (accessed 28 April 2020).

Child Rights International Network (CRIN) (2018) *CRC General Comments*. Available at: https://archive.crin.org/en/library/publications/crc-general-comments.html (accessed 3 March 2020).

Children's Commissioner for England (CCE) (2018) *Playing Out: A Children's Commissioner's Report on the Importance to Children of Play and Physical Activity*. Available at: www.childrenscommissioner.gov.uk/wp-content/uploads/2018/08/Play-final-report.pdf (accessed 26 March 2020).

Children's Commissioner for England (CCE) (2020) *Childhood in 2020: Business plan consultation with children 2020–2021*. Available at: https://www.childrenscommissioner.gov.uk/wp-content/uploads/2020/03/cco-childhood-in-2020.pdf (Accessed 8 March 2021).

Children's Rights Alliance England (CRAE) (2016) *The Concluding Observations of the UN Committee on the Rights of the Child*. Available at: www.crae.org.uk/media/118248/CRAE-Briefing-UN-Committee-Rights-of-the-Child-Concluding-Observations-2016.pdf (accessed 29 February 2020).

Children's Rights Alliance England (CRAE) (2018) *State of Children's Rights in England 2018: Education, Leisure and Cultural Activities*. Available at: www.crae.org.uk/media/126994/B6_CRAE_EDUCATION_2018_WEB.pdf (accessed 2 February 2020).

Conservative and Unionist Party (2019) *Get Brexit Done: Unleash Britain's Potential – The Conservative and Unionist Party Manifesto 2019*. Available at: www.conservatives.com/our-plan (accessed 13 May 2020).

Davey, C., & Lundy, L. (2011) Towards greater recognition of the right to play: An analysis of Article 31 of the UNCRC. *Children & Society*, 25(1), 3–14.

Department for Children, Schools and Families (DCSF) (2008) *The Play Strategy*. Nottingham: DCSF Publications.

Department of Health (DoH) (2009) *Healthy Child Programme: Pregnancy and the First Five Years of Life*. Available at: https://assets.publishing.service.gov.uk/ government/uploads/system/uploads/attachment_data/file/167998/Health_ Child_Programme.pdf (accessed 23 February 2020).

Fortin, J. (2009) *Children's Rights and the Developing Law*, 4th edition. Cambridge: Cambridge University Press.

Freeman, M.D.A. (2007) Why it remains important to take children's rights seriously. *International Journal of Children's Rights*, 15(1), 5–23.

Fronczek, V. (2009) Article 31: A 'forgotten article of the UNCRC'. *Early Childhood Matters* (Bernard van Leer Foundation), 113: 24–28.

González, A. (2016) Two children's writers from Latin America: The right to play. *The Lion and the Unicorn*, 40(2), 163–178.

Hodgkin, R., & Newell, P. (2002) *Implementation Handbook for the United Nations Convention on the Rights of the Child*. New York: UNICEF.

Holloway, S.L., & Pimlott-Wilson, H. (2014) Enriching children, institutionalizing childhood? Geographies of play, extra-curricular activities, and parenting in England. *Annals of the Association of American Geographers*, 104, 613–627.

Institute for Health Equity (IHE) (2020) *Health Equity in England: The Marmot Review Ten Years On*. Available at: www.instituteofhealthequity.org/resources-reports/ marmot-review-10-years-on/the-marmot-review-10-years-on-full-report.pdf (accessed 10 April 2020).

Institute of Health Visiting (IHV) (2019) *Health Visiting in England: A Vision for the Future*. Available at: https://ihv.org.uk/our-work/our-vision (accessed 2 May 2020).

International Play Association (IPA) (2010) *Promoting the Child's Right to Play: IPA Global Consultations on Children's Right to Play Report*. Farringdon: IPA.

International Play Association (IPA) (2013) *IPA Summary of United Nations General Comment No. 17 on the Rights of the Child to Rest, Play, Recreational Activities, Cultural Life and the Arts* (Article 31). Farringdon: IPA. Available at: http://ipaworld. org/childs-right-to-play/article-31/summary-gc17 (accessed 17 April 2020).

Lambert, V., Coad, J., Hicks, P., & Glacken, M. (2014) Young children's perspectives of ideal physical design features for hospital-built environments. *Journal of Child Health Care*, 18(1), 57–71.

Lester, S., & Russell, W. (2008) *Play for a Change: Play, Policy and Practice – A Review of Contemporary Perspectives*. London: Play England.

Lester, S., & Russell, W. (2013) *Leopard Skin Wellies, a Top Hat and a Vacuum Cleaner Hose: An Analysis of Wales' Play Sufficiency Assessment Duty*. Gloucester: University of Gloucestershire/Play Wales.

Lindkvist, L. (2019) 1979: A year of the child, but not of children's human rights. *Diplomatica*, 1(2), 202–220.

Long, A. (2017) It's not just about 'more': A research project exploring satisfaction with opportunities to play, for children in two Welsh neighbouring communities. *International Journal of Play*, 6(1), 24–39.

National Assembly for Wales (2010) *Children and Families (Wales) Measure 2010*. Available at: www.legislation.gov.uk/mwa/2010/1/section/11 (accessed 20 February 2020).

National Assembly for Wales (2011) *Rights of Children and Young Persons (Wales) Measure 2011*. Available at: www.legislation.gov.uk/mwa/2011/2/contents (accessed 20 February 2020).

Nicholson, J., & Shimpi, P.M. (2015) Guiding future early childhood educators to reclaim their own play as a foundation for becoming effective advocates for children's play. *Early Child Development and Care*, 185(10), 1601–1616.

Nolan, A. (2014) Economic and social rights, budgets and the convention on the rights of the child. In M. Freeman (ed.) *The Future of Children's Rights*. Leiden: Brill Nijhoff, pp. 121–150.

Northern Ireland Executive (2011) *Play and Leisure Plan*. Available at: www.education-ni.gov.uk/publications/play-and-leisure-plan-statement-and-implementation-plan-0 (accessed 30 April 2020).

Office of the High Commissioner for Human Rights (1997) *Manual on Human Rights Reporting: Under Six Major International Human Rights Instruments*. Geneva: United Nations.

Play England, IPA England, & The Playwork Foundation (2019) *A Manifesto for Play: Policy Proposals for Children's Play in England*. Available at: www.playengland.org.uk/wp-content/uploads/2019/09/Manifesto-for-Play.pdf (accessed 4 May 2020).

Play Wales (2015) *Advocacy and Communication*. Available at: https://issuu.com/playwales/docs/advocacy_and_communication (accessed 11 May 2020).

Play Wales (2020a) *Play Policy*. Available at: www.playwales.org.uk/eng/playpolicy (accessed 20 February 2020).

Play Wales (2020b) *Play and the Seven Core Aims*. Available at: www.playwales.org.uk/eng/playsevencoreaims (accessed 2 April 2020).

Powell, S. (2008) The value of play: Constructions of play in government policy in England. *Children & Society*, 23, 29–42.

Rico, A.P., & Janot, J.B. (2019) Building a system of indicators to evaluate the right of a child to play. *Children & Society*, 33(1), 13–23.

Scottish Government (2013) *Play Strategy for Scotland: Our Vision*. Available at: www.gov.scot/publications/play-strategy-scotland-vision (accessed 29 April 2020).

Siddique, H. (2020) Marcus Rashford forces Boris Johnson into second U turn on child food poverty, *Guardian*, 8 November. Available at: www.theguardian.com/education/2020/nov/08/marcus-rashford-forces-boris-johnson-into-second-u-turn-on-child-food-poverty (accessed 13 November 2020).

Starmer, K. (2019) *Rights without remedies seminar: Full speech by Sir Keir Starmer*, 2 May. Coram, London. Available at: www.coram.org.uk/resource/rights-without-remedies-seminar-full-speech-sir-keir-starmer (accessed 17 March 2020).

Towler, K. (2015) *The Right to Play is Central to Childhood*. Available at: http://ipaworld.org/uncategorized/towler-blog (accessed 12 May 2020).

United Nations Children's Fund (UNICEF) (1989) *The United Nations Convention on the Rights of the Child*. Available at: https://downloads.unicef.org.uk/wp-content/uploads/2016/08/unicef-convention-rights-child-uncrc.pdf (accessed 13 February 2020).

United Nations Children's Fund (UNICEF) (2007) *Implementation Handbook for the Convention on the Rights of the Child*, 3rd edition. Available at: www.unicef.org/publications/index_43110.html (accessed 20 April 2020).

United Nations Children's Fund (UNICEF) (2010) *Advocacy Toolkit: A Guide to Influencing Decisions that Improve Children's Lives*. Available at: www.unicef.org/cbsc/files/Advocacy_Toolkit.pdf (accessed 1 March 2020).

United Nations Children's Fund (UNICEF) (2020) *What are Human Rights?* Available at: www.unicef.org/child-rights-convention/what-are-human-rights (accessed 20 February 2020).

United Nations Commission on Human Rights (UNCHR) (1959) *Declaration of the Rights of the Child*. Available at: www.cirp.org/library/ethics/UN-declaration (accessed 13 February 2020).

United Nations Committee on the Rights of the Child (UNCRC) (2013) *General Comment No. 17 on the Right of the Child to Rest, Leisure, Play, Recreational Activities, Cultural Life and the Arts (Article 31)*, 17 April, CRC/C/GC/17. Available at: www.refworld.org/docid/51ef9bcc4.html (accessed 3 March 2020).

United Nations Committee on the Rights of the Child (UNCRC) (2015) *Consideration of Reports Submitted by States Parties Under Article 44 of the Convention: Fifth Periodic Reports of States Parties due in 2014, United Kingdom*. Available at: https://documents-dds-ny.un.org/doc/UNDOC/GEN/G15/044/91/PDF/G1504491.pdf?OpenElement (accessed 2 April 2020).

United Nations Committee on the Rights of the Child (UNCRC) (2016) *Concluding Observations on the Fifth Periodic Report of the United Kingdom of Great Britain and Northern Ireland*. Available at: http://docstore.ohchr.org/SelfServices/FilesHandler.ashx?enc=6QkG1d%2FPPRiCAqhKb7yhskHOj6VpDS%2F%2FJqg2Jxb9gncn UyUgbnuttBweOlylfyYPkBbwffitW2JurgBRuMMxZqnGgerUdpjxij3uZ0bj QBOLNTNvQ9fUIEOvA5LtW0GL (accessed 20 February 2020).

United Nations Committee on the Rights of the Child (UNCRC) (2020) *Monitoring Children's Rights.* Available at: www.ohchr.org/EN/HRBodies/CRC/Pages/CRCIntro.aspx (accessed 3 April 2020).

Voce, A. (2015) *Policy for Play: Responding to Children's Forgotten Right.* Bristol: Policy Press.

Welsh Government (2014) *Wales: A Play Friendly Country.* Available at: https://gov.wales/sites/default/files/publications/2019-07/wales-a-play-friendly-country.pdf (accessed 24 February 2020).

Whitebread, D., Basilio, M., Kuvalja, M., & Verma, M. (2012) *The Importance of Play: A Report on the Value of Children's Play with a Series of Policy Recommendations.* Brussels, Belgium: Toy Industries of Europe.

Wood, J. (2017) Planning for children's play: Exploring the 'forgotten' right in Welsh and Scottish policy. *Town Planning Review,* 88(5), 579–602.

9

LEARNING AND PLAY: CURRICULUM, PEDAGOGY AND ASSESSMENT

Su Wall and Sarah Roeschlaub

CONTENTS

This chapter explores learning, teaching and assessment and the role of play within both the Early Years Foundation Stage (EYFS) (DfE, 2017a) and the National Curriculum (DfE, 2014a).

THIS CHAPTER WILL...

- Explain the Early Years Foundation Stage and National Curriculum (KS1) frameworks in England
- Explore how play fits within curricular frameworks
- Consider the impact of assessment requirements
- Discuss differing perspectives on formalised learning and play in early years settings.

KEY TERMS

age-related expectations (ARE), assessment, early learning goals (ELG), Early Years Foundation Stage (EYFS), Key Stage 1, National Curriculum, observation, Office for Standards in Education, Children's Services and Skills (Ofsted), planning

INTRODUCTION

In the 1980s, the government introduced a new approach towards education that included a common curriculum for all publically funded schools. This led to the introduction of a national testing regime designed to support continuity and social mobility, but which also enabled comparison between schools and pupils on a local and national level. In combination, these had substantial ramifications for the profession in terms of curriculum and pedagogy. Many have suggested that play in schools has been a casualty of these reforms. Each of these factors will be explored as we present debates surrounding the historic and current position of play in education.

EARLY YEARS FOUNDATION STAGE

The Early Years Foundation Stage (EYFS) resulted in 2012 from the Tickell review (2011), which had brought together three key early years documents: *Birth to Three Matters*, *Full Care Requirements* and *Curriculum Guidance for the Foundation Stage*. It was subsequently updated (DfE, 2017a) and is mandatory for any setting or early years provider, including those in the private, voluntary and maintained sectors. The EYFS specifies both *welfare requirements* and *learning and development requirements* to ensure that children are healthy, and learn and develop within a safe environment.

The EYFS aims to provide:

- quality and consistency in all early years settings, so that every child makes good progress and no child gets left behind
- learning and development opportunities which are planned around the needs and interests of each individual child and are assessed and reviewed regularly; these should provide a sound foundation for future development
- partnership working between practitioners and parents/carers
- equality of opportunity and anti-discriminatory practice, ensuring every child is included and supported. (DfE, 2017a)

The EYFS specifies:

- the areas of learning and development which must shape activities and experiences (educational programmes) for children in all early years settings
- the **early learning goals**, which providers must help children work towards (the knowledge, skills and understanding children should have at the end of the academic year in which they turn 5)
- assessment arrangements for measuring progress
- requirements for reporting to parents and/or carers. (DfE, 2017a)

Play in the EYFS

The EYFS carries an expectation that activities should be play-based, and whilst many providers have embraced a child-led, play-rich approach, commentators have noted a lack of consistency (Roberts-Holmes, 2012). It would appear that ambiguity around how practitioners should implement the EYFS has led some to focus on formalised learning and outcomes (Torrance, 2018), in order to satisfy the early learning goals and ensure a smooth transition into the knowledge-rich National Curriculum (Palmer & Bayley, 2013). This clearly has a knock-on effect. Where 'learning' and achieving 'goals' are regarded as being of upmost importance, 'play' becomes something that must yield measurable outcomes rather than being simply a pleasurable activity or an end in itself. A survey of children and young people in England (NHS, 2020) found that the number of children diagnosed as having a probable mental disorder had increased substantially since 2017, suggesting a national need to pay careful attention to children's mental health and emotional wellbeing.

TIME TO CONSIDER

Should the early years be primarily about play or about preparing for formal schooling? To what extent do you think it is possible to combine the two?

Characteristics of effective learning

The *characteristics of effective learning* are central to the EYFS (Wood, 2014). Practitioners and teachers are expected to understand how these support children's learning and development, and their own role in providing an enabling environment. The enabling environment must be appropriate to the child's age and stage, yet challenging and engaging enough to drive development. Table 9.1 shows the characteristics of effective learning, as set out by the DfE (2012).

Table 9.1 Characteristics of effective learning

Playing and exploring engagement	Active learning motivation	Creating and thinking critically
Finding out and exploring	Being involved and concentrating	Having their own ideas
Playing with what they know	Keeping trying	Making links
Being willing to have a go	Enjoying achieving what they set out to do	Choosing ways to do things

Source: DfE (2012)

Ofsted, in its *Bold Beginnings Report* (Ofsted, 2017), highlighted the need for a smooth transition from Reception to Year 1. However, despite the best efforts of many practitioners, this has proved difficult due to a misalignment of the early learning goals and the increased expectations of the National Curriculum. The characteristics detailed above are notably absent from Year 1 onwards (DfE, 2014a).

USING VYGOTSKIAN PRINCIPLES

Vygotsky (1978) asserted that children learn naturally during play. Play would therefore appear to be the ideal means of maximising learning in the very young. However, his zone of proximal development theory (see Chapter 1) also suggests that appropriate support and challenge from more knowledgeable others (be they adults or peers) will aid understanding and development in any context. Moyles (2015), therefore, suggests that learning can be sensitively scaffolded (Bruner, 1978) and the characteristics of effective learning maintained, regardless of the apparent strictures of an imposed curriculum. Much is dependent on the ideals, ethos and pedagogy created by the individual classroom practitioner.

It must be remembered that children generally learn more from undertaking a process than they do from the outcome. With the correct environment and support, children will become creative, adventurous and active learners with a positive attitude towards learning. Children need opportunities to explore new materials and discover their own capabilities. Time must be allowed for children to apply these ideas, using the skills and techniques they have learned, and to refine such ideas through play and exploration.

Age-related expectations

The National Curriculum contains **age-related expectations (ARE)**. These are based on what 'the average child' should have learned, or be able to do, at the end of each Key Stage. Children are classed as:

- working *towards* the expected standard
- working *at* the expected standard
- working *above* the expected standard.

Pupils who fall into the middle bracket are meeting 'age-related expectations'.

 CASE STUDY 9.1

Ben attends the Reception class of a school in an affluent suburban area which has outdoor provision available. The early years practitioners from the onsite nursery class passed on transition documentation stating that Ben was on track to meet all of his early learning goals. He is a confident and energetic boy who thrives in the outdoor environment and learns well through self-motivated, exploratory play. Ben is also a very sociable, thoughtful and caring child, who excels in short-term tasks that require limited periods of concentration.

On entry to Reception class, the teacher assessed Ben in line with baseline testing and was surprised to note that Ben's progress trajectory indicated he would not meet his early learning goals in maths, reading and writing. This means that he may fall behind with the National Curriculum AREs in Year 1 and beyond.

Cases such as Ben's illustrate the importance of both task and environment when attempting to assess young children – a child may excel according to one set of criteria but fail according to another.

Reflective question

After reviewing the case study, what are your views regarding testing in the early years? You may find it useful to compare the differing viewpoints offered by the government (Reception baseline assessment framework; Gov.uk) and the campaign group 'More Than a Score' (www.morethanascore.org.uk).

THE NATIONAL CURRICULUM
What is the National Curriculum?

Although curriculum is synonymous in the UK with the centrally controlled National Curriculum, first implemented in 1988 (DfES, 1988), the term curriculum has been used to define academic studies since early Greek civilisation (Marsh, 2009). Marsh (2009) suggests it is a guide to what is taught in schools, whilst Alexander (2010) views it as that intended to be taught and learnt overall. The design of any curriculum is founded on a belief in the purpose of education. Marsh (2009) and Claxton (2008) argue that the purpose is to prepare the next generation for a future society; thus, the education system, as a social institution, needs to continually change (Kelly, 2009; Shelton, in O'Grady & Cottle, 2016) and predict the needs of the future society. Claxton (2008) argues that in this rapidly evolving society, education may be falling short. Eyre (2017, cited in Blatchford, 2013) expands this argument by acknowledging that the continual change and refinement of curriculum is a result of the uncertainty about what primary education should achieve or look like, suggesting it is subject to the political views of the government in power at the time, as with any social policy.

The content of any curriculum relies on a decision made about what it should, and should not, contain, which is often viewed as the body of essential knowledge to be taught and learnt (Shelton, in O'Grady & Cottle, 2016). The National Curriculum (DfE, 2014a) is centrally controlled, with the government deciding on the essential knowledge required for future society growth, adding a political (Claxton, 2008) and socio-economic influence (FitzPatrick, Twohig & Morgan, 2014) to policy associated with teaching and children's learning, rather than the child-led approach witnessed in the EYFS. Kelly (2009) acknowledges the important role teachers play in the implementation of any new curriculum, and the confidence and training practitioners have can either broaden or narrow a child's learning experience.

History of the National Curriculum

The National Curriculum was introduced in the UK in 1988 with a list of subjects, deemed essential by the government, to be studied at each Key Stage – subjects that resembled those taught in 1908 (Claxton, 2008), implying a lack of evolution in key knowledge for a changing society. Kelly (2009) argues that the centralisation of the curriculum was designed to meet society's needs rather than those of the individual, and it removed both pupil and teacher voice from education as teachers became operatives in a scientific activity. Shelton (in O'Grady and Cottle, 2016) argues that teachers, as facilitators of learning, are in a prime position to challenge the constraints of the National Curriculum, to push for teaching to be aligned to children's needs. Rose (2009) noted that, at the time, the National Curriculum (DfES, 1988) offered a national entitlement with general standards and continuity and cohesion for a more mobile society. The revised Curriculum (DfES, 1999), however, continued to set out the requirements of knowledge for the subjects to be taught and was criticised for being overcrowded, over-prescriptive and unmanageable (Alexander, 2010; Rose, 2009).

Pedagogy and practice within the National Curriculum: Room for play?

Although the National Curriculum (DfES, 1988) and its revision (DfES, 1999) did not dictate, or suggest how the content should be taught (the pedagogy), the introduction of assessments and league tables modified practice (Alexander, Willcocks & Nelson, 1996). With national tests and assessments leading rather than supporting the received curriculum (Kelly, 2009), the over-emphasis on results can lead to a narrowing of the curriculum, with assessed subjects given more time and emphasis over the school day. Leach and Moon (2008) warned that a curriculum focused on coverage of knowledge could be the enemy of understanding and have a detrimental effect on play within the **Key Stage 1** environment (Nicholson, 2019).

Since the introduction of the National Curriculum (DfES, 1988), education has witnessed many complex and overlapping reforms to its curriculum and practice (Brundrett, Duncan & Rhodes, 2010), in order to reflect a continual evolution of society. Many of these reforms are designed to raise standards whilst allowing teachers to develop new approaches to learning (Brundrett & Duncan, 2011). The revised National Curriculum (DfE, 2014a) is one of the most recent changes within the evolution and aspiration of higher standards that does not suggest pedagogy but may well influence it.

This heralded reform as a way to drive up standards and offer a world-class curriculum that would inspire the next generation (DfE, 2014b). This suggests that the motivation for revision of the National Curriculum was to increase the standards of education for all, as in the Ruskin Speech (Callaghan, 1976); yet Smith, Anderson and Blanch (2016) warn that the quest for increased standards often leads to a narrowing of the curriculum received by learners, a point supported by Kelly (2009). A focus on measurable knowledge takes the focus away from creativity and wider learning experiences (Shelton, in O'Grady & Cottle, 2016).

TIME TO CONSIDER

Thinking back to your own time at school, how much emphasis do you feel was placed on assessments? Do you feel that it impacted what or how you were taught in any way? Are there any changes you would have liked to see?

Play theory into practice

Classic theorists such as Vygotsky and Piaget advocated an approach which put exploration and play at the heart of education. Modern theorists have largely echoed this approach, suggesting a need for child-led provision facilitated by a supportive practitioner rather than the structured approach to learning seen in the National Curriculum.

Piaget's theory of play, based on cognitive development, would contest the politician's view of formal education as a means of providing the skilled workforce of the future, as Piaget saw learning as a lifelong journey of discovery. He suggested that there were two key processes in learning: assimilation (of new knowledge and experience) and accommodation (of the knowledge and experience into the child's existing patterns of thought and behaviour, otherwise known as schemas) (see Chapter 3).

It should be noted that modern psychologists have questioned Piaget's experimental methods and the inflexibility of his stages. Today, there is widespread recognition of the differences that exist between individual children, and the importance of environmental factors. Developments within cognitive psychology in the years since his death have also led to some amendments to and expansions of his theory. Piaget, however, remains one of the most influential theorists of the modern age and is recognised as having challenged previously accepted norms.

In later life, Piaget (1936) suggested that one of the major issues with education is the lack of agreement regarding its goal. In particular, he questioned whether we are attempting to form children who are only capable of learning what is already known. Perhaps, he suggested, we should try developing creative and innovative minds, capable of discovery throughout life?

Piaget theorised four distinct stages of development that revolve around play and learning, which can be seen in Table 9.2.

Table 9.2 Piaget's four distinct stages of child development

Stage	Age	Information
Sensorimotor	Birth–2 years	Children use their five senses and movement to explore and experience the word around them.
Pre-operational	2–7 years (approx.)	Children start to add pretend to their play, but such pretend is limited by the child's experience and imagination. Play and questioning play a vital role in the child establishing reasoning and identifying significant levels of schema already existing that need to be put into context with the world around them.
Concrete operational stage	7–11 years (pre-adolescence)	Children start to logically assemble schemas and consciously save them for reference; they can classify objects and become more adept at dealing with mathematical and more abstract problems.
Formal operational stage	11–18 years (adulthood or later)	Young people develop logical thinking and abstract reasoning based on their experiences.

Throughout Piaget's stages, play is seen to support cognitive development, and movement between stages is dependent on the provision of appropriate stimuli within the child's environment. Within Piaget's framework, the change from EYFS to National Curriculum sits in the middle of the pre-operational stage – and this requires play in order for children to explore and understand their world. Yet, at this point, we see a move from a play-based curriculum to a more formal, subject-led one. Indeed, 'play' is only mentioned 38 times in the 201-page National Curriculum document, mainly in the context of 'role-play', plays (as in play scripts), the spelling section, and one suggestion regarding playing mirror games within the notes section of the Year 3 programme of study for science (DfE, 2014a). It might be argued that, as the National Curriculum forms only one part of the school curriculum, schools are free to include other subjects in their own programme of education (DfE, 2014a), and therefore play can still be incorporated into learning. This relies on the teacher ensuring that play is at the heart of learning and experience for children. However, some feel that the statutory document is, in actuality, so overcrowded that it leaves little room for play (Alexander, 2010; Nicholson, 2019; Warwick Commission, 2015).

ASSESSMENT AND PLANNING CYCLES

Assessment has been asked to perform an increasing number of functions in recent years – from judging individual pupils to evaluating schools and monitoring national performance.

Current assessment tools

1   Checks carried out at 2 years old – this was introduced to identify any developmental needs potentially requiring early intervention. This process is carried out through observations of play. However, Nicholson and Palaiologou (2016) question:
    o   the reliability and usefulness of such a complex assessment at such an early age
    o   the training, qualifications and experience of the practitioners conducting the reviews.
2   *Reception baseline assessment* – this is conducted within three weeks of a child starting school and used as the starting point to measure progress through primary school (DfE, 2019).
3   *Early learning goals* – at the end of Reception, children are expected to have attained the early learning goals within the seven areas of learning (those children who require additional support may continue to be measured against them in KS1).
4   *Age-related expectations* at the end of every school year.
5   *Phonics screening* – conducted in Year 1 to test children's ability to de-code words using phonics.
6   *KS1 statutory assessment tests (SATS)* – tests at the end of Year 2/KS1 in:
    o   reading
    o   English grammar, punctuation and spelling (optional)
    o   maths.

Dowling (2010) suggests that many Reception and KS1 teachers feel pressurised by assessments and regard them as counterproductive for children. The current focus on formalised learning and assessment necessitates a daily routine that is more adult-led and less play-based. This is necessitating a reduction in creative and innovative teaching techniques, for instance the use of outdoor environments (see Chapter 4). It also commodifies children, paying scant regard to their individuality or feelings, with detrimental consequences for their emotional wellbeing.

Individual assessment

Ongoing formative assessment is fundamental within any early childhood or primary setting. The assessment cycle should support children's learning and development, whilst following their interest and planning for their next steps (see Figure 9.1).

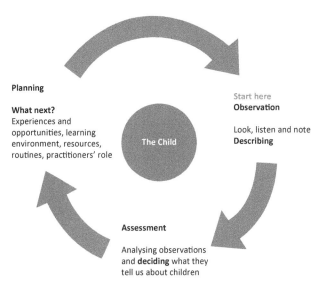

Figure 9.1 Observation, assessment and planning cycle

Source: DfE (2012)

Assessment in practice

The following considerations will support the effectiveness of assessment:

- Know and understand children fully
- Provide a supportive and positive attitude within a safe and calm enabling environment, both indoors and outdoors
- Provide a range of opportunities to engage with children, linked to their interests and needs
- Maintain high but realistic expectations

- Ensure a balance of adult-led and child-led opportunities
- Promote high quality adult interaction, knowing when to intervene and when to observe
- Ensure sufficient time and space. (Dubiel, 2016)

Davies (2011) expands the planning cycle into the learning environment by including the triangulation of observation, product and conversation to support a holistic approach to planning, learning and assessment.

As all sources of assessment offer insight into different aspects of learning, they should not be used in isolation; yet, in recent legislation such as the National Curriculum (DfE, 2014a), the emphasis appears to be on more formal testing. This means that practitioners need to ensure other sources are considered and encompassed within their practice as learning is multi-faceted and complex.

Including parents and children

Given that parents have knowledge and insights to offer, parental involvement must be valued and supported to ensure a holistic approach to assessment. To support development, it is important that practitioners and teachers listen if parents express concerns about their child's development, as well as listening to and addressing any concerns raised by the children themselves (SEND Code of Practice, DfE, 2015). Once children fully understand what they know (Whitebread, 2012), they should be encouraged to contribute to their own assessment. Whilst this is recognised in the EYFS assessment process, the formalised nature of standardised testing limits it somewhat. Furthermore, assessment within the primary years is often focused on SATs and phonics screening, leading to an emphasis on teaching the subjects being tested: English, maths and science. This has been further exacerbated by Ofsted's (2017) assertion that successful schools are those that teach reading, writing and maths to ensure children are equipped for year 1 and beyond, instead of ensuring that children are valued, supported and encouraged to follow their interests and learning through play.

We would seem to be moving towards the position Wood and Bennett (1999) feared may arise, wherein the child-centred principles which shape the early childhood curriculum are being eroded by the downward pressure of targets from the more formal Key Stage 1.

Observations

Observations are key to assessment and are utilised to:

- assess children's development
- inform future planning
- highlight any areas of concern
- identify children's interests
- provide information for parents and professionals.

The DfE (2014a) endorses the use of observations as a means of understanding children's level of achievement and interests, and thus allowing effective planning to take place. However, it is important that those conducting the observations are fully trained and confident that they know what to look for and how to evidence it, otherwise findings may be inaccurate. Yates et al. (2020) stress that observations must be completed in a non-judgemental manner, using unbiased and ethical protocols. For instance, due attention should be paid to:

- the rights of the child
- the child's voice
- prior consent being received
- the purpose of the observation (is it necessary?)
- confidentiality during observation and access to observational data.

Accurate observational data can highlight areas of individual need and enable early intervention to help address the issue. Early intervention has a demonstrable impact on life chances (Powell, 2019), health and wellbeing, and can prove transformative for both the child and their family (Action for Children, 2020). However, many settings fail to respond promptly, with significant consequences for the children involved (Action for Children, 2020).

 **TIME TO CONSIDER**

- Why do you think that in some situations, early intervention is still not fully embedded into practice?
- Do you think that children's autonomy is generally considered during observations?

 **SPECIAL STUDY: BARRIERS TO EFFECTIVE** ▬▬▬▬ **ASSESSMENT**

For decades, it has been recognised that the skills and expertise of the early years workforce vary drastically across the sector and that this variance impacts play-based learning and assessment. The minimum statutory requirement allows early years settings to have 50 per cent of their workforce as unqualified practitioners, 50 per cent of staff qualified to level 2 and only a manager holding a level 3 qualification (DfE, 2017b). This is despite clear evidence from research, such as the influential Effective Provision of Preschool Education (EPPE) project (Sylvia et al., 2004), that a highly qualified workforce and a recognition of the importance of play are strongly correlated with high quality settings. Given that half of the staff may be untrained in child development and unaware of the significance of learning through play, Nicholson and Palaiologou (2016) question how they can be expected to make accurate judgements and assessments. Progress remains patchy, with little evidence of any long-term vision for improving the skills of the workforce (Bonetti, 2020).

Although there is a need for a highly qualified workforce, it must be recognised that experience and knowledge are fundamental to accurate assessments in a play-based environment. Dubiel (2016) raises concerns that if practitioners and teachers consider an area to be of less importance or place no value on it, then provision and assessment are less likely to occur. Responsibility for a play-based pedagogy and accurate assessment therefore lies squarely with the individual teacher or practitioner.

THE IMPACT OF THE NATIONAL CURRICULUM ON PLAY AND CREATIVITY

Roeschlaub (2018) explored the views of Reception and Key Stage 1 teachers on how the revised National Curriculum (DfE, 2014a) had impacted practice, policy and pedagogy. Phenomenological analysis of questionnaire and interview data found that all participants agreed the following:

- Education has the power to transform lives and plays a vital role in social justice.
- The National Curriculum provides an outline of core knowledge from which practitioners can develop exciting and stimulating lessons.
- The National Curriculum can restrict child-led and play-based learning.
- The degree of constriction is substantially impacted by the practitioner's confidence and experience and the school's support network.
- The National Curriculum is over-prescriptive (in relation to the EYFS).
- This over-prescription means that lack of time is a key barrier to play, creativity and lessons beyond the core curriculum.

Participants stated:

> 'As a year 2 teacher the interim assessments have been very prescriptive this year, have left very little time to teach anything beyond the curriculum.'

> 'There is very little time to fit in anything else, explore the children's interest etc.'

However, teachers also believed that there is a need to *make time* for play and creativity. For instance, one participant stated: 'For those who are committed to it, time and space can be found *despite* NC2014, not because of it.'

The findings implied that responsibility for providing stimulating and interesting lessons lie with the school and the teacher, supporting Shelton's (in O'Grady & Cottle, 2016) view that teachers are in a prime position to challenge the constraints of the National Curriculum.

 **TIME TO CONSIDER**

Do you think the pressure placed on practitioners through testing impacts on play and creativity? Why?

How would you support child-led learning and a broader learning experience within a prescribed system?

FINAL REFLECTION

Teachers and practitioners are expected to operate within the curricular and assessment guidelines laid down by central government. The EYFS (DfE, 2017a) supports child-led, play-based learning; however, variations in interpretation mean that some settings focus on what is being learnt, to the exclusion of free, child-led play. The National Curriculum KS1 (DfE, 2014a) is viewed by many practitioners as being over-crowded, constricting, formalising and with little room for play-based learning. Despite its constrictions, with creative and careful planning, it is possible for teachers to utilise a pedagogy more closely aligned to the approaches seen within the EYFS.

Assessment, be it formative or summative, is a fundamental component of everyday practice. Given the significance ascribed to results, it is important that we have a highly trained workforce in order to ensure accuracy and reliability. We may also need to question whether the emphasis on assessments is leading practitioners and teachers to 'teach to the test' and, in doing so, to substantially reduce young children's access to play.

KEY POINTS

- The EYFS supports the notion of learning through play, but interpretations as to how this should be capacitated, vary widely.
- The National Curriculum offers a formalised approach but, with creativity, practitioners can introduce child-led and play-based aspects to teaching and learning.
- The importance of a highly trained and motivated early years workforce cannot be overestimated.
- The needs of children must take precedence in all decisions regarding curriculum, pedagogy and assessment.

QUESTIONS TO CONSIDER

1   Do you believe that play is important in learning in all stages of children's development?
2   How do you implement play for all children aged 0–8 years?
3   Do you believe that testing influences teaching within the EYFS and Key Stage 1?
4   What are your views on children being 'tested'?
5   What other ways can you think of to assess children?

FURTHER READING

The following academic sources will support further investigations into debates surrounding play, curriculum and assessment:

Alexander, R. (2010) *Children, Their World, Their Education: Final Report and Recommendations of the Cambridge Primary Review*. Abingdon: Routledge. (The Cambridge Primary Review offered an in-depth insight into educational provision in England with regards to teaching, curriculum and assessment, and provided an independent review of play and of the significance of role play in children's development.)

Gerver, R. (2014) *Creating Tomorrows Schools Today: Education – Our Children – Their Futures*. London: Bloomsbury. (Gerver offers a critical and insightful view of schools and educational provision from a practitioner's point of view.)

Tickell, C. (2011) *The Early Years Foundations for Life, Health and Learning*. London: DfE. (Tickell provides an independent review of the impact of the EYFS on children's learning and development, and on early years practitioners.)

REFERENCES

Action for Children (2020) *Early Intervention*. Available at: www.actionforchildren. org.uk/media/3456/afc_early_intervention_-_final.pdf (accessed 1 June 2020).

Alexander, R. (2010) *Children, Their World, Their Education: Final Report and Recommendations of the Cambridge Primary Review*. Abingdon: Routledge.

Alexander, R., Willcocks, J., & Nelson, N. (1996) Discourse, pedagogy and the National Curriculum: Change and continuity in primary schools. *Research Papers in Education*, 11(1), 81–120.

Blatchford, R. (ed.) (2013) *Taking Forward the Primary Curriculum: Applying the 2014 National Curriculum for KS1 and KS2*. Woodbridge: John Catt Educational Ltd.

Bonetti, S. (2020) *Early Years Workforce Development in England: Key Ingredients and Missed Opportunities*. London: EPI.

Brundrett, M., & Duncan, D. (2011). Leading curriculum innovation in primary schools. *Management in Education*, 25(3),119–124.

Brundrett, M., Duncan, D., & Rhodes, C. (2010) Leading curriculum innovation in primary schools project: An interim report on school leaders' roles in curriculum development in England. *Education 3–13*, 38(4), 403–419.

Bruner, J.S. (1978) The role of dialogue in language acquisition. In A. Sinclair, R.J. Jarvelle & W.J.M. Levelt (eds) *The Child's Concept of Language*. New York: Springer-Verlag

Callaghan, J. (1976) *Towards a National Debate*. Available at: http://education. guardian.co.uk/thegreatdebate/story/0,574645,00.html (accessed June 2020).

Claxton, G. (2008) *What's the Point of School? Rediscovering the Heart of Education*. Oxford: Oneworld Publications.

Davies, A. (2011) *Making Classroom Assessment Work*, 3rd edition. Bloomington, IN: Solution Tree Press.

DfE (2012) *Development matters in the Early Years Foundation Stage*. London, DfE

DfE (2014a) *The National Curriculum*. London: DfE.

DfE (2014b) *The National Curriculum in England Key Stages 1 and 2 framework document*. Available at: www.gov.uk/government/publications/national-curriculum-in-england-primary-curriculum (accessed May 2020).

DfE (2015) *Special Educational Needs and Disability Code of Practice: 0 to 25 Years – Statutory guidance for organisations which work with and support children and young people who have special educational needs or disabilities*. London: DfE.

DfE (2017a) *The Early Years Foundation Stage*. London: DfE.

DfE (2017b) *The Early Years Workforce Strategy*. London: DfE.

DfE (2019) *Early Years Foundation Stage Reforms Consultation*. Available at https://consult.education.gov.uk/early-years-quality-outcomes/early-years-foundation-satge-reforms/.

Department for Education and Skills (DfES) (1988) *The National Curriculum*. London: DfES.

Department for Education and Skills (DfES) (1999) *The National Curriculum: Handbook for Primary Teachers in England*. London: QCA.

Dowling, M. (2010) *Young Children's Personal, Social and Emotional Development*. London: Sage.

Dubiel, J. (2016) *Effective Assessment in the Early Years Foundation Stage*. London: Sage.

Eyre, C. (2017) *The Elephant in the Staffroom: How to Reduce Stress and Improve Teacher Wellbeing*. Abingdon: Routledge.

FitzPatrick, S., Twohig, M., & Morgan, M. (2014) Priorities for primary education? From subjects to life-skills and children's social and emotional development. *Irish Educational Studies*, 33(3), 269–228.

Kelly, A.V. (2009) *The Curriculum: Theory and Practice*, 6th edition. London: Sage.

Leach, J., & Moon, B. (2008) *The Power of Pedagogy*. London: Sage.

Marsh, C. (2009) *Key Concepts for Understanding Curriculum*, 4th edition. Abingdon: Routledge.

Moyles, J. (2015) *The Excellence of Play*. Maidenhead: Open University Press.

NHS (2020) *Mental Health of Children and Young People in England, 2020: Wave 1 follow up to the 2017 survey*. Available at https://digital.nhs.uk/data-and-information/publications/statistical/mental-health-of-children-and-young-people-in-england/2020-wave-1-follow-up (accessed 15 April 2020).

Nicholson, M. (2019) *Preschool Students Learning from Play Based Learning and Small Group Instruction*. Orange City, IA: Northwestern College.

Nicholson, N., & Palaiologou, L. (2016) Early years foundation stage progress check at the age of two for early intervention in relation to speech and language difficulties in England: The voices of the team around the child. *Early Child Development and Care*, 186(12), 2009–2021.

Office for Standards in Education, Children's Services and Skills (Ofsted) (2017) *Bold Beginnings*. Available at: https://assets.publishing.service.gov.uk/government/uploads/system/uploads/attachment_data/file/663560/28933_Ofsted_-_Early_Years_Curriculum_Report_-_Accessible.pdf (accessed June 2020).

O'Grady, A., & Cottle, V. (eds) (2016) *Exploring Education at Postgraduate Level: Policy, Theory and Practice*. Abingdon: Routledge.

Palmer, S., & Bayley, R. (2013) *Foundations of Literacy*. London: Featherstone.

Piaget, J. (1936) *Origins of Intelligence in the Child*. London, Routledge & Kegan Paul.

Powel, T. (2019) *Health and Well Being*. London: House of Commons.

Roberts-Holmes, G. (2012) 'It's the bread and butter of our practice': Experiencing the Early Years Foundation Stage. *International Journal of Early Years Education*, 20(1), 30–42.

Rose, J. (2009) *The Independent Review of the Primary Curriculum: Final Report.* London: DCSF Publications. Available at: www.education.gov.uk/publications/eOrderingDownload/Primary_curriculum_Report.pdf (accessed May 2020).

Roeschlaub, S. (2017) *The revised National Curriculum (2014) in practice: an analysis of current practice in a primary school in relation to current policy and teacher* [Unpublished Masters dissertation]. University of Derby.

Smith, L., Anderson, V., & Blanch, K. (2016) Five beginning teachers' reflections on enacting New Zealand's national standards. *Teaching and Teacher Education*, 54(2016), 107–116.

Sylvia, K, Melhuish, E., Sammons, P., Siraj-Blatchford, I., & Taggart, B. (2004) *The Effective Provision of Preschool Education (EPPE) Project*. Nottingham: DfES.

Tickell, C. (2011) *The Early Years Foundations for Life, Health and Learning*. London: DfE.

Torrance, H. (2018) The return to final paper examining in English National Curriculum assessment and school examinations: Issues of validity and politics. *British Journal of Education Studies*, 66(1), 3–27.

Vygotsky, L. (1978) *Mind in Society: The Development of Higher Psychological Processes*. London: Harvard University Press.

Warwick Commission (2015) *Enriching Britain: Culture, Creativity and Growth.* Available at: https://warwick.ac.uk/research/warwickcommission/futureculture/finalreport/warwick_commission_final_report.pdf.

Whitebread, D. (2012) *Developmental Psychology and Early Childhood Education.* London: Sage.

Wood, A. (2014) *The Characteristics of Effective Learning: Creating and Capturing the Possibilities in the Early Years*. London: Routledge.

Wood, E., & Bennett, N. (1999) Progression and continuity in early childhood education: Tensions and contradictions. *International Journal of Early Years Education*, 7(1), 5–16.

Yates, E., Twigg, E., Wall, S., & Appleby, M. (2020) The Emerging Practitioner in R. Oates (ed) *The Student Practitioner in Early Childhood Studies: An Essential Guide to Working with Children*. London: Routledge.

10

A HISTORICAL VIEW OF ANTHROPOLOGICAL, INTERNATIONAL AND INTERCULTURAL PERSPECTIVES

Marco Antonio Delgado-Fuentes

CONTENTS

This chapter explores how our current knowledge of play is framed by our historical and social context. Our understanding of play has been shaped mainly by the notions of psychology and education in English-speaking countries. However, other disciplines and cultures have also studied it. This chapter will explain how our conceptions and use of play, games and toys will continue to be contested and evolve.

THIS CHAPTER WILL...

- Explain some historical and anthropological perspectives on play
- Discuss how our culture shapes our understanding of play
- Introduce some of the different ideas of play that have been proposed in different parts of the world
- Help you to consider future developments in the knowledge and use of play.

KEY TERMS

anthropology, cultural artefact, cultural relevance, colonisation, culture, decolonisation, emancipation, inclusion, interculturalism, international perspectives, postmodernism, poststructuralism

INTRODUCTION

Anthropology is a social science that studies human beings from different perspectives. Social and cultural anthropology study culture. But culture itself is a complex and symbolic world: the words, narratives, institutions, spaces and relationships that shape knowledge, continuity of everyday life and changes in societies. Culture is not monolithic, static or total (Enriz, 2011). Play has been studied since the rise of the discipline, and understanding its development helps us to comprehend not only other cultures but ours too. Researching cultures gives us the possibility to collaborate in the construction of an inclusive world and to learn how play can be either a colonising activity or part of an emancipatory process – that is, using play to impose a vision of childhood on other cultures, or using it to create societies that are based on cultural diversity and diverse childhoods.

THE RISE OF ANTHROPOLOGY AND THE STUDY OF PLAY, GAMES AND TOYS

The interest in other cultures and play started early in human history. Plato in ancient Greece, for example, wrote at length about the relationships between play, sport, values and knowledge (Ardley, 1967).

Anthropology originated in the UK and the USA during colonial times in the late 19th century as it developed the ethnographic method and aimed to produce systematic knowledge of peoples and their cultures. Although modern-day anthropology tends to be based on observations and interviews and may also use quantitative techniques, in the beginning it relied more on observations focusing on the descriptions of everyday life, rites, ceremonies and social structures. In the early stage, the study of play considered the study of games and toys together. There was not widespread interest in distinguishing between adults' and children's leisure activities.

In a comprehensive historical review of anthropology and play written in Italian, de Sanctis Ricciardone (1994) reports on more than 20 ethnographies published before 1920. The primary sources of information were the journal *American Anthropologist* and *The Journal of the Anthropological Institute of Great Britain and Ireland*, mostly focusing on North American peoples. Amongst these were some studies of the Zuñi (Coxe Stevenson, 1903; Kroeber, 1916), Ojibwa (Hoffman, 1890; Reagan & Waugh, 1919), Tewa (Harrington, 1912), Seneca (Hough, 1888), Cherokee (Mooney, 1890) and Algonkian (Speck, 1917) peoples. Dorsey (1901) studied Klamath people's gambling games and made a relevant early distinction on gender differences in games.

Further from the US mainland, Culin (1899) reported on Hawaiian games. A few others focused on the native peoples of other countries, such as Culin (1900) and Simms (1908), who looked at games from the Philippines.

There were also some emerging attempts to formulate theories on the primordial sources of games, trying to find a common root amongst cultures, or evidence of cultural interchange through games, play and toys. Tylor (1879), for example, conducted one early attempt at transcultural analysis by trying to link an ancient Mexican game with some Asiatic games, and Stearns (1890) reported on how white people in Boston adopted a Nishinam people's game. There were also some attempts to establish a geographical categorisation, as Culin (1903) did with American games generally, or Kroeber (1920) with Californian games.

Research began to emerge elsewhere in other languages. Mauger (1915) studied Chinese games and their relationship to social and political structure; the work was published in French.

Nowadays, some of these papers are valuable as descriptions of objects and rules. Interestingly, the then-contemporary reviews give us a good idea of their limitations and the potential use of these reports as historical artefacts in their own right. These show the gradual consolidation of the discipline and the position adopted by the early authors, as white males who considered themselves to be at the pinnacle of human evolution.

Early examples of anthropological ideas on play

McGee (1899: 565–566), reviewing Culin's work (1898), stated:

> During recent years anthropologists have given much attention to games, especially those of primitive peoples. Various publications have resulted. The eminent Briton, Tylor, has described and discussed the games of the Amerinds; Cushing has brought out the exceeding significance of the arrow in primitive games; Director Culin has issued a luminous monograph on the games of Korea, China, and Japan, in addition to lesser writings of standard value; while contributors have added their quota to the growing literature subject. Some of the contributions … are essentially descriptive and comparative, Collectively, the publications, especially those of Messrs Culin and Cushing, have reduced the chaos of primitive to fairly satisfactory order, and have furnished a basis for further inquiry.

It is clear that anthropology, and other social sciences, have now moved away from some of the ideas and assumptions of past centuries. Early ethnography held the underlying assumptions that cultures were an evolutionary process in which white people of the USA and the UK were the most civilised; the rest of the world was primitive (Vidich & Lyman, 2000). Hence, the task of anthropology was to classify peoples and their cultures according to how primitive or civilised they were. As we shall see, anthropology and its focus on play evolved as this view died out.

 TIME TO CONSIDER

Do you think that future generations will look back at our current representations of different cultures and consider them unacceptable?

Is it possible to understand games, play and toys of other cultures by only observing and describing objects and activities?

Do you think that attempts to understand other cultures and improve understanding enrich our own culture?

Enriz (2011) explains that in the late 19th and early 20th centuries, the main narrative aimed to find a universal theory of culture and play. In their attempts to achieve this, some assumed there was a mythical, shared origin and tried to establish relationships between civilisations that may not have had contact with one another. Others looked for evidence of play's role in reproducing society and maintaining the status quo. According to Enriz's analysis, early anthropologists studying play failed to consider the opinions of the players themselves in terms of the social meaning of their interactions.

THE 20TH CENTURY: THEORETICAL PERSPECTIVES AND CONSOLIDATION OF THE FIELD

In her detailed review of the anthropology of play, written in Spanish, Enriz (2011) discusses how the interest in play, games and toys has had various waves in history, receiving more attention at different times. During the 20th century, anthropology experienced considerable development and provided enriching discussions by considering other disciplines such as sociology, history and philosophy. This in part directed the discipline towards a discourse in which play and games were deemed to be symbolic manifestations of culture, and by studying them it was possible to reveal certain views of class, gender and child-rearing practices. During the century, two lines of thought were salient in the study of play: phenomenology and hermeneutics.

Phenomenology and its contribution to anthropology

Phenomenology is a school of thought that emerged from philosophical thinking. It focuses on the individual's conscious perception of lived experience of external reality. French philosopher Merleau-Ponty wrote the influential book *Phenomenology of Perception* in 1946 (English version, 2012) and developed the notion that, through play, children come to understand their senses and the process of socialisation. As in the previous century, attempts to study play showed that merely describing objects and practices, failed to illuminate their meaning. The voice and feelings of players were crucial to understanding this. This realisation encouraged collaboration between psychology and anthropology and gave rise to the possibility of considering games as a means of education. Astrada (1942) continued to develop phenomenological ideas using the notions of occurrence, chance and risk to relate play to other aspects of society through more sophisticated means than simple observation. Through combining different disciplines, it became apparent that the study of play requires a complex framework that considers individual development (psychology) and the cultural environment (anthropology and sociology).

Hermeneutics and its contribution to anthropology

Hermeneutics is a methodology of interpretation initially used to reflect on how the Bible could be understood to give sense to human actions; later, some of its principles informed the process of systematic interpretation of data required by social sciences. By introducing this notion, the anthropologist's role turned from one of imposing her cultural assumptions upon others to that of deciphering the logic and symbols of other cultures as a non-judgemental enterprise, as language translators do with words. Shared meanings, such as values, roles and hierarchies, make sense in a symbolic arrangement that gives identity to members of a cultural community. Eliade (1959, 1964) employed hermeneutics to study myths, ceremonies and civil and religious roles that make sense in a given culture and its social structure. In the study of play, hermeneutics was useful to relate games to general social symbolisms. Mauss (1926) did so whilst examining young children's play; Fink (1969) and Bereau (1976) examined how play was influenced by the gender biases of storybooks and literature. Brougère (1998, 2004) argued that studying games requires a consideration of the artefacts – toys, the system of rules, the players' experience, and the discourse that unifies and makes sense of all of these components. This perspective allows us to understand how the symbolic nature of play links to the broader culture and how children use it to share their representation of the word.

Play as a crucial component of culture: *Homo Ludens*

Perhaps the best-known theory on play, culture and society is found in the book *Homo Ludens* ('The Playing Human') (Huizinga, 1955), originally published in Dutch in 1938. Here, Huizinga theorises that games and playfulness are essential to the emergence and development of culture and are therefore a crucial component of civilisation. The author argues that play is not a manifestation of culture but instead one of its foundations. Creativity, ingenuity, innovation, art and creation have a ludic characteristic in common. A significant development is Caillois's (1958) analysis on how culture has been impoverished as play and playfulness have been restricted in modern Western culture.

The traditional description and classification of play and games continued through the 20th century with some notable examples, such as Béart and Monod's (1955) inventory of some 1500 games and toys of West Africa, and Opie and Opie (1969) bringing together over 2500 games from the UK.

TIME TO CONSIDER

Current literature on culture and globalisation has suggested that the process has eroded the cultural richness of other cultures. Has the culture in the West and in the UK been impoverished too? Are we playing less than past generations and, if so, why?

The consolidation of the cultural study of play

The second part of the 20th century stood out with the creation of the Cultural Anthropology of Play Reprint Society in 1973 in the USA, which, in 1974, became the Association for the Anthropological Study of Play and, finally, in 1987, the Association for the Study of Play, now an interdisciplinary association (TASP, no date). The Association has a journal, *Play & Culture Studies*, that a few years ago celebrated 40 years of research on play, publishing a retrospective on its research output (Patte & Sutterby, 2016). In this work, the Association discusses the multidisciplinary nature of the field. It highlights how the topics of anthropology have remained focused on – and continued to develop around – cross-cultural comparisons and the relationship between play and culture, such as gender and race issues and the study of toys. These socially constructed artefacts reflect the industrialisation of games and its possible repercussions for children's socialisation. Intergenerational and geriatric play emerge as current issues in the field.

One of the best-known authors on anthropology from this Association was Brian Sutton-Smith, who also pointed out the need to consider the biological component of play (Sutton-Smith, 1997). He studied children's play during school breaks (Beresin & Sutton-Smith, 2010b); play and gender (Beresin & Sutton-Smith, 2010a); and other general cultural issues surrounding children's play (Beresin & Sutton-Smith, 2010b; Sutton-Smith, 1981, 1989). He argued that children's play should not be analysed separately from that of adults.

Toys have also received some attention (Castillo-Gallardo, 2015). While the relationship between toys and gender has been a popular topic since almost the beginning of anthropology, Pope Jr., Olivardia, Gruber and Borowiecki (1999) studied the notion of ideal gender and body images through toys. Denieul (1992) explored how board games and other toys introduce children to capitalism and competitive behaviour. Berg (1986) examines how dolls reflect social order and add psychological components such as touch, textures and identities. These and similar studies mark a promising turning point, as anthropology focused on the authors' very own culture.

Porter's (1971) famous – and contested – study of contemporary multicultural context and its conflicts used dolls of different skin colours to explore children's perceptions and racial attitudes, concluding that attitudes towards skin colour are developed between 3 and 5 years of age. Children of all skin colours showed a preference for white-skinned dolls and negative feelings towards black dolls. The study was based on a previous experiment conducted by Kennet and Mamie Clark, that was used to dispute school segregation in the USA during the 1940s. Chin (1999), however, concludes that toys as **cultural artefacts** cannot transmit sociocultural values and ideas, but, rather, these are transmitted by the social and symbolic environment in which play takes place.

Play, games and toys are embedded in a cultural and historical context. Some services providing for children and their families have tried to use play as a means to encourage children's learning and development (see Chapter 9). However, such services share the values and ideals of the dominant culture too.

 TIME TO CONSIDER

Can play help to promote ideas about gender, race and social stratification?

Is it possible to use play to promote good relationships and to help minority children to love themselves and appreciate their culture, body and skin colour?

THE 21ST CENTURY AND POSTMODERN AND CRITICAL VIEWS

In the final decades of the 20th century, as with most social sciences, anthropology went through a process commonly referred to as a **postmodern** crisis. Through a process of self-reflection, the discipline began to adopt **poststructuralist** thinking. In this new understanding of the discipline, anthropology is socially constructed and is therefore historically and socially situated; hence, much of its results are also culturally and historically limited. Ethnographies could not be neutral; they would always reflect, to some extent, the ethnographer's political, ethical, racial, gender and cultural preconceptions. Revisiting the discipline's historical output meant that it was necessary to accept that 19th and early 20th century ethnography reflected colonial views, and that only white men were allowed to interpret and construct reality, using anthropology to justify racism and domination (Vidich & Lyman, 2000). Social sciences, anthropology and ethnography had been developing in other countries for a long time by this point. Colonised peoples would start using anthropology as a means of reaffirmation, self-representation and **emancipation**: in short, to decolonise their culture and identity. Essentially, the postmodern turn means that there cannot be representation without participation.

A distinction can be made between the rise of postmodern views in colonised and colonising countries even in current times, perhaps a reflection still of the relationships of power that continue to underpin much of the contemporary world. While the former actively undertook to reclaim traditional identities and resist acculturation, the latter reflected on the development of interdisciplinary studies, focusing on their local context, with novel cross-cultural collaboration at times. Also, play and games in the emerging digital media began to be studied.

Critical views on ex-colonising countries

In English-speaking countries, postmodern play discusses the blurring of notions of space–time and labels. Nikolajeva (2008), for example, analyses play and storybooks and how narrative styles and types of game have spawned new ways of writing that reflect children's non-linear conception of narrative, something which videos or digital media can achieve more readily. The use of literature and games as understood in this postmodern sense have been adopted in play therapy (see, for example, Gallerani & Dybicz, 2011; Taylor, Clement & Ledet, 2013).

Regarding play in the preschool and Reception years, Rogers (2010) and a team of culturally diverse authors have reflected on play and the use of power in analysing the use of play and games in other parts of the world. Play as pedagogy is discussed, along with its alignment to the representation of the Western child. It is noted that, within education, play is juxtaposed between being regarded as educationally useful and at odds with 'serious' work in school. Brooker (2010) reports on how the notion of play in preschool makes no sense to some peoples from Bangladesh. Conversely, Nordic countries reject the idea of play to promote school readiness and therefore dissociate it from assessment or the curriculum. Hence, the concept of exporting play-based pedagogy or indeed of implementing a national curriculum in a multicultural nation, presents issues of acculturation and is most probably attempting to impose notions of childhood across cultures.

THE STUDY OF PLAY IN EX-COLONISED COUNTRIES

Perhaps some of the most exciting contributions to the anthropological study of play in current times come from the previously silenced voices, because they help us to contest some of the notions taken for granted in the West.

What is play?

As with many concepts, other cultures use different words that do not necessarily match the meanings in English. Bantulà i Janot (2006), for example, discusses how different cultures think about playing: sometimes there is no distinction between 'play' and other activities such as *fiestas*, carnivals and other festivities. Such activities involve interactions amongst children of different ages but also adults. In other cultures, play also takes place with animals, and other beings considered to be part of nature, for example in the Colombian jungle (Carreño Cardozo, 2003). A different word and concept are used to refer to 'play' as an activity taking place in school and imposed by teachers.

Similarly, Enriz (2012), whilst studying play amongst the *Mbya Guaraní* people (a group that inhabits Paraguay, Brazil, Argentina and Uruguay), discusses how some children's games involve dances and songs, some related to rituals. Certain community activities can also be classified as 'play' and valued by the wider community of all ages. The make-believe involved, which avoids harming others during play, seems to be an effective way of defining what play and games mean for these people. The author also discusses how children differ from adults in classifying what play is; for children, play can be a serious activity. Fantasy, liberty and creativity are closely related to play, art and festivities in other cultures (Gutiérrez Párraga, 2004).

In Colombia, Molina Bedoya (2015) argues that much of the understanding of 'play' in the West seems to be framed by space and power relationships. The phrase 'work hard and play hard', for example, contrasts with indigenous everyday life, where 'work' and family life blur, hence 'play' occurs spontaneously amongst people of all ages. In the West, playing seems to be allowed in specific spaces and situations, contrary to indigenous life, where play is not forbidden whilst 'working', or limited chronologically by institutions (preschool, Reception year, primary school) or relationships (line managers, supervisors) (Panqueba Cifuentes, 2015). Similarly, in Mexico, the indigenous notion of *buena vida* (the good life) conceives the meaning of life as being in harmony with others and with nature. Fun, wellbeing and joy are essential to life (Delgado Ramos, 2014; Peña-Ramos, Vera-Noriega & Santiz-Lopez, 2018; Quick & Spartz, 2018); why should school promote play if it is everywhere? What kind of society has taken play away from children in the first place?

In various indigenous cultures, the idea of separating children from families to attend preschool means that play is being restricted from intergenerational relationships by imposing the limited notion that play only happens between children of the same age and in confined spaces.

 TIME TO CONSIDER

In the English language, play means several things too. Children play games; all of us can play an instrument, play a role in performing acts; we use the 'play' button to activate devices. Why do you think we use the same word with all of these meanings? Could it be that, in past times, play was a more crucial and ever-present component of our society and, if that was the case, why have we lost it?

Visit the online etymology dictionary to see one version of how the meaning of the word play has evolved in the English language – www.etymonline.com/word/play.

The notion of individualism and competitive behaviour

One commonly contested Western notion is that of the individualistic and competitive idea of Western games. Most of the references cited here refer to it. Marfo and Biersteker (2010) contest Western descriptions and understandings of African games, discussing how the former have overlooked relevant meanings such as collaboration and community values, and how older children help to shape younger children's games by promoting relevant relationships. Hunleth (2019) also relates play and make-believe to children's strategies for caring for themselves and their families in difficult times, including epidemics in Zambia, showing a profound interest in community. It seems that the concept of individual development and play is a Western cultural production. Competition, it would seem, is not fun in the West.

 TIME TO CONSIDER

Read the following Mailonline article about fathers who cannot stand losing games when playing with their young children – www.dailymail.co.uk/news/article-2247310/Board-game-dads-hate-lose-Study-finds-fathers-win–mothers-happy-children-victory.html.

Since its early days, anthropology has related play and games to the social structure and broader culture they are found in. Try to connect some of the issues raised by this newspaper article with the values of our society. Why do we think that winning games is so important for adults? What do children learn from playing competitive games with other children and adults? What might you interpret from those fathers who cannot stand to lose? Can you identify any gender issues?

 CASE STUDY 10.1

In the jungle of Colombia, *Embera* people have their own conception of body parts and their relationship to nature. Most wear few clothes and children are usually naked; they speak their own language in which 'play' refers to particular activities in school, but they have a different word that applies to all ludic activities of all ages. Laughs and fun seem to characterise their games. Although some games have rules, part of the fun is that these rules can change, and observing the usual beginning and ending is not necessary as long as laughs continue. *El imamá* (The tiger) requires one child to assume the role of the tiger; she imitates the movements and sounds of the animal and chases all the other children. The others run away, and if the tiger gets tired, the children come back to tease the tiger. Participants will run, tumble, scream, tease each other, and many spend a considerable amount of time laughing. Spontaneously, other children can adopt the role of the tiger or of another jungle animal and plot against one child or a group of them. The rain, the mud and the river are considered to participate in the game. No one knows when the game will end, no one gains, and older children and adults can join in at any time.

Reflective question

In our society, do adults other than relatives tend to engage spontaneously with children in their play? Are our games framed in a specific space and time with a clear end? Are the forest and other living beings considered to be related to us and do they form part of our games? What do your answers tell us about the culture in the UK?

Source: Carreño Cardozo (2003)

Toys, culture and industrialisation

Castillo-Gallardo (2015) has analysed the evolution of toys from a critical perspective. She discusses how toy mass production has led to an impoverished range of materials and possibilities of use. Modern toys tend to present narrow cultural conceptions and prescribe how the toy can be used. Many toys are simply objects to be switched on and admired rather than explored and used to encourage innovation and surprise. Industrialisation seems to limit interactions, fantasy and creativity, ignore cultural differences and conceive children as consumers.

CASE STUDY 10.2

The game of *cañute* (coloured sticks) is played amongst various indigenous peoples who inhabit ancient Mexico, part of what is nowadays the southern USA. The game requires a series of hollow sticks with perforations. The sticks are handcrafted and show colours and intricate symbols and usually belong to the person who made them. Some have passed through several generations. A series of beans and a metal pin are placed inside the sticks which are grounded on a pile of sand. The game consists of guessing where the pin is. Two groups play the game, and part of the game is cheating, singing, teasing each other about what is going to happen, and the way the sticks are ordered is related to local stories and mythology.

Reflective questions

Imagine that your ancestors crafted your toys and the symbols on them; these have meaning and messages for you. Some of these symbols are also represented in your handmade clothes, in your relatives' tattoos and other objects. If you were a child, how would you relate to a toy made by your parents or grandparents? If you were a parent, would using these objects change the way you played with your children?

Imagine that as a child you are allowed to use valuable objects like toys. You can touch them, manipulate them, share them with others, lend them to your relatives, friends and neighbours for a long time, even years; lend the history of your family, knowing that the toy will come back and be passed to the next generation. What kind of relationships do you think this kind of toy promotes?

What games or toys in your community could be playing a similar role?

Source: Harrington (1912)

Colonising practices through play

Contemporary play, games and toys and their use in education and public spaces seem to be part of a colonising process, which involves the imposition of notions which have originated within large Western companies. In Serbia, Marija (2019) discusses how the design of playgrounds and playrooms follows a commercial rationale that does not consider local ideas. Jiménez Becerra (2018) focuses on the historical transformation of games and toys and their use in schools in Colombia. Similarly, Castillo-Gallardo (2015) discusses the manufacturing of toys and their relationship with inequalities in Chile. However, she argues that the notion that toys can transmit social meanings may be wrong, as social interactions frame interpretations and hence there is always a process that filters social practice and makes resistance possible.

Molins-Pueyo (2012) analyses schoolyards in Spain. Although widely accepted as being an essential part of education, the relevance of play has been considered when improving classrooms, where adults control play activities, but not when it comes to improving children's spaces; schoolyards remain poor environments for children to play in autonomously. **Colonisation** seems to run through play within the West through school and teaching activities, with the wealthy classes imposing their views on the less fortunate.

Play as a place for cultural resistance

The identification of colonising practices leads naturally to questions regarding the need to **decolonise** such practices: that is, how to use local knowledge to value and reinforce local identities. This is what Galeano Lopez and Giraldo Duque (2019) and Useche González (2003) do whilst exploring indigenous and Afro-Colombian peoples in Colombia, along with other researchers in Brazil (Medeiros Nogueira, 2015; Neves, Castanheira & Gouvêa, 2015; Rocco Gruppi, 2016; Ruiz Vicente & Hernández Vázquez, 2016).

Alomía Riascos (2015) makes a case for thinking more comprehensively and profoundly about play, arguing that, as cultural artefacts, games and toys reflect values, hopes and identities, play, seen as a human right, needs to be aligned to the rights of vulnerable minorities and therefore should be considered as a form of non-material human heritage. Not only does play reclaim identities but it also functions as a means of emancipation. Play and its use in schools, therefore, should be negotiated with communities and children to avoid colonising processes. This is possible only through the use of intercultural processes, meaning respectful cross-cultural collaboration that prevents colonisation, whilst promoting the value of co-existing in harmony (Dietz, 2009; Mendoza-Zuany & Delgado-Fuentes, 2019).

Anthropology and play seem to have come closer to the end of the colonising process than previously. This has happened through an intercultural approach to cultural studies, rather than simply cross-cultural or multicultural collaborations. However, there are also some new issues to consider such as digital play.

Some previously established ideas are still valid. Digital play reflects the industrialisation of games, the values of the Western world and controls on social interaction (Duek & Enriz, 2015; Duek, Enriz, Muñoz Larretta & Tourn, 2013), such as the opportunity to negotiate rules (Jiménez Vélez, 2013). It seems, however, that as long as other forms of play and interaction are available, this should not be demonised (Castillo-Gallardo, 2015).

FINAL REFLECTION

Play is an essential part of a culture; for that reason, in schools and other spaces, play, games and toys should be encouraged, as should the participation of children, families and communities in their choice and use. Such decisions can influence processes far beyond the uses envisaged by practitioners in particular settings. Play can be useful for improving **interculturalism**, that is, meaningful cross-cultural relationships, and the modern world could benefit from promoting elements of play in everyday life at all ages. For positive intercultural relationships to exist, dialogue and participation must take place.

KEY POINTS

- Play is a **cultural artefact**, and as such is framed within historical and social conditions.
- The study of play, games and toys in the English-speaking world has, by and large, ignored the ideas and practices of other cultures.
- Anthropological developments offer the possibility for a collaborative, cross-cultural understanding of play and its use in school and other institutions.

QUESTIONS TO CONSIDER

1 Watch this video reproducing Potter's dolls experiment with US children in 2016: www.youtube.com/watch?v=QRZPw-9sJtQ.
2 What role do you think play in preschools has had in promoting race relationships?
3 In the UK, play is highly valued in early childhood education, and there is an expressed emphasis on respecting all cultures in a contemporary culturally diverse society. Who decides what play, games and toys are used in preschool education? Do you think there is an awareness of the cultural meanings, values and relationships that play, games and toys promote in our contemporary society?
4 Imagine that you are a young child from a cultural minority and your background values collaboration, sharing and multigenerational play. You get to a nursery where different values are promoted. How do you feel, integrate and perform? Do practitioners have the time, resources and methods to understand and mediate the various meanings of the culturally diverse context in which they work?
5 Do you think that other areas of knowledge, such as psychology and education, are socially and historically framed? Can theories emerging from these fields have a colonising effect too?

FURTHER READING

You can read more about the Association for the Study of Play by visiting its website at www.tasplay.org.

Visit the multilingual open journal *Anthropochildren* at https://popups.uliege. be/2034–8517/index.php?id=918 for current and recent research.

You can also watch a short documentary about aboriginal games, produced by the Department of Premier and Cabinet Victoria, Australia, at https://youtu.be/ kiTtHUaCtT4.

REFERENCES

Alomía Riascos, M.Á. (2015) Una reflexión crítica desde la educación intercultural. hacia la pedagogía de la recreación. *Lúdica Pedagógica*, 2(22).

Ardley, G. (1967) The role of play in the philosophy of Plato. *Philosophy*, 42(161), 226–244.

Astrada, C. (1942) *El juego metafísico*. Buenos Aires: El Ateneo.

Bantulà i Janot, J. (2006) Los estudios socioculturales sobre el juego tradicional: una revisión taxonómica. *Revista de Dialectología y Tradiciones Populares: Consejo Superior de Investigaciones Científicas*, 61(2), 19–42.

Béart, C., & Monod, T. (1955) *Jeux et jouets de l'Ouest africain*. Dakar: IFAN.

Bereau, J. (1976) *Les Eglogues et aultres œuvres poétiques*. Edited by M. Gautier. Paris: Librairie Droz.

Beresin, A.R., & Sutton-Smith, B. (2010a) *The Grown-Ups Giveth, the Grown-Ups Taketh Away: Misunderstanding Gendered Play. Recess Battles: Playing, Fighting, and Storytelling.* Jackson, MS: University Press of Mississippi, p. 62.

Beresin, A.R., & Sutton-Smith, B. (2010b) *Play and Children's Culture. Recess Battles: Playing, Fighting, and Storytelling.* Jackson, MS: University Press of Mississippi, p. 88.

Berg, D. (1986) 'Transformers', Barbie dolls and the cabbage patch kids: Toys, technology, and human identity. *ETC: A Review of General Semantics*, 43(2), 207–211.

Brooker, L. (2010) Taking play seriously. In S. Rogers (ed.) *Rethinking Play and Pedagogy in Early Childhood Education: Concepts, Contexts and Cultures*. London: Routledge Taylor & Francis Group, pp. 152–164.

Brougère, G. (1998) *Jogo e educação*. Porto Alegre: Artes Médicas.

Brougère, G. (2004) *Brinquedo e companhia*. São Paulo: Cortez.

Caillois, R. (1958) *Les jeux et les hommes: le masque et le vertige*. Paris: Gallimard.

Carreño Cardozo, J.M. (2003) El cuerpo y el juego en los Embera de Tumburrulá. *Lúdica Pedagógica*, 1(8).

Castillo-Gallardo, P. (2015) Historia de la infancia observada desde los ejes del juego, juguete y desigualdad. *Educación en Foco*, 20(3), 289–322.

Chin, E. (1999) Ethnically correct dolls: Toying with the race industry. *American Anthropologist*, 101(2), 305–321.

Coxe Stevenson, M. (1903) Zuñi games. *American Anthropologist*, 5(3), 468–497.

Culin, S. (1898) *Chess and Playing Cards*. University of Pennsylvania, University Museum. Available at: http://archive.org/details/chessplayingcard00culi (accessed 7 May 2020).

Culin, S. (1899) Hawaiian games. *American Anthropologist*, 1(2), 201–247.

Culin, S. (1900) Philippine games. *American Anthropologist*, 2(4), 643–656.

Culin, S. (1903) American Indian games 1902. *American Anthropologist*, 5(1), 58–64.

Delgado Ramos, G.C. (ed.) (2014) *Buena Vida, Buen Vivir: imaginarios alternativos para el bien común de la humanidad*. Mexico: UNAM. Available at: http://buenvivir.signisalc.org (accessed 29 May 2020).

Denieul, P.-N. (1992) Jeu de Societe. In R. Jaulin, *Jeux et jouets*. Paris: Aubier Montaigne, pp. 182–192.

Dietz, G. (2009) *Multiculturalism, Interculturality and Diversity in Education: An Anthropological Approach*. Edited by U. Neumann and W. Weisse. Münster: Waxmann Verlag GmbH, Germany.

Dorsey, G.A. (1901) Certain gambling games of the Klamath Indians. *American Anthropologist*, 3(1), 14–27.

Duek, C., & Enriz, N. (2015) Les jeux, les enfants et les nouvelles technologies: une relation culturelle et complexe. *Revue française des sciences de l'information et de la communication*, 6.

Duek, C., Enriz, N., Muñoz Larretta, F., & Tourn, G. (2013) Juego, redes sociales e infancia: hacia la definición de nuevos escenarios comunicativos. *Lúdica Pedagógica*, 2(18).

Eliade, M. (1959) *The Sacred and the Profane: The Nature of Religion*. New York: Harcourt Brace Jovanovich (A harvest book: HB144).

Eliade, M. (1964) *Myth and Reality*. London: Allen & Unwin (World perspectives: 21).

Enriz, N. (2011) Antropología y juego: apuntes para la reflexión. *Cuadernos de Antropología Social*, 34, 93–114.

Enriz, N. (2012) Ceremonias lúdicas mbyá guaraní. *Maguaré*, 26(2), 87–118.

Fink, E. (1969) *Il gioco come simbolo del mondo*. Roma: Lerici Editori.

Galeano Lopez, Y., & Giraldo Duque, E. (2019) Características de los Juegos tradicionales de la comunidad Embera Chamí de Pueblo Rico, Risaralda. *Lúdica Pedagógica*, 1(30), 1–13.

Gallerani, T., & Dybicz, P. (2011) Postmodern sandplay: An introduction for play therapists. *International Journal of Play Therapy*, 20(3), 165–177.

Gutiérrez Párraga, M.T. (2004) *La significación del juego en el arte moderno y sus implicaciones en la educación artística*. Universidad Complutense de Madrid. Available at: www.google.com/url?sa=t&rct=j&q=&esrc=s&source=web&cd=33&ved=2ahUKEwi4lNrWrJDpAhXJMMAKHe1BC9I4HhAWMAJ6BAgDEAE&url=https%3A%2F%2Feprints.ucm.es%2F7209%2F1%2FT28325.pdf&usg=AOvVaw1NbfAEpZiRUZYgZPBhmM3E.

Harrington, J.P. (1912) The Tewa Indian game of 'Cañute'. *American Anthropologist*, 14(2), 243–286.

Hoffman, W.J. (1890) Remarks on Ojibwa ball play. *American Anthropologist*, 3(2), 133–136.

Hough, W. (1888) Games of Seneca Indians. *American Anthropologist*, 1(2), 134–134.

Huizinga, J. (1955) *Homo Ludens: A Study of the Play Element in Culture*. Boston, MA: Beacon Press. Available at: http://ezproxy.derby.ac.uk/login?url=http://search.ebscohost.com/login.aspx?direct=true&db=cat01750a&AN=udc.81451&site=eds-live (accessed 11 May 2020).

Hunleth, J. (2019) Zambian children's imaginal caring: On fantasy, play, and anticipation in an epidemic. *Cultural Anthropology*, 34(2), 155–186.

Jiménez Becerra, A. (2018) Los tiempos de la infancia en Colombia a través de la transformación del juego y del juguete a finales del siglo XX e inicios del XXI. *Humanidades*, 4. Universidad de Montevideo.

Jiménez Vélez, C.A. (2013) La lúdica y los nativos digitales. *Lúdica Pedagógica*, 2(18).

Kroeber, A.L. (1916) The speech of a Zuñi child. *American Anthropologist*, 18(4), 529–534.

Kroeber, A.L. (1920) Games of the California Indians. *American Anthropologist*, 22(3), 272–277.

Marfo, K., & Biersteker, L. (2010) Exploring culture, play, and early childhood education practice in African cultures. In S. Rogers (ed.) *Rethinking Play and Pedagogy in Early Childhood Education: Concepts, Contexts and Cultures*. London: Taylor & Francis Group, pp. 73–85. Available at: http://ebookcentral.proquest.com/lib/derby/detail.action?docID=667847 (accessed 21 May 2020).

Marija, M. (2019) The pedagogical implications of the commercialization of children's playgrounds in urban environments (Pedagoško društvo Srbije i Institut za pedagogiju i andragogiju Filozofskog fakulteta Univerziteta u Beogradu). *Nastava i Vaspitanje*, 68(1), 51–70.

Mauger, G.E. (1915) Quelques considérations sur les jeux en Chine et leur développement synchronique avec celui de l'Empire chinois. *Bulletins et Mémoires de la Société d'Anthropologie de Paris*, 6(5), 238–281.

Mauss, M. (1926) *Manuel d'ethnographie*. Available at: http://classiques.uqac.ca/classiques/mauss_marcel/manuel_ethnographie/manuel_ethnographie.html (accessed 11 May 2020).

McGee, W.J. (1899) Review of chess and playing cards. *American Anthropologist*, 1(3), 565–568.

Medeiros Nogueira, G. (2015) Cultura de pares e cultura lúdica: brincadeiras na escola. *Poiésis: Revista do Programa de Pós-Graduação em Educação*, 9(15), 117–131.

Mendoza-Zuany, R.G., & Delgado-Fuentes, M.A. (2019) Bilingualism and multilingualism in early childhood education (Mexico). In A. Alcantara, M.A. Delgado-Fuentes and M. Waniganayake (eds) *Bloomsbury Education and Childhood Studies*. London: Bloomsbury Academic.

Merleau-Ponty, M. (2012) *Phenomenology of Perception*. London: Taylor & Francis Group. [Originally published 1946] Available at: http://eds.a.ebscohost.com.ezproxy.derby.ac.uk/eds/detail/detail?vid=2&sid=8fd43ba8–1022–40cb-8721–6179714d70a0%40sdc-v-sessmgr03&bdata=JnNpdGU9ZWRzLWxpdmU%3d#AN=udc.1023127&db=cat01750a (accessed 11 May 2020).

Molina Bedoya, V.A. (2015) Tiempo, juego y cronología escolar indígena. ¿interculturalidad? *Lúdica Pedagógica*, 2(22).

Molins-Pueyo, C. (2012) School playgrounds and socio-cultural diversity in Catalonia: A study on the uses and possibilities for playing and learning. *Papers*, 97(2), 431–460.

Mooney, J. (1890) The Cherokee ball play. *American Anthropologist*, 3(2), 14–32.

Neves, V.F.A., Castanheira, M.L., & Gouvêa, M.C.S. (2015) O letramento e o brincar em processos de socialização na educação infantil brincadeiras diferentes. *Revista Brasileira de Educação*, 20(60), 215–244.

Nikolajeva, M. (2008) Play and playfulness in postmodern picture books. In L.R. Sipe & S. Pantaleo (eds) *Postmodern Picturebooks: Play, Parody, and Self-Referentiality*. London: Taylor & Francis Group, pp. 55–74. Available at: http://ebookcentral.proquest.com/lib/derby/detail.action?docID=332068 (accessed 21 May 2020).

Opie, I., & Opie, P. (1969) *Children's Games in Street and Playground*. Oxford: Clarendon Press.

Panqueba Cifuentes, J.F. (2015) Patrimonios corporales ancestrales del pueblo indígena zenú: el cargamento e' casa como escenario del montucuy entre bailes, juegos, pito atravesao y gaitas. *Lúdica Pedagógica*, 2(22).

Patte, M.M., & Sutterby, J.A. (2016) *Celebrating 40 Years of Play Research: Connecting Our Past, Present, and Future*, Vol. 13. Falls Village, CT: Hamilton Books. Available at: https://rowman.com/ISBN/9780761868163/Celebrating-40-Years-of-Play-Research-Connecting-Our-Past-Present-and-Future-Volume-13 (accessed 19 May 2020).

Peña-Ramos, M.O., Vera-Noriega, J.A., & Santiz-Lopez, J.E. (2018) Childhood and child-rearing in a Tzeltal indigenous rural area in Los Altos de Chiapas/Ninez y crianza en una zona rural tseltal en Altos de Chiapas/A infancia na zona rural indigena tseltal em Altos de Chiapas. *Revista Latinoamericana de Ciencias Sociales, Ninez y Juventud.* Centro Internacional de Education y Desarrollo Humano (Cinde) y Universidad de Caldas, 1, 149.

Pope Jr., H.G., Olivardia, R., Gruber, A., & Borowiecki, J. (1999) Evolving ideals of male body image as seen through action toys. *International Journal of Eating Disorders*, 26(1), 65–72.

Porter, J.D.R. (1971) *Black Child, White Child: The Development of Racial Attitudes.* Cambridge, MA: Harvard University Press.

Quick, J., & Spartz, J.T. (2018) On the pursuit of good living in highland Ecuador: Critical indigenous discourses of Sumak Kawsay. *Latin American Research Review*, 53(4), 757–769.

Reagan, A.B., & Waugh, F.W. (1919) Some games of the Bois Fort Ojibwa. *American Anthropologist*, 21(3), 264–278.

Rocco Gruppi, D. (2016) Trajetórias dos jogos escolares brasileiros para os jogos dos povos indígenas. *ATHLOS: Revista Internacional de Ciencias Sociales de la Actividad Física, el Juego y el Deporte*, X(10).

Rogers, S. (2010) *Rethinking Play and Pedagogy in Early Childhood Education: Concepts, Contexts and Cultures.* London: Routledge.

Ruiz Vicente, D., & Hernández Vázquez, M. (2016) Conceptualización de los juegos de los pueblos indígenas. *ATHLOS: Revista Internacional de Ciencias Sociales de la Actividad Física, el Juego y el Deporte*, 24 July. Available at: http://museodeljuego. org/athlos-revista/athlos-no-10/conceptualizacion-de-los-juegos-de-los-pueblos-indigenas (accessed 30 April 2020).

Sanctis Ricciardone, de, P. (1994) *Antropologia e gioco.* Napoli: Liguori.

Simms, S.C. (1908) Bontoc Igorot games. *American Anthropologist*, 10(4), 563–567.

Speck, F.G. (1917) Game totems among the northeastern Algonkians. *American Anthropologist*, 19(1), 9–18.

Stearns, R.E.C. (1890) On the Nishinam game of 'Ha' and the Boston game of 'Props'. *American Anthropologist*, 3(4), 353–358.

Sutton-Smith, B. (1981) *A History of Children's Play: New Zealand, 1840–1950.* Philadelphia, PA: University of Pennsylvania Press.

Sutton-Smith, B. (1989) Children's folk games as customs. *Western Folklore*, 48(1), 33–42.

Sutton-Smith, B. (1997) *The Ambiguity of Play.* Cambridge, MA: Harvard University Press. Available at: http://ezproxy.derby.ac.uk/login?url=http://search.ebscohost.

com/login.aspx?direct=true&db=cat01750a&AN=udc.652618&site=eds-live (accessed 11 May 2020).

Taylor, E.R., Clement, M., & Ledet, G. (2013) Postmodern and alternative approaches in genogram use with children and adolescents. *Journal of Creativity in Mental Health*, 8(3), 278–292.

The Association for the Study of Play (TASP) (n.d.) *History of TASP*. Available at: www.tasplay.org/about-us/history (accessed 11 May 2020).

Tylor, E.B. (1879) On the game of Patolli in ancient Mexico, and its probably Asiatic origin. *The Journal of the Anthropological Institute of Great Britain and Ireland*, 8, 116.

Useche González, G. (2003) Etnoeducación. *Lúdica Pedagógica*, 1(8).

Vidich, A.J., & Lyman, S.M. (2000) Qualitative methods: Their history in sociology and anthropology. In N.K. Denzin, & Y.S. Lincoln (eds) *Handbook of Qualitative Research*, 2nd edition. Thousand Oaks, CA: Sage, pp. 37–84.

11

AUTISM AND PLAY

Trevor Cotterill

CONTENTS

This chapter examines the importance of play for autistic children – how core issues of impaired socialisation and communication with restricted, repetitive and stereotyped behaviours or interests impact on pretend play in particular. It will allow you to relate key topics identified in the other chapters of the book and compare and contrast these in relation to autism.

 THIS CHAPTER WILL...

- Explain some of the differences relating to play for autistic and typically developing children
- Invite you to examine research which critically evaluates these differences
- Focus on aspects of imaginary, symbolic and pretend play
- Introduce you to cognitive perspectives underpinning issues with play, such as theory of mind, executive functioning and learned helplessness
- Help you to consider the impact of intervention strategies to support play and social skills.

KEY TERMS

autism spectrum disorder (ASD), executive function, integrated play groups, pretend play, social stories, symbolic play, theory of mind

INTRODUCTION

Autism spectrum disorder (ASD) is a pervasive neurodevelopmental disorder characterised by impairments in social communication and restricted, repetitive patterns of behaviour, interests or activities (American Psychiatric Association, 2013). These issues also result in significant adaptive deficits (Kanne et al., 2011) and cause difficulties in play (Mastrangelo, 2009). They impact on the ability to copy simple actions, explore the surroundings, share objects and attention with others and take turns. Autistic children therefore play differently from other children. From a very young age, they are more likely than their typical peers to line objects up, play by themselves and repeat the same actions over and over again. They are also less likely to engage in play that requires make-believe, collaboration or social communication with peers and family. Autistic children may be unaware of others' activities and preferences, meaning that they find it difficult to join in, learn new play skills or collaborate during play.

Early research

Kanner (1944) described how several of the children that he identified as autistic demonstrated unusual or limited play skills. For example:

- Donald T. resented being urged to play with certain things, never seemed glad to see any playmate and his play was repetitive.
- Alfred L. played with trains by connecting and disconnecting the carriages in a slow, monotonous manner and repeatedly counted the windows.

Kanner noted that, for these children, play involved repetitive interactions with objects that seemingly caught their attention, their play skills generally lacked pretend qualities, and they rarely engaged in social play with others.

PRETEND PLAY

Pretend play is composed of both conventional imaginative play and symbolic play. As discussed in Chapter 2, pretending may provide children with practice in navigating symbolic relationships (Weisberg, 2015), which may strengthen their language skills. It enables children to enact different social roles (Singer & Singer, 1990), practise differing interactions and develop an understanding of how social rules operate. This generally necessitates skills such as sharing, taking turns and verbally interacting with peers and adults.

Pretend play in autism

Imaginary or pretend play is an activity that typically developing (TD) children engage in frequently and spontaneously; however, children diagnosed with an ASD show deficits in this behaviour (Rutherford, Young, Hepburn & Rogers, 2007). Hobson et al. (2013) found that autistic children show less playful pretending, and suggested that this may be correlated with individual differences in communication, social interaction, restricted interpersonal communication and engagement. Symbolic and pretend play emerge slowly, if at all, in autistic children, and a key difference from their typically developing peers is that this lacks fun and enjoyment. The question is whether the absence of pretend play is attributable to neurological, cognitive and social differences *preventing* engagement, or whether the child understands but *chooses* not to participate.

Wing, Gould, Yeates and Brierly (1977) found that in a sample of children aged 3–14, the majority of children with no symbolic play, or with stereotyped play, had autism.

This was supported by Rutherford and colleagues (2007), who found that children with ASD found it significantly more difficult than TD children to participate, and that their spontaneous pretend play was more impaired.

Imaginative and symbolic play

Symbolic play is common amongst TD children aged 2–3 years. However, such play behaviour is weak or nearly absent in children with ASD.

Symbolic and imaginative play involves perceiving objects (or conventional toys) as real and using them in a functionally correct way outside the usual context. Examples include feeding a doll using a toy spoon, using an empty cup to pretend to drink, rolling a toy car on the floor whilst making engine noises, using a banana as a telephone, or making an imagined cup with the hands and pretending to drink. It may involve using objects as something else, attributing properties to them, or pretending an absent object is present. Imaginative and symbolic play provides an opportunity for children to practise events occurring in their daily lives or social worlds. This type of play reflects and facilitates the development of emotions, language, cognition, social skills, social awareness and perspective-taking ability.

Symbolic play in autism

Many aspects of development differ between those with autism and those who are typically developing. Some skills emerge a little later and some may not appear at all. Functional skills generally do emerge (albeit sometimes slowly); however, many children with autism struggle to make the shift from functional to symbolic play. Symbolic play may not appear at all, or it may appear infrequently (Jarrold, Boucher & Smith, 1996). It is unclear as to whether the issues are attributable to difficulties in acquiring the skills or whether they relate to performance problems. Studies find that when children with autism receive prompts to perform, they engage in the same level of pretend play as typically developing children at the same developmental level (Rutherford et al., 2007).

 **TIME TO CONSIDER**

What impact do you think the differences noted so far will have on:

- The child
- The family
- Playmates?

COGNITIVE FACTORS IN PRETEND PLAY

Pretend play is important in developing the ability to use symbols for thought, to provide an arena for examining social interactions amongst people and their emotional concomitants, as well as allowing for the practising of social roles. Pretend play often involves the construction of verbal narratives, an activity that involves complex planning, sequencing and organisation, in addition to well-developed language skills. Typically developing children spend a great deal of time engaged in pretend play, and, for them, pretend play may be an early area of cognitive competence. In a small longitudinal study, Nicolich (1977) found that there was strong evidence for structural levels of pretend games.

Cognitive factors in autistic pretend play

Children with autism demonstrate atypical play preferences and a preoccupation with certain features of objects, and their play often lacks creativity, imitation and flexibility. As identified previously, autistic children use more repetitive play than TD peers. Neuropsychological theories of autism shed some light on the play deficits exhibited by children with autism. Some theories propose that specific impairments in socio-cognitive abilities lead to an absence of higher levels of play or to unusual behaviours. For example, theory of mind (Baron-Cohen, Leslie & Frith, 1985) posits that because children with autism have difficulty taking another's perspective, the meaning of play exchanges between children is missed, resulting in solitary play. Hobson and Lee (1998) found that compared with control subjects, those with autism were less likely to offer spontaneous verbal and nonverbal gestures of greeting and farewell, and were less likely to establish eye contact even when they were offered a greeting. There were also fewer autistic subjects who smiled, or waved goodbye, which may reflect a relative lack of intersubjective engagement by autistic individuals.

Theory of mind, autism and play

Researchers have suggested that impairment in theory of mind (ToM) may be associated with pretend play deficits. The term is currently used to explain a related set of intellectual abilities that enable us to understand that others have beliefs, desires, plans, hopes, information and intentions that may differ from our own. ToM involves memory, joint attention, complex perceptual recognition (such as face and gaze processing), language, executive functions (such as tracking of intentions and goals and moral reasoning), emotion processing recognition, empathy and imitation (Korkmaz, 2011), along with an understanding of social skills.

It is also important for children to understand emotional states, beliefs and complex social information (Baron-Cohen et al., 1985). Chan, Chen and Feng (2016) examined the relationships of theory of mind (ToM) to both pretend play and playfulness in children with ASD. They showed that children's ToM was significantly associated with their pretend play, and supported the idea that some autistic children have better ToM which does allow them to develop pretend play, but not better playfulness, which might be more strongly related to their autistic severity. A discrete theory of mind mechanism (ToMM) may be a core feature of this cognitive function (Byom & Mutlu, 2013). According to this model of cognitive development, children's engagement in pretend play relies on the development of a ToMM. Leslie, Friedman and German (2004) suggest that our ability to understand the thoughts and feelings of other people does not initially develop as a theory but as a mechanism (ToMM); in other words, part of the architecture of the human brain is specialised for learning about mental states. Impaired development of this mechanism can have a drastic effect on social learning. Rutherford and Rogers (2003) suggest that the autistic-specific deficit may have to do with performance rather than competence. Pretend play deficits may have to do with imitation, flexibility or, more generally, executive function.

Executive functioning, autism and play

Another prominent model, the executive function theory, offers an explanation for the complex picture of pretend play seen in children with autism. Executive function (EF) includes working memory, inhibition, generativity and planning, which underlie goal-directed thought and behaviour (Hill, 2004). Executive dysfunction is defined as impairments in socio-communication and stereotypical behaviours. According to Rutherford and Rogers (2003), pretend play requires three EF processes: inhibition (disengagement from reality), generativity (scenario creation) and set shifting (shifting attention from one interpretation of toys or objects to another). Autistic individuals exhibit deficits in cognitive flexibility, planning, organising, predicting and anticipating situations, with Ozonoff, Pennington and Rogers (1991) suggesting that this lack of planning and flexibility in problem solving and a lack of goal-directed action, result in autistic play behaviours.

Thus, autistic children may have the cognitive ability necessary to engage in pretend play, but cannot consistently do so due to a lack of organisation or planning. Executive functions begin to mature at the end of the first year and the beginning of the second year of life, meaning that differences may become evident in a lack of novel acts with play objects in children with autism during the 9–12-month period. Deficits, particularly in the initiation or generation of spontaneous pretend play, might therefore be related to executive dysfunction. Faja and colleagues (2016) suggest that EF and play skills are linked to cognitive and language ability. Subsequently, early EF skills may be critical in order for verbal children with autism to develop their play behaviours.

Other cognitive features in autism and play

Weak central coherence theory (Happé, 1997) argues that autism involves a piece-meal processing style, resulting in an inability to perceive complex stimuli as meaningful wholes. Thus, a tendency to focus on parts of play objects and to display unusual preoccupations with objects, occurs. Based on this theory, it is assumed that children with autism display more repetition of the same play behaviours, and are therefore expected to remain in the lower levels of object play (e.g. simple manipulation) rather than independently moving on to higher levels.

Learned helplessness in a child with ASD can be another inhibitor if the child has had negative experiences with pretend play. Learned helplessness is achieved when the individual views aversive events as being out of their control, and results in the individual being unable or unwilling to have encounters with negative stimuli (Mastrangelo, 2009). When events are uncontrollable, the child learns that their behaviour and the outcomes of that behaviour are independent, and this learning produces the motivational, cognitive and emotional effects of uncontrollability (Maier & Seligman, 1976). Learned helplessness can further exacerbate a problem in behaviour or pretend play because the child can develop low confidence in their abilities and lose the motivation to learn or try to use their imagination (Mastrangelo, 2009).

SPECIAL STUDY: PLAY, THE AUTISTIC CHILD AND PARENTAL EXPERIENCES

Much research has been carried out on the differences in play between autistic children and their typically developing peers. However, it is equally important to examine the role of parents and the view that, whilst play serves as an essential medium for parent–child interaction, engaging children with ASD through play can be a challenge for parents.

An interesting study using a phenomenological approach by Román-Oyola et al. (2018), explored the perspectives of parents with children on the autism spectrum regarding play experiences and self-efficacy during play encounters. They found that fathers and mothers had different experiences of playing with their child. Mothers tended to insert play moments into daily routines, whilst fathers had opportunities for play that were not necessarily embedded within other daily tasks.

The parents recognised that there were challenges related to engaging the child in pretend play situations, with one mother verbalising significant frustration about not being able to actively engage her daughter in pretend play.

Fathers' motivations for playing with their children had an emotional emphasis, such as creating laughter or smiles. The mothers' motivators were more outcome-oriented, for instance stressing the importance of play as a means of socialising in school. The researchers also found that fathers were more inclined to judge themselves as competent during play than mothers.

Whilst this is only one study, it provides some useful insights into the role of parents in facilitating play and the impact that play (or its absence) with offspring can have on parents.

WHY IS PLAY IMPORTANT TO THE DEVELOPING CHILD?

Throughout the book, we have explained that play has a number of functions. For example, during play children can develop symbolic understanding about the real world using toys; copy behaviours seen in real life, such as fixing a car or cooking a meal; work out how to behave in social situations such as visiting a hospital; and express imagination and creativity. However, some of these examples may be difficult for the autistic child, who may play with toys in unusual ways, doesn't learn incidentally during play and needs support to develop play skills.

Gray (2013) suggests that there are five characteristics of play and these can be seen in Table 11.1.

Table 11.1 Five characteristics of play

1	Play is self-chosen and self-directed. Play may be a means by which children learn how to take control of their own lives and learn to negotiate, compromise and cooperate.
2	Play is intrinsically motivated. Play is carried out for its own sake, not for some extrinsic reward.
3	Play is guided by mental rules and boundaries, but the rules leave room for creativity. Players may change the rules as play progresses.
4	Play is imaginative. The ability to think hypothetically, or about anything that is not immediately present, involves imagination, and children continuously practise imagination in play.
5	Play is conducted in an alert, active but relatively non-stressed frame of mind. Because the ends do not have immediate real-world consequences, the person at play is relatively free from pressure or stress.

Source: Gray (2013)

 TIME TO CONSIDER

Taking each of Gray's (2013) characteristics of play, discuss why autistic children may have difficulties in addressing the points identified.

STRATEGIES TO SUPPORT PLAY
The Integrated Play Group model

The Integrated Play Group (IPG) model provides intensive guidance for autistic children to participate with TD peers in play activities which are mutually engaging. Based on **social constructivism** it aims to improve the social and symbolic play skills of autistic children from ages 3 to 11.

Wolfberg, Bottema-Beutel and DeWitt (2012) suggest that both developmental and sociocultural factors place children with ASD at risk of being excluded from essential play experiences. Without explicit guidance by adults, they are in jeopardy of being neglected and rejected by peers, especially when play contains social aspects.

The IPG model maximises each child's developmental potential and intrinsic motivation to play, socialise and form meaningful relationships with peers. Equal emphasis is placed on supporting peers to be accepting of, responsive to and inclusive of children's unique differences. Given their disparities, autistic children are highly vulnerable to being ignored, rejected and judged as social outcasts by those children who lack an understanding of their autistic peers.

Procedure

A typical group consists of the autistic children (novice players) and competent peer partners (expert players) who are led by a qualified adult facilitator (IPG guide), within a specially designed play environment. The activities are embedded with the symbolic and social domains of play, including sensory, functional and symbolic/pretend play, along with playing alongside and collaborative play with peers. Using sensitive assessments, IPG sessions are tailored to children's unique interests, abilities and needs. Play activities may include pretending, constructing, movement, interactive games, art, music, drama, video and other creative pursuits. Guided participation is used to facilitate mutually engaging experiences that encourage increasing capacities for socialisation, communication, play and imagination. Gradually, novice and expert players mediate their own social play experiences with minimal adult guidance.

Objectives

The primary objectives of the IPG model are to promote social communication, reciprocity and relationships with peers, whilst also expanding the play repertoire to include symbolic play. It is also important that peers gain the knowledge, empathy and skills to be accepting of and responsive to the unique differences of their playmates with ASD.

The IPG model differs from other peer-mediated and play therapy interventions in that its principles and practices are grounded in sociocultural theory. It draws from the social constructivist work of Vygotsky (1967, 1978), who ascribed prime importance to the role of play as both mirroring and leading development, with imaginary play being a collective social activity through which children learn and develop social skills together. Rogoff (1990) refers to guided participation whereby children's learning and development are mediated through active engagement in culturally relevant activity (namely play), with the assistance and challenge of responsive social partners (adults and peers) who vary in skill and status.

The following are key aspects of guided participation as they relate to IPG:

- nurturing play initiations in which novice players express their interests and intentions to play in the company of peers
- scaffolding play and adjusting the amount and type of support
- guiding social communication supports novice and expert players in using verbal and nonverbal social communication cues, through the ZPD.

The guide adjusts the amount of support given during the play group sessions, according to the needs of the children, and builds on the interests and abilities of the group members. Initially, the guide directs the play activity. As the children become more capable of creating play themes, initiating interactions and setting up play events, the guide fades support until no direct guidance is provided.

Transitions are often challenging for children with autism. Consistency in schedule and routine are important components of the IPG model because they help participants anticipate future events. The same groups meet regularly in natural settings, 2–3 times a week for 30–60 minutes each time. Opening and closing rituals are utilised and visual cues provide additional support.

Research into IPG

Wolfberg and Schuler (1993) examined the efficacy of the IPG model. The researchers were interested in determining whether the model would increase the functional and symbolic use of objects and social play of individuals with autism. Using play group settings, consisting of two novice players and three expert players, results indicated that all participants with autism engaged in a greater percentage of functional and symbolic toy use and social play after the IPG intervention.

Wolfberg, DeWitt, Young and Nguyen (2015) examined the effects of a 12-week IPG intervention on the symbolic and social play of 48 children with ASD, using a repeated measures design. The findings revealed significant gains in symbolic and social play that generalised to unsupported play with unfamiliar peers. Consistent with prior studies, the outcomes provide robust and compelling evidence that further validate the efficacy of the IPG model.

The Floortime model

Greenspan and Wieder's (2009) Floortime model offers another play intervention for preschool-aged children with ASDs. Interventions are designed according to the child's developmental level and individual characteristics. Greenspan explains that, although affective engagement such as showing pleasure, sharing emotions and reciprocating interactions is secondary to the primary symptoms of autism (e.g. cognitive deficits), affect and relationships are more amenable to intervention. Greenspan believes that through affective interaction, children with autism will concurrently experience cognitive and emotional growth.

Procedure

The play partner gets down on the floor and, for 20 or more minutes, works with the child to master each of their developmental capacities. It can be thought of as a specific technique and a general philosophy that characterises all of the interactions with the child (Lanz, 2020). The parent or carer is a constructive helper who does not offer prescriptive solutions, but follows the child's lead and interests in a way that encourages the child to interact. It is important to join the child in their world in order to help them master each of their functional, emotional and developmental capacities (Hess, 2013).

Objectives

Floortime is child directed and adult supported. It provides an opportunity to transform perseverative play into more meaningful and developmentally beneficial behaviour, and works to expand the play themes of children with ASDs. At the same time, it is designed to help the child develop relationships with others.

Lanz (2020) identifies five steps involved in Floortime:

1 Observe: The adult observes the child playing in order to determine how to approach him/her.
2 Approach, with open circles of communication: The adult approaches the child and joins in the activity, whilst trying to match the child's emotional tone.
3 Follow: The adult follows the child's lead where the child directs the action.
4 Expand: The adult extends and expands the child's chosen play theme without being intrusive.
5 Close: Finally, the child closes the circle of communication when they build on the adult's input and start a new circle.

Research into Floortime

Liao et al. (2014) researched the effects of Floortime on social interaction and the adaptive functioning of autistic children. The participants were 11 children, aged 45–69 months, and their mothers. Mothers were instructed in the principles of the approach by an occupational therapist. All 11 children and their mothers completed the 10-week, home-based intervention programme, undergoing an average of 109.7 hours of intervention.

Children made significant changes in mean scores for emotional functioning, communication and daily living skills. Moreover, the mothers perceived positive changes in their parent–child interactions.

Greenspan and Wieder (2009) reviewed the charts of 200 children diagnosed with ASDs and found that most children who received Floortime intervention for at least two years made significant improvement in all areas of development. All children in the study received 2–5 hours of Floortime interaction at home, in addition to comprehensive services such as speech therapy, occupational therapy and special or general education services. The researchers claimed that 58 per cent of the participants made significant improvements in social behaviour, cognitive skills, symbolic play and creative behaviour. However, the findings should be critically evaluated, for example the results cannot be generalised, and more controlled scientific studies would provide further information on the efficacy of the intervention.

 CASE STUDY 11.1

Oliver is 4 years old, has no functional language and does not appear to have the interest or the capacity to play with toys. When he leaves home, he carries a car which he will not let go of. His play is mostly aimless, and he does not engage with anyone playing with toys for any length of time. He waves his arms around but seems to want to hold his car out as a gesture.

Taking each of the two key features of Floortime and the five steps, suggest how an adult might support Oliver during play.

Reflective question

The IPG and Floortime models have strengths and weaknesses. The primary advantage of both models is that they allow children with ASDs the opportunity to explore relationships with others on their own terms and without the imposition of adult demands. What do you think are the issues with both interventions? How important is it that children have relationships with others?

Social stories

Many individuals with autism experience difficulties with social interaction; they struggle to interpret other people's actions (Power & Jordan, 1997, cited in Ozdemir, 2010) and this can have an effect on play.

Social stories are one of many strategies that professionals can use to support children with ASD (McCann, 2016) and help them deal with ambiguous situations (Plimley & Bowen, 2006).

Objective

It is a system to support children in understanding social information, using social cues, perspectives and common responses (Gray, 2007). Ali and Frederickson (2006) describe a social story as being a system that uses patience and accuracy to support children, as a simple narrative to teach an autistic child how to respond to certain behaviours (Reynhout & Carter, 2011). Social stories, developed by Carol Gray (1994), are short stories written from the perspective of the target participant to help him or her have a better understanding of 'the what, when, who, and why aspects of social situations' (Sansosti, Powell-Smith & Kincaid, 2004: 195). They are considered to be evidence-based interventions for school-aged children (National Autism Center, 2011; National Professional Development Center on ASDs, 2008).

Procedure

Gray (2016) identifies the following steps when writing a social story:

1 Picture the goal. What is the purpose of the social story? What does the child need to understand to achieve this goal?
2 Gather information. Collect information about the situation you want to describe in your social story. Where does the situation occur? Who is it with? How does it begin and end? How long does it last? What actually happens in the situation and why? What are the age, interests, attention span, level of ability and understanding of the individual? It is important that the child's age and ability are taken into account (Khantreejitranon, 2018). Use age-appropriate photographs, picture symbols or drawings with text to help people who have difficulty reading, or for younger children.
3 Tailor the text. A social story needs to have a title, an introduction, a body and a conclusion, and should use patient and supportive language. It should answer six questions: where, when, who, what, how and why?

CASE STUDY 11.2

Clara is 5 years old and she has few friends in her class. She wants to be liked by her peers, but they ignore her and tease her. She finds it difficult to make friends and she has no one to play with during breaks. She misinterprets their gestures and expressions, as well as not understanding how to join in with the games that they play. Clara feels isolated and thinks that her peers have given up asking her to play with them.

Reflective question

Using a social story, explain how you could support Clara to join in with her peers during break times.

Research into social stories

Reynhout and Carter (2009) researched the efficacy of social stories, using teachers as participants. All teachers within the study admitted to using the social stories within their classroom, with 92 per cent of them stating that they use social stories for a wide range of behaviours as well as to support the child's social skills. However, Gray and Garand (1993) concluded that for a social story to benefit the child, they must have some communication skills.

The cognitive theories discussed earlier in the chapter may also relate to our understanding of the impact of social stories. For example, Baron-Cohen et al. (1985) and Frith (2003) hypothesise that autistic children lack theory of mind and therefore struggle to understand other people's perspectives or what they are thinking. As daily life depends heavily on an ability to understand the behaviour of others (Tager-Flusberg, 2007), social interaction may be difficult, unpredictable and confusing for individuals with autism (Ali & Frederickson, 2006). Delano and Snell (2006) suggest that interventions should therefore be focused on social functioning, and the development of socially appropriate responses and behaviours. Scattone, Tingstrom and Wilczynski (2006) regard social stories as being unique as they are written from the child's perspective and give control to the child, allowing them to feel part of the story.

SPOTLIGHT ON RESEARCH

Youn Kang, V., & Sunyoung, K. (2020) Social stories with self-modeling to teach social play behaviors to Korean American children with autism. *Child & Family Behavior Therapy*, 42(2), 73–97.

Objective

The research sought to evaluate the effectiveness of social stories with self-modelling (SSSM) on the social skills of three Korean-American children with ASD.

Method

Mothers and researchers designated a play area for the study in the living room. Researchers observed the mother–child interaction and completed data collection. All sessions were video recorded. Sessions occurred 3–4 times every week over approximately two months. A social story was created for each participant and each child, and the mother read a story illustrating appropriate social initiations and responses in their preferred language and played with a designated set of toys for 10 minutes. The frequency of children's verbal and nonverbal initiations and children's verbal and nonverbal responses to adults' initiations during the 10 minutes of play, were measured separately.

Findings

The results showed a functional relation between reading SSSM and children's use of appropriate initiations and responses. All three participants showed improvement in their initiations, responses and affect after the introduction of the SSSM. Participants continued to show increased initiations and responses without the intervention package during a short-term follow-up. There was a positive affect (greater interest and engagement in the activity) during the intervention and follow-up conditions.

Conclusion

Reading a social story with self-modelling that is responsive to families' language and culture improved children's initiations, responses and affect. These changes were maintained during a short-term follow-up and generalised to a novel adult. Parents expressed high satisfaction with the intervention procedures and outcomes.

Reflective question

Do you think that intervention strategies, such as those considered in this chapter, are best administered by a parent or a practitioner?

FINAL REFLECTION

In this chapter, we have examined how play undertaken by an autistic child may differ from that of a typically developing peer, often having a persistent sensorimotor or ritualistic quality together with an inclination towards repetitive behaviour and interests, and an adherence to rules. Symbolic and pretend play are liable to prove particularly difficult for someone on the autism spectrum.

Playing alone and with friends allows children to rehearse social interactions, generate novel ideas and develop narratives. These skills are beneficial throughout life, but many children with autism have difficulties in all of these areas. However, through interventions such as Floortime and IPG, the autistic child can be supported in play activities, and social stories may aid social skills, play and communication.

KEY POINTS

- Autistic children play differently from other children.
- Imaginative, symbolic and pretend play are particularly impaired in autistic children, compared to their typically developing peers.
- Cognitive factors in pretend play, such as theory of mind and executive functioning, play a part in understanding these differences.
- It remains unclear whether the play skills of autistic children develop more slowly, or whether differences in play are due to other factors such as the repetitive, overly focused attention they pay to objects.
- There are a number of interventions and strategies which can be used to support play skills.

QUESTIONS TO CONSIDER

1 What might parents and schools do to support collaborative play between an autistic child and their typically developing peers?
2 Do you think that interventions such as those discussed in this chapter work, or should we accept that autistic children will play differently to their peers?
3 What do you think may be the longer-term social and academic consequences of the issues discussed in this chapter, on the life of an individual on the autism spectrum?

FURTHER READING

Beyer, J., & Gammeltoft, L. (2000) *Autism and Play.* London: Jessica Kingsley Publishers. (This accessible handbook describes different play sequences which encourage the integration of social, emotional and cognitive development in autistic children. The easy-to-follow play strategies focus on the four key skills of visualising, imitation, mirroring and turn-taking. The book is illustrated throughout with photographs, and includes a questionnaire for observing and assessing play interventions as an appendix.)

Conn, C. (2016) *Play and Friendship in Inclusive Autism Education: Supporting Learning and Development.* London: Routledge. (Taking an innovative approach to autism and play, this practical text focuses on the particular form that play and friendship take for children with autism and their peers.)

LeGoff, D.B. (2017) *How LEGO-based Therapy for Autism Works: Landing on my Planet.* London: Jessica Kingsley Publishers. (Through a series of case histories of children with ASDs who participated in LEGO therapy, this volume shows how and why this therapy is so effective. It provides practical guidance and inspiration for professionals working with children to improve their social interaction skills.)

REFERENCES

Ali, S., & Frederickson, N. (2006) Investigating the evidence base of social stories. *Educational Psychology in Practice*, 22(1), 355–317.

American Psychiatric Association (APA) (2013) *Autism Spectrum Disorder.* Available at: www.apa.org/topics/autism (accessed 19 May 2020).

Baron-Cohen, S., Leslie, A., & Frith, U. (1985) Does the autistic child have a 'theory of mind'? *Cognition*, 21(1), 37–46.

Byom, L., & Mutlu, B. (2013) Theory of mind: Mechanisms, methods, and new directions. *Frontiers in Human Neuroscience*, 7, 413.

Chan, P.-C., Chen, C.-T., & Feng, H. (2016) Theory of Mind deficit is associated with pretend play performance, but not playfulness, in children with autism spectrum disorder. *Hong Kong Journal of Occupational Therapy*, 28(1), 43–52.

Delano, M., & Snell, M. (2006) The effects of social stories on the social engagement of children with autism. *Journal of Positive Behaviour Interventions*, 8, 29–42.

Faja, S., Dawson, G., Sullivan, K., Meltzoff, A.N., Estes, A., & Bernier, R. (2016) Executive function predicts the development of play skills for verbal preschoolers with autism spectrum disorders. *Autism Research: Official Journal of the International Society for Autism Research*, 9(12), 1274–1284.

Frith, U. (2003) *Autism: Explaining the Enigma.* Oxford: Blackwell Publishing.

Gray, C. (1994) *The New Social Story Book.* Arlington, TX: Future Horizons.

Gray, C. (2007) *Social Stories.* Available at: www.thegraycentre.org (accessed 14 April 2020).

Gray, C. (2016) *What is a Social Story?* Available at: http://carolgraysocialstories. com/social-stories/what-is-it (accessed 4 May 2020).

Gray, C., & Garand, J.D. (1993) Social stories: Improving responses of students with autism with accurate social information. *Focus on Autistic Behavior*, 8, 1–10.

Gray, P. (2013) *Definitions of Play.* Available at: www.scholarpedia.org/article/ Definitions_of_Play (accessed 11 August 2020).

Greenspan, S.I., & Wieder, S. (2009) *Engaging Autism: Using the Floortime Approach to Help Children Relate, Communicate, and Think.* Philadelphia, PA: Da Capo Lifelong Books.

Happé, F. (1997) Central coherence and theory of mind: Reading homographs in context. *British Journal of Developmental Psychology*, 15, 1–12.

Hess, E. (2013) DIR/Floortime: Evidence based practice towards the treatment of autism and sensory processing disorder in children and adolescents. *International Journal of Child Health and Human Development*, 6(3), 267–274.

Hill, E.L. (2004) Executive dysfunction in autism. *Trends in Cognitive Sciences*, 8(1), 26–32.

Hobson, J.A., Hobson, R.P., Malik, S., Bargiota, K., & Caló, S. (2013) The relation between social engagement and pretend play in autism. *British Journal of Developmental Psychology*, 31(1), 114–127.

Hobson, R.P., & Lee, A. (1998) Hello and goodbye: A study of social engagement in autism. *Journal of Autism & Developmental Disorders*, 28, 117–127.

Jarrold, C., Boucher, J., & Smith, P. (1996) Generativity deficits in pretend play in autism. *British Journal of Developmental Psychology*, 14(3), 275–300.

Kanne, S., Gerber, A.J., Quirmbach, L.M., Sparrow, S.S., Cicchetti, D.V., & Saulnier, C. (2011) The role of adaptive behavior in autism spectrum disorders: Implications for functional outcome. *Journal of Autism and Developmental Disorders*, 41, 1007–1018.

Kanner, L. (1944) Early infantile autism. *The Journal of Pediatrics*, 25(3), 211–217.

Khantreejitranon, A. (2018) Using a social story intervention to decrease inappropriate behavior of preschool children with autism. *Kasetsart Journal of Social Sciences*, 39, 90–97.

Korkmaz, B. (2011) Theory of mind and neurodevelopmental disorders of childhood. *Pediatric Research*, 69, 101–108.

Lanz, J. (2020) *Play Time: An Examination of Play Intervention Strategies for Children with Autism Spectrum Disorders*. Available at: www.iidc.indiana.edu/irca/articles/play-time-an-examination-of-play-intervention-strategies-for-children-with-autism-spectrum-disorders.html (accessed 6 May 2020).

Leslie, A., Friedman, O., & German, T. (2004) Core mechanisms in 'theory of mind'. *Trends in Cognitive Sciences*, 8(12), 528–533.

Liao, S.T., Hwang, Y.S., Chen, Y.J., Lee, P., Chen S.J., & Lin, L.Y. (2014) Home-based DIR/Floortime intervention program for preschool children with autism spectrum disorders: Preliminary findings. *Physical and Occupational Therapy in Pediatrics*, 34(4), 356–367.

Maier, S.F., & Seligman, M.E. (1976) Learned helplessness: Theory and evidence. *Journal of Experimental Psychology: General*, 105(1), 3–46.

Mastrangelo, S. (2009) Play and the child with autism spectrum disorder: From possibilities to practice. *International Journal of Play Therapy*, 18(1), 13–30.

McCann, L. (2016) *Social Stories for children with autism* [online]. Available at: https://reachoutasc.co./wp-content/uploads/2020/09/Social-stories-SC228.pdf (accessed 10 July 2020).

National Autism Center (2011) *Where are the Autism Teaching Competencies?* Available at: www.edweek.org/ew/articles/2011/09/21/04martin.h31.html?tkn=TSSFkQLvOpCzb3%2Baf4xxPghb01iNnkne0dkA&cmp=clp-edweek (accessed 5 May 2020).

National Professional Development Center on Autism Spectrum Disorders (2008) *Evidence-Based Practice: Autism in the Schools.* Available at: www.unl.edu/asdnetwork/documents/guidelines_resources/nac_guide.pdf (accessed 5 May 2020).

Nicolich, L.M. (1977) Beyond sensorimotor intelligence: Assessment of symbolic maturity through analysis of pretend play. *Merrill-Palmer Quarterly*, 23(2), 89–99.

Ozdemir, S. (2010) Social stories: An intervention technique for children with autism. *Procedia: Social and Behavioral Sciences*, 5, 1827–1830.

Ozonoff, S., Pennington, B.F., & Rogers, S.J. (1991) Executive function deficits in high-functioning autistic individuals: Relationship to theory of mind. *Journal of Child Psychology & Psychiatry*, 32(7), 1081–1105.

Plimley, L., & Bowen, M. (2006) *Supporting Pupils with Autistic Spectrum Disorders: A Guide for School Support Staff.* London: Paul Chapman Publishing.

Powell, S., & Jordan, R. (1997) *Autism and Learning: A guide to good practice.* London: Fulton

Reynhout, G., & Carter, M. (2009) The use of social stories by teachers and their perceived efficacy. *Research in Autism Spectrum Disorder*, 3, 232–251.

Reynhout, G., & Carter, M. (2011) Evaluation of efficacy of social stories using three subject metrics. *Research in Autism Spectrum Disorder*, 5, 885–900.

Rogoff, B. (1990) *Apprenticeship in Thinking.* New York: Oxford University Press.

Román-Oyola, R., Figueroa-Feliciano, V., Torres-Martínez, Y., Torres-Vélez, J., Encarnación-Pizarro, K., Fragoso-Pagán, S., & Torres-Colón, L. (2018) Play, playfulness, and self-efficacy: Parental experiences with children on the autism spectrum. *Occupational Therapy International*, Article 4636780.

Rutherford, M.D., & Rogers, S. (2003) Cognitive underpinnings of pretend play in autism. *Journal of Autism and Developmental Disorders*, 33, 289–302.

Rutherford, M.D., Young, G.S., Hepburn, S., & Rogers, S.J. (2007) A longitudinal study of pretend play in autism. *Journal of Autism and Developmental Disorders*, 37(6), 1024–1039.

Sansosti, F.J., Powell-Smith, K.A., & Kincaid, D. (2004) A research synthesis of social story interventions for children with autism spectrum disorders. *Focus on Autism and Other Developmental Disabilities*, 19(4), 194–204.

Scattone, D., Tingstrom, D.H., & Wilczynski, S.M. (2006) Increasing appropriate social interactions of children with autism spectrum disorders using social stories. *Focus on Autism and Other Developmental Disabilities*, 21, 211–222.

Singer, D.G., & Singer, J.L. (1990) *The House of Make Believe: Children's Play and the Developing Imagination*. Cambridge, MA: Harvard University Press.

Tager-Flusberg, H. (2007) Evaluating the theory-of-mind hypothesis of autism. *Current Directions in Psychological Science*, 16(6), 311–315.

Vygotsky, L.S. (1967) Play and its role in the mental development of the child. *Soviet Psychology*, 5(3), 6–18.

Vygotsky, L.S. (1978) Interaction between learning and development. In *Mind in Society*. Cambridge, MA: Harvard University Press, pp. 79–91.

Weisberg, D.S. (2015) Pretend play. *WIREs Cognitive Science*, 6(3), 249–261.

Wing, L., Gould, J., Yeates, S.R., & Brierly, L.M. (1997) Symbolic play in severely mentally retarded and in autistic children. *Journal of Child Psychology and Psychiatry*, 18(2), 167–178.

Wolfberg, P., & Schuler, A.L. (1993) Integrated play groups: A model for promoting the social and cognitive dimensions of play. *Journal of Autism and Developmental Disorders*, 23(3), 1–23.

Wolfberg, P., Bottema-Beutel, K., & DeWitt, M. (2012) Integrated play groups: Including children with autism in social and imaginary play with typical peers. *American Journal of Play*, 5, 55–80.

Wolfberg, P., DeWitt, M., Young, G.S., & Nguyen, T. (2015) Integrated play groups: Promoting symbolic play and social engagement with typical peers in children with ASD across settings. *Journal of Autism and Developmental Disorders*, 45, 830–845.

Youn Kang, V., & Sunyoung, K. (2020) Social stories with self-modeling to teach social play behaviors to Korean American children with autism. *Child & Family Behavior Therapy*, 42(2), 73–97.

CONCLUSION: THE REAL PROBLEM WITH PLAY

Kay Owen

In the Introduction to this book, Owen and Turvill discussed some of the issues facing us when we attempt academic discourse about play. In the first instance, there is the definitional imprecision – although many have tried, and some have managed to isolate broad criteria, there is still no agreed definition as to what constitutes play. Throughout the course of this book, we have considered some of play's many formats and invited readers to ponder what they believe characterises true play. What has become clear is that the generic term 'play' covers an incalculable number of variations, each of which is amenable to further moulding and amendment in response to the child's internal and external circumstance. Gray's (2013) criteria, vague as it might seem, may therefore constitute the closest we can come to a working definition. Despite the prevailing fashion for definitive delineation, we believe that this ambiguity is a cause for celebration. At a time when children are increasingly required to comply and conform, play gives the imagination and the spirit free rein to creatively explore possibilities. Play enables discovery, joy, wonder, silliness and hilarity. Childhood is brief and precious. We would contend that, even if play had no outcomes beyond its capacity to make early childhood fun, then it would still be of immeasurable value.

This leads us to the second issue we considered – the relationship between play and development. Having considered a vast array of evidence, it appears clear that the two are inexorably linked. Some associations are obvious – for instance, the link between physically rousing outdoor play and muscular strength. However, we have come to recognise that many of these obvious connections are only the first wave that triggers an even more significant ripple effect. For instance, in this example, physical activity also initiates chemical, emotional and neurological change; it enables children to grasp cultural tools such as language, which aid psychological development and help transmit cultural norms. Furthermore, the range and variety of potential play behaviours means that play is uniquely placed to affect every aspect of human development. The human body cannot flourish solely on a diet of chocolate or apples. As with food, a balanced diet of different play activities promotes good health, emotional wellbeing and, ultimately, longevity.

As we noted at the very beginning of this book, most people would agree that young children need to play and should be allowed to play. What we have discovered is that opportunities for play are diminishing, and that there is an inequality of access. There is a human tendency to assume that our own lived experience is the norm and that the experiences of childhood are broadly homogenous. However, this is not the case; children's experiences vary according to their own individual strengths, limitations and drives, and in response to their immediate and wider environment. Even if your family has lived in the same place for generations, your childhood experience there will differ from those of your parents, grandparents and children. We live at a specific point in history that necessarily shapes our lived experience. Every generation is impacted by government decisions regarding funding priorities, housing, education and everything else that filters down to affect daily life. Currently, UK residents are also facing the particular challenges associated with government responses to Brexit and Covid-19. Politics therefore impacts play because it determines what happens in school, the community and the family home.

In recent decades, society has witnessed an increase in urbanisation, enabled in part by building on what had previously been school fields and other green spaces. Add to this the increase in car ownership and the result is a substantial reduction in the availability of safe spaces where children can play. Whilst this may be considered generally lamentable, it is of particular concern for children growing up in urban areas, where they are less likely to have access to private gardens. Due to land costs, some children now find themselves with neither private nor public play spaces and insufficient money to travel beyond their area. The loss of green spaces is thus serving to further disadvantage those who are born into the most disadvantaged communities. These differences are not new. We noted in Chapter 1 that from the late 1700s, moneyed children had an option on play and education, whilst working-class children had more limited opportunities. What is perhaps surprising is that, 300 years later, there are still children in Britain (such as those visiting Forest School; see Chapter 4) who have reached the age of 4 without ever having walked on grass.

These communities contain pockets of further disadvantage and groups whose sense of disenfranchisement or exclusion serves to limit access to play. Many adults from ethnic minorities regard local parks and play spaces as 'white areas' where they and their children feel unwelcome. Access issues and the absence of suitable equipment prohibit many parents of children with physical atypicalities from using parks and other resources. The tendency to stim or flap, Cotterill notes in Chapter 11, means that children with autism often receive unwelcome attention from the broader population, sufficient to dissuade parents and carers from utilising shared spaces. In combination, these factors mean that most shared play spaces are largely the preserve of the white, middle-class, typically developing child (Harwood et al., 2018).

We have noted that social attitudes have changed over the years, and the sense of being watched and judged is not limited to parents from minority groups. This, along with safety concerns and a reduction in safe spaces, has led to children increasingly playing within the home. The development of new technology has ensured that those under 25 are the most digitally skilled generation in history. Whilst recognising the potential benefits this may bring, Turvill (Chapter 5) points out that digital devices provide multiple opportunities to make further purchases in order to improve or extend the play experience. Like so many other formats, children thus experience an inequality of access based on their socio-economic status.

Primarily in Chapter 9, but throughout the book, we have discussed the impact of the National Curriculum, SATs and league tables on children's education. The climate of accountability and successive governments' desire to 'drive up standards' has led to an increasing formalisation and narrowing of the early years curriculum. Although government documentation promotes 'learning through play', we have noted that what is on offer frequently lacks any of Gray's (2013) hallmarks and, as such, is a misrepresentation that instrumentalises play. The emphasis on testing and assessment places increased pressure on those settings situated in disadvantaged communities, where baseline scores are inclined to be depressed. In order to counter this, skill acquisition is emphasised still further. Hence, those children with reduced access to play and green space at home, are also less likely to have play opportunities at school.

We have determined that the development of play behaviours is attributable to a mixture of experiential and biological factors. It thus follows that those children who are not exposed to a variety of experiences, and who are denied the opportunity to participate in the socially enriching experiences of pretend play, will lack vital developmental drivers. As Chapter 8 discusses, play is enshrined as a basic right of the child. Whilst it may be claimed that this right is satisfied in the 'learning through play' agenda, in many settings play is adult led and used to assess and measure external behaviours – particularly where the workforce lacks training regarding the nature and value of play. Play is therefore subject to curriculum demand, meaning young children's use of time and space are increasingly regulated, monitored and controlled by adults (Wyness, 2018). In this way, the meaning of play is contested and 'becomes a specific form of investment for adults', rather than children (Wyness, 2000: 16). Children's opportunities to deploy their agency are minimised. We would assert that a sense of agency is fundamental to true play. What is important is the child's ownership and experience of the play, not the practitioner's assessment of it.

As Boldrin notes in Chapter 3, and Fenton in Chapter 7, an outcomes-based approach is particularly unhelpful for children who have suffered neglect, trauma or abuse. In such instances, it is, at best, inappropriate to monitor and regulate children's experiences in order to measure them against universal norms. Instead, we must recognise their individual needs and enable the child to play out feelings and start to address painful experiences in a safe and autonomous fashion.

The real problem with play is therefore not that we as adults find it difficult to define, or that we are unable to provide definitive evidence of, its developmental impact. The real problem is that one of the fundamental rights of childhood is slipping away from the current generation of children, and that those who start their lives in a position of disadvantage are losing out most of all.

REFERENCES

Gray, P. (2013) *Definitions of Play*. Available at: www.scholarpedia.org/article/ Definitions_of_Play (accessed 11 August 2020).

Harwood, S.A., Mendenhall, R., Lee, S.S., Riopelle, C., & Browne Huntt, M. (2018) Everyday racism in integrated spaces: Mapping the experiences of students of color at a diversifying predominantly white institution. *Annals of the American Association of Geographers*, 108(5), 1245–1259.

Wyness, M.G. (2000) *Contesting Childhood*. Oxon: Routledge.

Wyness, M.G. (2018) *Childhood, Culture and Society in a Global Context*. London: Sage.

GLOSSARY

Age-related expectations (ARE): These identify what is expected of a pupil by a specified age or year group.

Anthropology: The study of human societies, cultures and their development.

Attention economy: The creation of profit by commercial entities by selling people's attention and time to advertisers.

Autism spectrum disorder (ASD): A developmental disorder/atypicality that primarily affects communication and some aspects of behaviour.

Barrier to engagement: The degree of effort, input or complexity that is required to do something.

Cognitive constructivism: A broad term covering a variety of different theories. In general, it suggests that knowledge is the result of an individual's cognitive processing.

Cognitive development: A process whereby individuals gain, organise and learn to use knowledge.

Colonisation: The action or process of establishing control over indigenous people and appropriating the area for one's own use.

Commercial influence: The guiding or design of artefacts by entities motivated by commercial gain.

Cultural artefact: An item created by humans that provides information about their culture.

Decentration: The ability to consider multiple elements of a situation at the same time. Younger children often lack this ability. In Piagetian theory, it is also the process whereby children become less egocentric and begin to understand that others may perceive and experience the world differently to them.

Decolonisation: The process of analysing and interpreting the ways in which concepts and social practices have been socially constructed, favouring Western views over indigenous traditions. After the analysis, the act of revindicating the local knowledge and values is used to strengthen the minority communities.

Digital migrant: The term applied to someone who was not born into or brought up within a significantly digital environment or society, but has learned and adopted digital behaviours later in their lives.

Digital native: The term applied to someone born into and brought up within a significantly digital environment or society.

Early learning goals (ELGs): The targets children should achieve at the end of the Reception year and at the end of the Early Years Foundation Stage.

Early Years Foundation Stage (EYFS): Sets out the statutory standards for all registered provision regarding learning development from birth to the end of Reception.

Emancipation: This refers to the process of identifying and changing the social practice that subjugated certain groups of the population, aiming to balance the power relations.

Emotional intelligence: The ability to react to emotionally arousing information and manage one's own emotions in an appropriate manner.

Emotional wellbeing: The extent to which an individual is emotionally comfortable, healthy and happy.

Empathy: An awareness and understanding of other people's emotions. In discussion about emotional and moral development, the term is used to denote taking on another's perspective.

Executive function: Generally used as a collective term for all of the processes involved in self-regulation, planning and goal-directed activities. There is some disagreement as to which processes it includes.

Extrinsic reward: A reward given by an external source, rather than for the intrinsic value of the thing itself.

Forest School: An educational model which aims to develop personal (particularly self-esteem), social and technical skills through use of natural spaces.

Inalienable rights: Rights that cannot be given up or taken away.

Indivisible rights: Rights that are equally important.

Inherent rights: Rights that exist at birth.

Interculturalism: A philosophy which challenges the tendency to focus on cultural differences, believing that this can lead to segregation. Instead, it recognises similarities and differences in order to support and promote dialogue between cultures.

Interdependent and interrelated rights: The realisation of one or more rights depends wholly or in part on the realisation of others.

Key Stage 1: The phase of primary education for pupils aged 5 to 7 in England.

Mediation strategies: Actions taken by a parent or caregiver to control or limit a child's engagement with a particular activity or object.

Mental health: A person's psychological and emotional wellbeing.

Meta-cognition: The processes people use in order to plan, monitor and assess their own understanding and performance; also the individual's ability to be aware of their own thought processes and learning.

National Curriculum: Used by primary and secondary schools in identifying a set of subjects and standards, ensuring all children have the same opportunities and learn the same subjects. The NC covers which subjects are taught and what standard children should be able to achieve by each age.

Nature connection: An individual's sense of their relationship with the natural world.

Neurology: A branch of medicine that attempts to diagnose, treat and manage disorders of the central nervous system.

Nurture groups: A short-term, targeted, psychosocial intervention run within schools by trained teachers. Through supporting children with social, emotional and/or behavioural difficulties, the groups help children to develop positive relationships and remove barriers to learning.

Office for Standards in Education, Children's Services and Skills (Ofsted): The body responsible for inspecting a range of educational settings and reporting directly to parliament.

Pedagogy: The methods and practice of teaching.

Persuasive design: The deliberate use of specific features to increase the likelihood that someone's attention will be grabbed and held.

Play cues: The physical, facial or spoken signals children give to show they want to play.

Play cycles: Within the discipline of playwork, a conceptual understanding of play as a process.

Play frame: The environment or situation that the play exists within, whether it be physical boundaries, rules, narrative or themes.

Play therapy: A psychological intervention that utilises children's ability to express and explore difficult thoughts and feelings through play and the creative arts.

Positive Play: An early intervention programme developed by Derbyshire County Council to build self-esteem and emotional wellbeing.

Postmodernism: A broad, largely philosophical movement, generally marked by a rejection of modernist ideologies, particularly with regard to those aimed at maintaining political or economic power.

Poststructuralism: Whilst ideas and themes vary, it generally rejects notions that the world can only be understood through fixed, binary or socially constructed means.

Pretend play: Involves using one object to represent another, or enactment of another's role or behaviours. Its emergence represents an important milestone in the development of symbolic thought.

Schemas (Piaget): A repeated pattern of play or behaviour expressed through physical action, language or thought.

Sedentary behaviour: Behaviour that does not involve significant physical movement or effort.

Social constructivism: Within social psychology, the term suggests that knowledge is not directly perceived by the individual, but is shaped by cultural factors and the constructs of others within the social system.

Social stories: Individualised short stories depicting social situations the child may encounter. Used particularly as a means of supporting social understanding in children with autistic spectrum disorder.

Social and emotional development: The domain of functioning relating to how children experience, express and manage their emotions and develop relationships with others.

Spotlight attention: A psychological theory of human attention, which posits that we have a conscious 'spotlight' which is directed by the unconscious processing of salient environmental information, as well as individual autonomy.

Taxonomy: A system or set of principles used to organise or classify information.

Theory of mind: The ability to reason about the beliefs, intents, desires, emotions and knowledge of others.

Unconditional rights: Rights that do not have to be earned.

Unconscious processing: Psychological processing of information which we are not directly aware of.

Universal rights: Rights that apply to all children.

Zone of proximal development: Introduced by Vygotsky to refer to the conceptual space between what a child can do unaided and what they can do with the help of an adult or a more capable peer.

INDEX

PLAY IN THE EARLY YEARS provides an accessible overview of key concepts, debates and approaches to children's play.

This book:

- considers play from a variety of perspectives
- offers expert insights into theory and research
- encourages the reader to critically reflect on both theory and practice.

With features including key terms, case studies, reflective questions, spotlights on research and an accompanying glossary, this text is perfect for everyone who is interested in play – from those just starting undergraduate degrees through to those with more advanced knowledge or experience.

KAY OWEN is a Lecturer in Early Childhood at the University of Derby.

⊛SAGE www.sagepublishing.com
Los Angeles I London I New Delhi I Singapore I Washington DC I Melbourne

Cover image © Getty Images I Cover design by Wendy Scott

ISBN 978-1-5297-1622-1

9 781529 716221